Veil and Vow

Veil and Vow

Marriage Matters in Contemporary African American Culture

Aneeka Ayanna Henderson

The University of North Carolina Press CHAPEL HILL

This book was published with the assistance of the Authors Fund of the University of North Carolina Press and with the support of Amherst College.

Set in Merope Basic by Westchester Publishing Services
Manufactured in the United States of America

The University of North Carolina Press has been a member of the Green Press Initiative since 2003.

Library of Congress Cataloging-in-Publication Data

Names: Henderson, Aneeka Ayanna, author.
Title: Veil and vow : marriage matters in contemporary african american culture / Aneeka Ayanna Henderson.
Description: 1. | Chapel Hill : The University of North Carolina Press, 2020. | Series: Gender and american culture | Includes bibliographical references and index.
Identifiers: LCCN 2019047734 | ISBN 9781469651750 (cloth) | ISBN 9781469651767 (paperback) | ISBN 9781469651774 (ebook)
Subjects: LCSH: African Americans—Marriage—History. | Marriage—Government policy—United States—History. | Income distribution—United States—History. | African American families—History.
Classification: LCC E185.86 .H4625 2020 | DDC 306.85/08996073—dc23
LC record available at https://lccn.loc.gov/2019047734

Cover illustration: Shawn Theodore, *The Hope for a Gift*, 2016.
Used by permission of the artist.

MIX
Paper from
responsible sources
FSC
www.fsc.org   FSC® C008955

To my ancestors and
to the beautiful, nurturing forms of
biological and chosen Black family.

Contents

Figures

Color photographs of each figure appear in the gallery located after page 115.

Veil and Vow

Invocation

We are gathered here today
in the presence of friends and loved ones,
to join this man and this woman.

As I rode the train to high school at the ghastly hour of 7 A.M. in Chicago during the 1990s, I grew accustomed to seeing women outfitted in sneakers and notched-collar trench coats, schlepping dog-eared novels with cover art featuring striking images of Black women and men. These novels that peeked out of tote bags and coat pockets on the train platform seemed to emerge in unison as the train departed from the station. The chorus of texts by Terry McMillan, Sandra Kitt, and Sister Souljah, among others, heralded a late twentieth-century reawakening in the African American cultural imagination and revealed that writers and consumers had a keen interest in the representation of African American romance and marriage.

As the women on the train migrated from what I presume to be their suburban homes to their jobs in the city, McMillan also experienced her own migration as her readership expanded, with her work moving from small, cramped corners to vast, lucrative sections in bookstores. McMillan's novels are often categorized as "Romance" in the few remaining brick-and-mortar bookstores that exist, while similar kinds of novels by African American authors are given less profitable real estate in "General Interest" or "African American Fiction" sections. Nevertheless, these hard-and-fast classifications belie the nuanced ways that these novels muddle what constitutes traditional "romance." While they are not prototypical Harlequin texts or titillating bodice-rippers, they use romance tropes, and the protagonists are often in search of a husband or a monogamous partner. References to expensive vehicles, designer handbags, high-priced clothing, and other luxury items are interwoven in the texts, preceding and reflecting the reverence for Jimmy Choo, Manolo Blahnik, and other upscale designers in chick lit and mainstream romance, such as *Sex and the City*.

These accoutrements not only attract a growing middle-class African American readership but provide added pressure for main characters to have successful heteronormative relationships with satisfying endings, culminating in the marriage proposal. Political achievements such as the civil rights movement redouble assumptions about the inevitable marriage proposal, and it is an assumption about African American people that has come to follow a historical pattern. Much like the expectation for wedlock and socioeconomic progress imposed on newly emancipated African American people who found that slavery supposedly could "no longer be blamed for social ills that plagued the black community," political and popular culture suggests that the last definitive hurdle for late twentieth-century African American middle-class protagonists enjoying the spoils of the civil rights movement is securing a monogamous heterosexual relationship.[1]

Many of the late twentieth-century books I saw on the train, such as McMillan's 1989 novel *Disappearing Acts*, employ romance tropes but pivot away from or revise the classic "Reader, I married him" or "happily ever after" (HEA) finale that characterizes romance and chick-lit genres, urging new modes of examining the representation of courtship and marriage in Black cultural production. The uncharacteristic rejection snarls the delicate line between the institution of marriage operating, albeit ostensibly, as a form of protection against racism, sexism, and poverty for some of the most vulnerable members of society and that same institution working as a mechanism that can make those members more vulnerable to state and intimate partner or domestic violence.

Taking this delicate line as its centerpiece, *Veil and Vow: Marriage Matters in Contemporary African American Culture* argues that portraits of courtship and marriage in the popular and political imaginary are an indispensable mode of reassessing family formation and the ways in which matrimony has become an increasingly politicized endeavor. I "worry" this delicate but jagged line, to use Cheryl Wall's term, by moving across and between print, sonic, and visual culture to explore what the representation of romance, courtship, and marriage means in the late twentieth and early twenty-first centuries.[2] I analyze films such as *The Best Man*, songs by Anita Baker, fiction by McMillan, book covers, and other cultural ephemera. Rather than rehearse the sweeping generalizations in cultural production pronouncing marriage as wholly "good" or "bad," I read against the grain an archive that registers as supposedly apolitical and unimportant, countering the assumption that romantic desires occupy a space of frivolity and escape. Underexamined and undertheorized, these texts mask the ways in which they have become central to our understanding of late twentieth- and early twenty-first-century African American and American cultural imaginaries.

I build on work by scholars such as Candice M. Jenkins, who argue that the "collection of historical tensions and suppressions surrounding black

erotic and domestic behavior suggests . . . that intimacy in general has political significance for black people, and is related to who African Americans
are as civic subjects, to the very shape of the black 'body politic.'"[3] In her research on African American literature, Jenkins elucidates the ways in which
African American political subjectivity and progress are firmly tethered to
the so-called private sphere of domesticity, courtship, and marriage. The nation has used this domain to threaten African American people, but writers
have also depicted African American characters ingeniously using the private
sphere as a tool for survival. Nevertheless, the use and misuse of these tools
spiral and curve across time and space, including to popular forms of creative expression. Belinda Edmondson maintains that broadly defined categories of "romance" and "erotic love" have long "been fraught with social
implications for black literature of almost every kind, from 'serious' antira-
cism novels to frothy Hollywood screenplays, from female-authored fiction
to male."[4] Edmondson deftly plots an expansive, pliable conceptualization
of "romance" because of its profound social implications for writers and artists navigating antiblackness. I use these theoretical frames as an entry
point for analyzing depictions of romance in the late twentieth- and early
twenty-first century, a period of time in which black popular culture grew
exponentially.

I establish *Veil and Vow*'s methodological intervention through a close
reading of print, visual, and sonic culture and by outlining a complex cartography for understanding how political and popular culture express overt
and latent anxieties about the institution of marriage. I critically examine
these eras and this polyamorous archive precisely because of what their kinship veils and unveils as well as vows and disavows. At the same time that
Black popular culture was undergoing a reinvention and its discursive reach
was rapidly expanding, it was generating angst about Black women's subjectivity and family formation in political culture. I demonstrate the ways in
which the fast-paced plots by prolific writers such as Sister Souljah (née Lisa
Williamson) career toward the future, but also articulate fears about what
the future might mean and bring forth. I unveil the old and new sociopolitical demands for "order" exemplified by legislation such as the 1996 Defense
of Marriage Act and the ways in which these fictional narratives imaginatively
endorse, diffuse, and disavow these pressures.

Political legislation can function as a blunt tool, so I have assembled this
triptych of film, fiction, and music because they provide shades of complexity despite glossy packaging and high-spirited plot twists. Situating popular
texts against and alongside their political landscape also unsheathes

dangerous political handiwork and legislative sleight of hand in the public sphere. This political and cultural consanguinity exposes the discrepancy between the vows that political leaders ask of their constituents and the vows they pledge to those they consider legitimate citizens. My analysis uncovers the fiction and fairy tale in political policy and the political stakes of fictional texts. The print, sonic, and visual culture that I examine in *Veil and Vow* affords a new opportunity to grapple with old questions, including who is imagined as a citizen—a designation bound to who is imagined as a "wife" and "marriageable." As I will explain, state apparatuses sanction broad forms of punishment for African American people whether they desire these labels or not. By stitching together cultural studies, African American studies, and feminist studies alongside political debates and landmark policies, this book illuminates the seam binding the ways in which political and popular texts refashion the notion of family.

Without question, Harriet Jacobs's 1861 slave narrative, *Incidents in the Life of a Slave Girl*, foreshadows the marriage refusal in late twentieth-century fiction and epitomizes the fragile relationship between African American women and wedlock, with her protagonist Linda Brent proclaiming, "Reader, my story ends in freedom; not in the usual way, with marriage."[5] An understudied and unique text among nineteenth-century narratives about enslaved people, Jacobs's narrative creates a hierarchy, prioritizing freedom from sexual and physical exploitation over obtaining a marriage proposal. Jacobs deploys sentimental tropes but disrupts the reader's expectation that the protagonist will end her narrative with a marriage proposal or matrimony, most famously exemplified by Charlotte Brontë's "Reader, I married him" finale in *Jane Eyre* (1847) a little more than ten years earlier.[6] Buried in Jacobs's bold declaration is a rupture dividing freedom and wedlock that continues to haunt Black women's relationship to the institution of marriage, resonating with Lucille Clifton's later prosody that "America made us heroines / not wives" in her poem "Black Women."[7] Jacobs recognizes "that the appropriate conclusion for a domestic novel is marriage" but instead ends her novel with her protagonist marrying "freedom by explicitly asserting moral legitimacy and political autonomy."[8]

Incidents in the Life of a Slave Girl precedes the 1865 establishment of the Freedmen's Bureau, which encouraged newly freed Black women and men to establish citizenship through wedlock, but echoes African American women who began to articulate their concerns about the institution of marriage hindering their self-possession and political authority. Although marriage and slavery cannot be conflated as identical institutions, some African American people expressed fears about the ways in which marriage could jeopardize their liberation. In 1867, Sojourner Truth declared that marriage meant "colored men will be masters over the women, and it will be just as bad as it was before. . . . You [men] . . . think that, like a slave-holder, that you own us. . . . I have plead with all the force I had that the day might come that the colored people might own their soul and body."[9] Truth disproves the prevailing assumption that all African American women covet marriage and maintains that formerly enslaved women have visceral testimonies about the abject violence of patriarchy and Black women's sui generis vulnerability under its regime.

Emancipated African American women were worried about what marriage would mean for their political sovereignty and grew uneasy about the pro-vincial and heavy-handed way the state defined "family" and the imminent danger associated with binding citizenship to owning property, which men could achieve by obtaining a wife and signing a marriage contract. African American women were also vexed by the false construction of marriage as impervious to the ways in which white supremacy blight its formation and preservation. A dangerous pendulum, marriage became highly politicized as proof of national belonging at the same time that systemic obstructions to its accessibility were understated.

African American people — enslaved and free — also worked within and on the fringes of what the state constituted a "proper" marriage. African American families envisioned marriage as a "malleable . . . institution formed as a synthesis of memory and imaginations, needs and options, de-sires and realities, theories and theologies, pragmatism and practicality."[10] Memoirs and family histories attest that a "synthesis of memory and imagi-nation" inspired African American people to construct kinship and diverse family structures despite white supremacy and its insistence on marriage as a lifeless, static entity. Tera W. Hunter points out that African American people understood that the "stakes for mating and marrying according to dominant standards were literally life and death. . . . Black marriage, family, and homes became the source of political imaginings of a disenfran-chised people."[11] These political imaginings and this gravitas elicited com-plex feelings and hypotheses. African American people celebrated and critiqued matrimony as well as reckoned with it as a form of citizenship or "a route to repudiating white supremacist discourse and admittance into full inclusion in the nation-state."[12]

Ribbons of fear remained amid the spools of familial love and sacrifice in African American communities. Economic upheaval and deceptive sociopolitical claims stalled and distorted political sovereignty in the twentieth century. Jim Crow racial apartheid laws, the Great Migration, and the Great Depression—among other late nineteenth- and early twentieth-century sociopolitical shifts—influenced familial patterns and structures. The urgency for robust, dependable institutions and social services did not deter politicians and leaders from amplifying the need for patriarchal family and trivializing the effect of systemic economic downfall and racist and sexist employment practices on African American socioeconomic mobility. In the second half of the twentieth century, Daniel Patrick Moynihan published his tendentious 1965 report, *The Negro Family: The Case for National Action*, reprising existing myths outlined in E. Franklin Frazier's *The Negro Family in the United States* (1939). Moynihan declares, "At the heart of the deterioration of the fabric of Negro society is the deterioration of the Negro family. It is the fundamental source of the weakness of the Negro community at present. . . . Unless this damage is repaired, all effort to end discrimination and poverty and injustice will come to little."[13] His hypothesis, which alleges that a pathological Black matriarchy and an inadequate Black patriarchy fuel racial inequality, is conspicuously in accord with his admission that his father's abandonment let him "down badly."[14] Prominent leaders such as Stokely Carmichael and Pauli Murray disputed Moynihan's claims and Robert Staples verified that Black women earned an annual wage of $2,372 compared to $3,410 for white women and $3,789 for Black men in 1960.[15] Nevertheless, Moynihan's hyperbole about "black family life was carried on through manifestoes and journalistic essays" in the 1970s.[16] The legacy of Moynihan's report continues to loom large in contemporary political and popular culture; it has asphyxiated the diverse and complex theories by women about their desire for and ambivalence about heteropatriarchal family in the cultural imagination.

Moynihan's report eclipses the creative folds and pleats of African American family and kinship, stitched outside the state's limited patriarchal conceptualization, as late twentieth-century political and popular imaginaries sustained his legacy. President Ronald Reagan lamented the "breakdown of the family" and deified patriarchal family as print and visual culture reaffirmed Moynihan's claims by outlining the boundaries of so-called proper family and delineating myopic guidelines for its maintenance. In 1983, *Ebony* magazine published "What Black Men Should Know about Black Women," which preceded relationship agitprop such as Shahrazad Ali's 1989 book *The Blackman's Guide to Understanding the Blackwoman*, published by the ironically named Civilized Publications.[17] Haki R. Madhubuti published a collection of essays that condemned Ali's wild theories, but Ali was able to build a strong following and attract a lot of attention.[18] The *Washington Post*, the *Los Angeles Times*, *Newsday*, and *Newsweek* magazine printed stories featuring her self-published book.[19] In it, Ali declared that when Black women become "viciously insulting it is time for the Blackman to soundly slap her in the mouth," implicitly corroborating Moynihan's fear of "emasculating" Black women.[20]

In concert with President Reagan's "breakdown of the family" rhetoric, Bill Moyers highlighted Black teenage pregnancy and indifference to marriage, declaring that "Black teenagers have the highest pregnancy rate in the industrial world, and in the inner city, practically no teenage mother gets married" in his 1986 docudrama, *The Vanishing Black Family: Crisis in Black America*.[21] Though there is a linguistic tie between Moyers's use of "vanishing" and McMillan's "disappearing," McMillan's novel eschews the misconception that Black marriage is universally accessible as well as imperative, while Moyers's title and reproach claim that the "Black family" is suddenly fading and patriarchal family is the nonpareil. Shahrazad Ali and Moyers exemplify "a range of gatekeeping responses from those committed to restricting the circulation of certain kinds of information within black communities and maintaining 'order.'"[22]

Historical amnesia about Black families animates discourse about a bygone era of idealized Black patriarchal family, denying the ways in which marriage functions as a hollow political remedy in the United States. Rather than addressing the mounting inequality within incarceration, unemployment, health care, and welfare reform, crisis-ridden discourses about Black families bolstered the assumption that patriarchal family and marriage could confer national belonging and remedy poverty. This rhetoric ignores research proposing that "single and living-alone households (and living with another adult) are making steady progress into the middle-class," as it troubles "neoconservative claims . . . of marriage as an anti-poverty measure."[23] Diffuse and homogenizing, this conservative deceit cultivated a generative landscape for fiction, film, and music, which complicated platitudes about family formation in the late twentieth and early twenty-first centuries.

The ascent of neoliberal logics and legislation illuminate the "fairy-tale" premises undergirding political and cultural demands for "order" in Black communities. Neoliberalism emerged as a multipronged new world order that began corroding post–World War II social programs and movements, such as the Head Start program for low-income families and the civil rights movement. Its corrosive work is propelled by a reliance on "deregulation, privatization, and the dismantling of social services—or what is commonly referred to as 'getting government out of the way.'"[24] These principles mobilize punishment of nonconformity and rebellion while championing privatization and monetization. Marlo D. David traces the maneuvers of racial neoliberalism through its insistence on advocating that "the state should be removed from any substantial corporate oversight or market regulation and that the government has no place . . . eliminating poverty as targeting forms of racial redress."[25] As the state purportedly relinquished its responsibility for establishing equity, the prison-industrial complex became a "thriving sector (alongside personal security services) in the US economy."[26] The state's so-called hands-off approach proves to be a fairy tale, masking its fixation on using private entities to police and control disenfranchised people. Without government assistance and oversight, citizens are left with the spindly, tattered threads of "personal responsibility" and "family values" as the requisite materials for survival and success.

The deepening intimacy and courtship between political dictum and cultural production urgently call for fresh ways of theorizing about sex and gender politics and African American family formation. There is a pressing need to "develop theories of corrective racial justice that explicitly attend to the history of racial injustice on both sides of the public/private divide and address the legacy of racialized disadvantage in the black intimate sphere" precisely because "the sphere of intimate relations is a significant realm in which black women experience injustice."[27] As such, I propose theories that reorient our conceptualization of racial injustice. Alongside visual, print, and sonic culture, public policy uses a powerful neoliberal logic for constructing a fictitious "marriage market" with covert but dangerous implications. These implications are animated by an ideological assumption I call "marriageocracy." A portmanteau of *marriage* and *meritocracy*, marriageocracy suggests that a free, unregulated, and equitable romance market animates marriage and the idea that it can be obtained with the cogent but misleading trinity of individual hard work, resilience, and moxie. It unmasks the neoliberal fantasy that marriage, much like the American dream, is a fair and equally accessible competition and exposes it as a cultural logic pervading self-help relationship books, political policy, and broader cultural discourse about marriage, while upholding bootstrap courtship politics and rendering institutional structures—such as unemployment, health care, and education—entirely inconsequential.

For African American women specifically, this nefarious line of thinking disregards their diminished and unequal capital on the marriage market, their queer identities, structural inequalities, and the compelling political and historical pressure placed on them to buckle and succumb to a legal heteropatriarchal union. The texts I examine in this project suggest that no amount of respectability is able to reverse reports and representations implying that Black women are considered the least desirable on the marriage market or capable of erasing the racialized sexual and gender pathology appended to Black women's flesh. The texts confirm that "The reputation for depraved sexuality was [and is] one that belong(s) first and solely to black women."[28]

The marriage market is a useful concept because it helps illuminate how "the 'free market' as a theoretical framework depends on the 'unfreedom' of those who are on the margins or outskirts of market activity."[29] Black women's unfreedom is made plain through the fictional depiction of domestic or intimate partner violence, rape, and sexual assault and the state's violent intervention in their private lives. These interventions, from both political and cultural institutions, often rehearse neoliberal discourse, bolstering familial order and privatized solutions as they reduce female subjectivity to marital status. They surreptitiously encourage African American women, imagined as the least desirable, to suffer through abuse and assault in order to sustain a facade of bourgeois nuclear family, made politically important for African American people.

In order to examine the distorted political urgency tethered to African American women's marital status in the popular imaginary, I reach back to W. E. B. Du Bois's prescient theory of the veil as a "shadow" of "double-focus" for Black people, while drawing on the veil's unmistakable gendered connotation to reimagine it as a *bridal veil*.[30] Du Bois contends that "within and without the sombre veil of color vast social forces have been at work"; thus, as a metaphor and lexical groundwork for this project, the bridal veil symbolizes a coverture or concealment of the tension between and seeming convergence of nationalist nostalgia and civil rights–era nostalgia, coupled with neoliberal ideology augmenting the pressure to marry.[31] I trace how a bricolage of music, film, and fiction, including the novels I saw on the train, is responding to, on one hand, Black nationalist and civil rights–era nostalgia in contestation with neoliberalism as they diverge in their construction of antiblackness and racial inequality. That is, as Black political nostalgia is being used to call attention to racial injustice, neoliberal logics are deracializing disparity and justifying inequality. At the same time, I untangle the ways in which forms of nostalgia and neoliberalism can work in tandem as political paramours through an insistence on substituting assistance from the state with seductive and romantic notions of self-determination and patriarchal family. The peculiar ideological intimacy between political nostalgia and neoliberal fantasy materialize around supposedly universal discourses of love, romance, and family formation in the texts I examine, veiling the ways in which structural hindrances produce inequitable results for African American female characters.

The bridal veil casts two silhouettes in the popular imaginary: *black bridal pathos* and *masculine veneer*. I developed these neologisms to index the repertoire of commonsense messages about family formation in the popular imaginary, ranging from McMillan's *Disappearing Acts* (1989) to the 2000 film *Love & Basketball*. Black bridal pathos has dual valences; it identifies the widespread presumption that Black women desperately hunger for and require heteropatriarchal marriage and makes visible the latent fear and anxiety that "unbridled" queer and heterosexual Black women want nothing to do with marriage. Hoary scripts about Black women as promiscuous and inept single mothers exemplify the former, while texts encouraging single heterosexual women to see themselves as "lonely" and queer women to see themselves as "deviant" and "destroying" the Black family confirm the latter. Such an analysis foregrounds the fear-based politically overburdened critiques of African American intimacy mobilized by a national preoccupation with supposed pathological unmarried women, absentee fathers, and the "breakdown of the family." Pathos draws out the cultural and political pity for "unwed" African American women as well as privileges the struggles and social death they negotiate as a result of marital conscription.

The second term, *masculine veneer*, outlines a common cultural trope of African American heterosexual male characters depicted as working class, racially oppressed, and possessing traditional gender and sex politics, but covered by a hermetic seal of striking good looks, a strong work ethic, and a circumscribed racial consciousness. This neologism is borne out of a cultural nostalgia for the previous era's beloved African American (male) political figures, movements, and iconography. As Nikol G. Alexander-Floyd, Madhu Dubey, Farah Jasmine Griffin, Wahneema Lubiano, Tracye Matthews, Barbara Ransby, and E. Frances White have illuminated, Black political nostalgia began acutely shaping late twentieth-century political and popular imaginaries. Albeit inspiring, this political nostalgia resulted in grossly oversimplified and highly distorted Black Power and civil rights pantomimes of

FIGURE I.1 "This Is What We Call Black Power."
Image from the SanCopha League Facebook page.
Established in 2012, the SanCopha League is a
nonprofit organization based in New Jersey.

racial solidarity and obligations to resuscitate idealized Black patriarchal figures in the public and private spheres (see figure 1.1).

Black authors and artists producing work specifically for a Black audience help bolster the power of and fascination with masculine veneer through re-fashioned, untenable Black political maxims lauding patriarchal figures as an effective political strategy. Under this dictum, the private sphere, often through the guise of patriarchal family, is venerated as a form of empowerment and "Black power" against unwieldy systemic hurdles in the public sphere. Idealized "prince charming" figures both are saddled with and assume the charge of symbiotically reestablishing Black political power in the public sphere and restoring the "Black family" as patriarchal figures in the private sphere, making marriage more desirable. Political hand-wringing about the so-called epidemic of absent Black fathers magnifies these figures and calcifies patriarchal scripts applauding fathers who are "present" but may be emotionally absent and damaging. By conceptualizing masculine veneer, I demonstrate how print, sonic, and visual culture encode impossible meritocratic goals for African American love and marriage.

Kissing Political Frogs

The neoliberal pivot to outsourcing policing and incarceration to for-profit enterprises and the subsequent rising rates of Black male incarceration not only strengthened political nostalgia and masculine veneer but also made ubiquitous directives for African American women to secure intraracial patriarchal family as a key form of financial support in the 1990s a cruel hoax. As a presidential candidate, "Bill Clinton vowed that he would never permit any Republican to be perceived as tougher on crime than he," and accordingly, in 1994 he introduced the Violent Crime Control and Law Enforcement

Act, a $30 billion bill radically accelerating mass incarceration in the United States.[32] Influenced by President George H. W. Bush's political arc, Clinton approved new federal capital crimes, sanctioned more than $16 billion for state prison grants and expansion of state and local police forces, and authorized life sentences for some three-time offenders.[33] African American people were incarcerated at disproportionate rates, and Black women have since been made increasingly vulnerable to the prison state, as Sandra Bland's fatal story evinces. Cultural institutions encouraged the preservation of Black love and patriarchal family as the prison industrial complex's violence against African American communities made Black women's search for intraracial heterosexual relationships a herculean task.

The 1994 Violence Against Women Act, part of the 1994 crime bill, created yet another impediment to matrimony and underscored the link between intimate and state violence. It provided funding for rape kits and mandated enforcement of victim protection orders in all states, but also established a set of laws that made Black women more susceptible to police brutality and incarceration. Coalescing with the crime bill's dependence on police and incarceration as a comprehensive remedy for social problems, the Violence Against Women Act encouraged mandatory arrests for all domestic violence calls. Black women have confessed to feeling apprehensive about calling the police on Black men, and activists were uneasy about police officers mediating assault, pointing to the high rate of intimate partner violence among law enforcement. In calls and reports concerning Black women, police officers frequently refused to see them as victims; they blamed Black women for their abuse and treated them as "social deviants and criminals," putting them in closer proximity to the carceral state.[34] Analogous to these constructions, African American female protagonists in the fiction I analyze are not only represented as "social deviants" who "provoke" abuse but also criminalized because they attempt to exploit patriarchal ideals of financial support, exemplified in the cult classic The Coldest Winter Ever (1999). My interrogation of texts by Souljah and others is an attempt to nuance and deepen our understanding of how intimate partner and state violence constrict African American girls and young women.

Working in tandem with the crime bill, Clinton's 1996 Personal Responsibility and Work Opportunity Reconciliation Act (PRWORA), or the Welfare Reform Act, further debilitated African American family formation as it reinforced marriageocracy. Exemplary of neoliberalism and its fidelity to bootstrap individualism and personal responsibility, the Welfare Reform Act enacted $55 billion cuts to welfare over six years, reducing spending on childcare, nutrition, food stamps, Supplemental Security Income, and the Social Services Block Grant. It affirmed a looming panic about the fictional "welfare queen," imagined as a poor, lazy Black woman bankrupting the state and averse to the ideals of personal responsibility and "proper" marriage. The Welfare Reform Act further villainized Black women and attributed their perceived failures to their "shortcomings rather than [to] interlocking, unequal structural forces."[35] It promoted "personal responsibility" by placing stricter regulations on who could receive benefits, drastically reducing its rolls, but it also declared that "marriage is the foundation of a successful society" and overstated claims that families with children born out of wedlock suffer "negative consequences," veiling the importance of structural obstacles.[36]

My analysis throws into sharp relief the subtle and rather shrewd connection between PRWORA and its political doppelgänger, the 1996 Defense of Marriage Act (DOMA), which denied same-sex couples federal rights and privileges and defined marriage as a union between a man and a woman, implicitly strengthening the power and authority of heterosexual marriage. As the state unceremoniously reduced and eliminated financial assistance for some of the poorest African American women in the United States via the PRWORA, the DOMA encouraged them to seek out an alternative "safety net" in the private sphere in the form of the symbolic veil and literal patriarchal family. Clinton advocated for and politicized heterosexual marriage and criminalized same-sex marriage in the DOMA during the same year that he decreased welfare assistance and argued for "personal responsibility" for families. Women, especially fictional freeloading "welfare queens," were expected to exchange a patriarchal nation for a patriarchal family. Deflecting from the state's culpability, politicians vigorously championed heteropatriarchal family as a privatized solution for vast forms of inequality.

Writers and other creative artists tried to make sense of this new world order as they engaged in new forms of world-making. Various forms of print, visual, and sonic culture represented and explored intimacy and desire alongside the heinous repercussions of 1990s legislation, including the political palimpsest of the DOMA, the PRWORA, and the crime bill. The tenderloin genre of "street fiction" or "street lit" by Sister Souljah and Teri Woods was a direct product of the crime bill and the Welfare Reform Act. The depiction of domestic violence and incarceration by Souljah and Woods bolsters the connective tissue between intimate partner and state violence. These authors explore the anxieties produced by the shrinkage in state support and the neoliberal pressure to marry contrasted with the prison state's decimation of Black communities.

They also fit within a broader realm of sonic and visual culture teeming with responses to these new political phenomena. Jodeci's 1993 hit love song "Feenin'" explores the pleasure and pathos of "fiends" who are addicted to love.[37] In doing so, they synchronize the compulsory heteronormativity and marriage produced by the DOMA and Welfare Reform Act with the growing "war on drugs" and proliferation of crack cocaine in Black communities, which made the figure of the "crackfiend" popular. Hip-hop artists such as Public Enemy, Boss, and N.W.A. chronicled the violent consequences of Clinton's legislation in impoverished urban neighborhoods. Films such as *New Jack City* (1991), *Boyz n the Hood* (1991), and *Menace II Society* (1993) visually rendered the hostility and disenfranchisement created by the growing police state and the "war on drugs."

In addition to its more conspicuous work in the crime bill and other government policy, neoliberalism shapes the contours of intimacy and marriage in less conspicuous ways. With intense competition, Janus-faced meritocracy, and bleak individualism at its fulcrum, neoliberalism has deeply permeated cultural and political logics and fostered bluesy feelings of despair, inadequacy, and loneliness, making wedlock simultaneously more daunting and appealing. As the saying goes, when white America catches a cold, Black America already has the flu, and analogously, when white Americans get despondent, African Americans have already descended into a blue funk. Neoliberalism helped thrust African American people into resounding pits of deep sadness, and marriage was called upon to do immense work yet again. Sustaining a healthy marriage becomes more daunting as citizens are urged to sacrifice leisure time in order to spend more time working, but neoliberal policy and cultural texts revamped quixotic portraits of marriage, making it an appealing, tacit remedy to the growing feelings of loneliness and melancholy. It would seem, then, that the labor consigned to marriage is complicated and infinite.

Still, the evolving political terrain in the second half of the twentieth century and early twenty-first century meant that cultural production had to begin working hard to sell marriage as an amorphous cure to "lonely" African American women, energizing Black bridal pathos. Since the 1950s, marriage has become less compulsory for women, owing to the reduced control men have had over their reproduction, sexual pleasure, employment, finances, and housing. The Food and Drug Administration approved the birth control pill as a contraceptive in 1960; growth of the sex-toy industry mirrored the rise of second-wave feminism; Congress passed the Equal Pay Act in 1963; the Civil Rights Act of 1964 prohibited racial discrimination in schools and employment; the 1968 Fair Housing Act ended racial discrimination in housing; California passed President Ronald Reagan's Family Law Act in 1969, sanctioning the no-fault divorce and setting the stage for the rest of the country; *Roe v. Wade* gave women the right to abortion in 1973; women could finally apply for credit in 1974; and in 1978, women could no longer be fired for being pregnant. This list, though not comprehensive, transformed the way African American women began envisioning the perils and privileges of marriage. "Marriage," according to Michael Warner, is "nothing if not a program for privilege," availing a host of rights and entitlements, and women began grappling with those long-established entitlements against new options.[38] "In 1990, the median marital age for women jumped to nearly twenty-four-years-old, the highest it had been in the century in which it had been recorded."[39]

This new social fabric, carefully unfurled by the nation, simultaneously began to pucker and wrinkle. Grassroots organizing and federal statutes made marriage less compulsory for women, but other legislative acts facilitated the dissemination of racialized gender clichés and superfluous references to marriage in cultural production. In the same year that Clinton signed the DOMA and the PRWORA, he also passed the Telecommunications Act of 1996, a neoliberal political project removing economic regulatory hurdles, resulting in large-scale corporate mergers. Since Clinton's legislation, there has been a "relentless push for consolidation within and across technological platforms, carving the market into national and regional oligopolies."[40] Though there is an illusion of choice in news and entertainment, just a few billion-dollar companies own and control the nation's largest studios and television networks. As fewer companies controlled cultural discourse and creative expression, politicians found another way to restrict creative content by demanding that the government phase out funding to agencies such as the National Endowment for the Humanities, which the Trump administration has threatened. African American creative artists were able to release an eclectic mix of songs, films, and television shows during the 1990s, but the attack on government-funded humanities projects and the ill-boding Telecommunications Act was a phantom thread strangling artistic innovation and representations of coupling and family formation.

Like the DOMA and the PRWORA, the Telecommunications Act became instrumental in parroting caricatures about African American people. In 1996, the same year Clinton passed the Telecommunications Act, the DOMA, and the PRWORA, Rupert Murdoch's Fox Entertainment Group, a subsidiary of Twenty-First Century Fox, Inc., launched its infamous Fox News Channel, triggering a perfect storm. Fox News, a network deemed a "refuge for racists," along with other forms of media, began to disseminate fake news about crises concerning teenage pregnancy and queer sexualities.[41] Print news and television venerated matrimony and antiquated guidelines for sex and gender comportment, while resuscitating misleading myths about Black women as supposed emasculating matriarchs and so-called promiscuous welfare queens. The media's histrionics conveyed as much angst about the past and present as it did about the future. The nation reached back to illusory images of the past in order to express nascent fears about a new queer future. Not only were people unnerved about the year 2000 as a date that would activate an earth-shattering Y2K software glitch, they were also terrified about the kind of so-called futuristic changes that might occur within the family.

Scholarship on the Telecommunications Act often focuses on television, film, music, and the internet, but the law also massively retooled the book publishing industry. Corporations absorbed publishing firms, creating monopolies and weakening editorial power and autonomy. Samuel Irving "Si" Newhouse Jr. was exemplary of this change. He inherited a publishing empire and "built it into one of the largest privately held fortunes in the United States, with estimates of the family wealth running over $12 billion" in the early aughts.[42] He was the former owner of Advance Publications and former chair of Condé Nast, which owns *Brides* magazine, the *New Yorker*, and countless other brands and media and his magazines were "criticized for exalting the rich and famous."[43] Upon purchasing Random House, he "insisted that Random House pay a huge advance to Donald Trump" and demanded that Random House "stop publishing 'so many books on the left' and instead publish more on the right."[44]

Right-wing magnates like Newhouse completely overhauled renowned publishing companies and typify how newly built conglomerates are able to switch their focus and circulate more conservative content. As many of these companies grew into massive corporate giants, they were also able to heavily promote conservative self-help relationship books to female readers across multiple networks. It seems to be how we were able to get derivative texts such as *Why Men Don't Listen and Women Can't Read Maps: How We're Different and What to Do About It* (1998) in libraries and on bookshelves. There are more than fifty editions of this book, but Broadway Books, a division of Random House, has published at least one edition. Self-proclaimed marriage and relationship experts championed superannuated models of courtship and domesticity, undergirded by the belief that marriage was a vital

"American institution and that its fortunes paralleled those of American society at large."[45] "The knowledge that every marriage had the potential to end in divorce (the United States has one of the highest divorce rates in the world . . .) clearly influenced the efforts to strengthen the institution" and compounded fears about the future of heteropatriarchal family as a tool to disenfranchise and empower.[46]

The despotic control of fiction and print culture also gnarled Black cultural imaginaries as "major publishers were . . . less interested in publishing more black authors."[47] Writers who had the opportunity to work with publishing conglomerates were frequently producing work under the daunting constraints of dictatorial monopolies, but a "rapidly growing independent press . . . aggressively pursue[d] new voices."[48] As new voices emerged, familiar problems reappeared. Writers feared that popular texts became "dangerously close to flooding their newly created market with hackneyed plots, gratuitous sexuality, and uninspiring characters."[49] In 2007, McMillan sent a widely publicized email to publishing executives condemning their endorsement of Black popular fiction depicting "exploitative, racist, and sexist" content, arguing that it "show[s] black people in a negative and stereotypical light."[50] Nevertheless, some African American readers, perhaps warding off a swelling blue funk, applauded the visceral depictions of lust, love, and emotional fulfillment. Other critics insist that contemporary depictions of Black romance and love highlight that "black people, too, can experience transcendent emotion, sublime emotion, and not just sentimental, mindless emotion."[51] In *Veil and Vow*, my aim is to trace these discordant responses, while critically examining the problematic and the progressive depictions of Black romance, coupling, and love as well as map the continuities between them.

Literary Histories and McMillan's Migrating Work

I open the book with Terry McMillan and transient female readers and return to McMillan, travel, and wanderlust here because they are a bellwether for the merging debates I map in chapter 1 and are paradigmatic of the book's thematic itinerary. As a case study, McMillan's literary history, lived experience, book covers, and the political terrain she maneuvers, are the anchoring hems of *Veil and Vow*. McMillan is often celebrated as a patron saint of late twentieth-century Black commercial fiction, especially because "the success of *Waiting to Exhale* helped change the publishing industry's approach to Black authors, leading to the careers of Bebe Moore Campbell,

Tina McElroy Ansa, and Connie Briscoe, among others, and opening doors for current writers from Kimberly Lawson Roby to Eric Jerome Dickey."[52] McMillan's remarkable success gestures toward an intricate and revelatory genealogy. Her corpus echoes the meaning historically consigned to wedlock as it moves from rendering Black women's private lives and depictions of romance and courtship as simultaneously serious and frivolous, highly politicized and apolitical.

In the 1970s, before McMillan's fame, second-wave feminism and its "the personal is political" rallying cry stimulated growth in the popular romance market and directed more attention toward female authors and the interior lives of women. Of the 1970s, Adrienne Rich writes, "Personal narrative was becoming valued as the true coin of feminist expression. At the same time, in every zone of public life, personal and private solutions were being marketed by a profit-driven corporate system, while collective action and even collective realities were mocked at best and at worst rendered historically sterile."[53] Feminists were drawn to stories featuring the once-hidden interior lives of women, who were exploring "fluid gender roles, expansive notions of sex and sexualities, [and] elastic notions of propriety and dignity."[54] As Rich surmises, profit-driven corporate systems made these images fit within a neoliberal ethos of exaggerating private solutions and diminishing collective action.

Simultaneously, the Black Power movement, Black Arts Movement, and burgeoning African American studies and women's studies departments and programs across the country fomented interest in novels and poetry grappling with the rich textures of Black female subjectivity by writers such as Toni Morrison, Alice Walker, and Lucille Clifton. Though readers were excited to see poetry and fiction centering Black female subjectivity, all was not well within literary circles. About Morrison's *Sula* (1973), Sara Blackburn claimed in the *New York Times* that "Toni Morrison is far too talented to remain only a marvelous recorder of the Black side of provincial American life. If she is to maintain the large and serious audience she deserves, she is going to have to address a riskier contemporary reality than this beautiful but nevertheless distanced novel."[55] Female and male critics condemned female writers for what they deemed as "unrealistic" and "stereotypical" portrayals of Black men and "irreproachable" depictions of Black women. Confessing the sales numbers for his book, writer Ishmael Reed claims that "the book only sold 8000 copies. I don't mind giving out the figure: 8000. Maybe if I was one of those young female Afro-American writers that are so hot now, I'd sell more. You know, fill my books with ghetto women who can do no wrong. . . .

But come on, I think I could have sold 8000 copies by myself."[56] Black women writers experienced a double ostracism, "largely 'disenfranchised' from critical works on the 'female tradition'" and often "excised from those on the Afro-American literary tradition by black male scholars."[57]

Although she was mentored by Ishmael Reed as an undergraduate student, McMillan did not shy away from centering working-class and middle-class African American female protagonists in her short stories and novels, eventually joining the ranks of the young female writers that Reed lambasts. Her first novel, *Mama* (1987), published by Washington Square Press (now a subsidiary of Simon and Schuster), depicts Mildred Peacock, a mother of five children in the small town of Point Haven, Michigan, who navigates racism and sexism during the 1960s. Subsequent glowing book reviews of *Mama* situate McMillan and her work within a respected and well-regarded literary topography.[58]

As McMillan continues to publish short stories and novels, her work becomes more itinerant and difficult to pigeonhole. In her sophomore novel, *Disappearing Acts*, McMillan eschews the small town 1960s setting of *Mama* and pens a contemporary story set in 1980s New York City. Viking Press (now owned by Penguin Random House) published the first edition of the novel and had also published fiction by acclaimed authors such as Saul Bellow and Jack Kerouac. McMillan depicts a fast-paced but tumultuous romance between Zora and Franklin in *Disappearing Acts*, implying that she sought a more commercial audience. The novel had more commercial appeal, but the Art Deco–inspired image on the 1989 hardcover edition and McMillan's protagonist Zora subtly links it to the Harlem Renaissance and Alice Walker's scholarly reclamation of Zora Neale Hurston's work (see figure 1.2).

Though *Disappearing Acts* partially adheres to the typical romance trajectory—beginning with a woman and man dating, breaking up, and then achieving a (somewhat) happily-ever-after resolution, signified by their reconciliation with no accompanying promise of monogamous commitment— the novel is untraditional in that the male suitor, Franklin, is allotted first-person narration and full chapters to recount his side or version of the romance. This creative antiphonal narrative tailoring helped shield McMillan from some of the criticism about the so-called one-dimensional depiction of Black male characters but also helped her straddle the muddled lines dividing the "literary" from the "popular." Publishers strategically used the cover art to avail McMillan's fiction a place among supposed high-brow literature and to disguise the so-called popular content and form of the novel, enabling the book to both obscure and make visible contemporary depictions

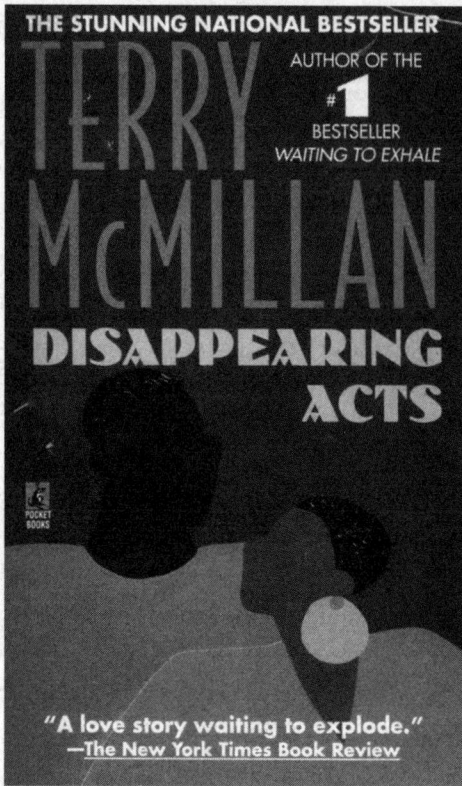

FIGURE I.2 Cover for Terry McMillan's novel *Disappearing Acts*, 1989.

of Black women's private lives. But by also riffing on Harlem Renaissance iconography, publishers signaled McMillan as a figure who would launch a rebirth of another kind of fiction by Black women.

Her book jackets, as itinerant veils, index ideological tensions at play across and within historical contexts and spaces but also embody what Black studies scholar Howard Rambsy II calls an "interrelated graphic narrative."[59] The interrelated graphic narrative of McMillan's work is a twisting and winding one. Attesting to their popularity, *Disappearing Acts* has seventeen editions and *Waiting to Exhale* has forty-three editions. The women pictured on the popular fiction covers I saw on the train, including Viking's 1992 edition of *Waiting to Exhale*, *Disappearing Acts* (editions from 1990, 1991, and 1993), and Lolita Files's *Scenes from a Sistah* (1997), are all shrouded in work similar to or designed by visual artist Synthia Saint James (see figures 1.3, 1.4, and 1.5).

Coincidentally, Saint James's artwork was also commissioned for the cover of a 1990 collection, published by Quality Paperback Book Club, containing three of Alice Walker's novels, anointing McMillan and her peers with a hint

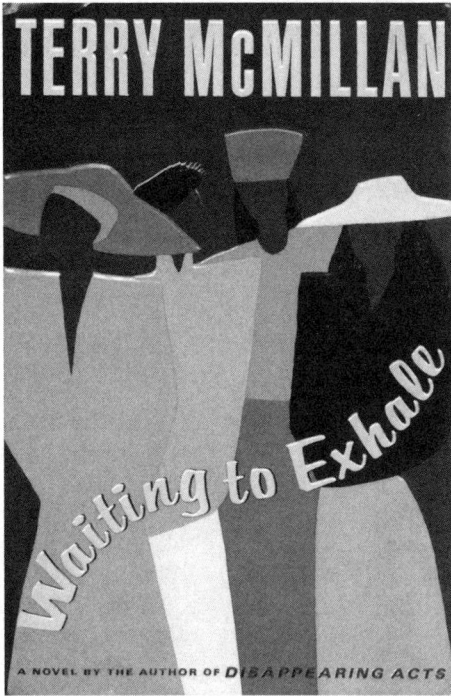

FIGURE 1.3 Cover for Terry McMillan's novel *Waiting to Exhale*. Viking hard cover edition, 1992. Cover image, *Ensemble*, by Synthia Saint James.

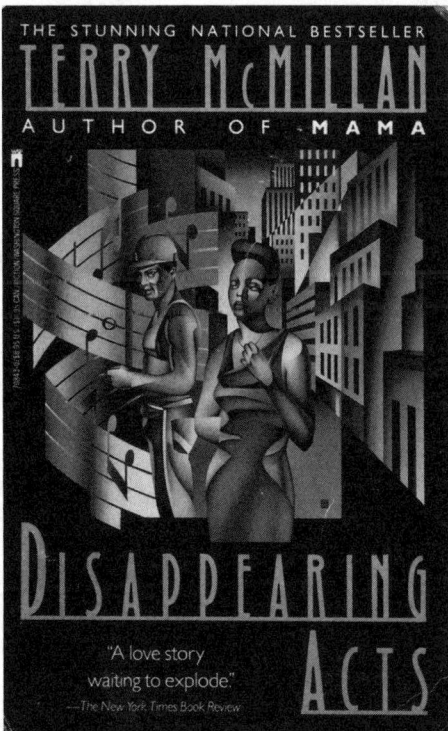

FIGURE 1.4 Cover for Terry McMillan's novel *Disappearing Acts*, 1991.

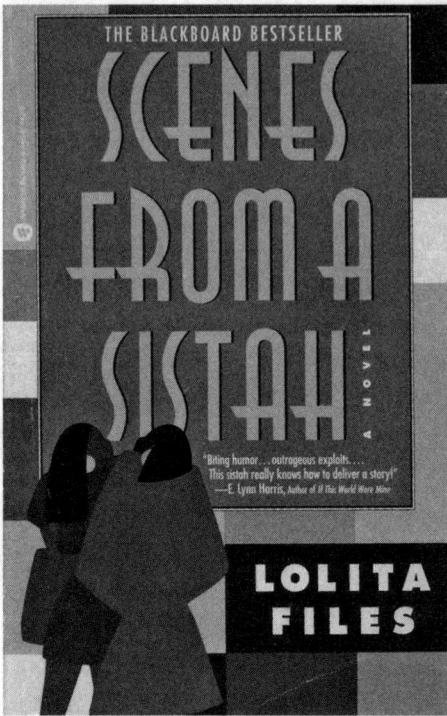

FIGURE 1.5 Cover for Lolita Files's novel *Scenes from a Sistah*, 1998.

of literary credibility (see figure 1.6). Famous for her 1997 Kwanzaa stamp, children's books, and commercially successful art, Saint James also encodes a tinge of commercial viability as well as racial solidarity, marshaled by Kwanzaa's cultural nationalism, to McMillan's work. So while the bright covers, or paratexts, appeared fresh and modern, they simultaneously conveyed nostalgia for cultural rituals and traditions celebrating racial unity and cooperation.

Although commercial, Saint James's artistic rendering of faceless Black women contrasting dramatic and coruscating attire seem to be influenced by, or in conversation with, the color-blocking techniques in Jacob Lawrence's 1941 modernist *Migration Series*, in which austere African American faces juxtapose blithesome apparel, availing Saint James, and by relation McMillan, an important link to critically acclaimed and "serious" visual artists in the popular imaginary (see figure 1.7). The polysemous facade shrouding McMillan's prose grants it a capacious movement that allows her to straddle "literary" and "popular" categories yet again. These kaleidoscopic cultural and aesthetic valences also illuminate the ways in which Black women's private lives and depictions of romance and courtship are rendered as benign

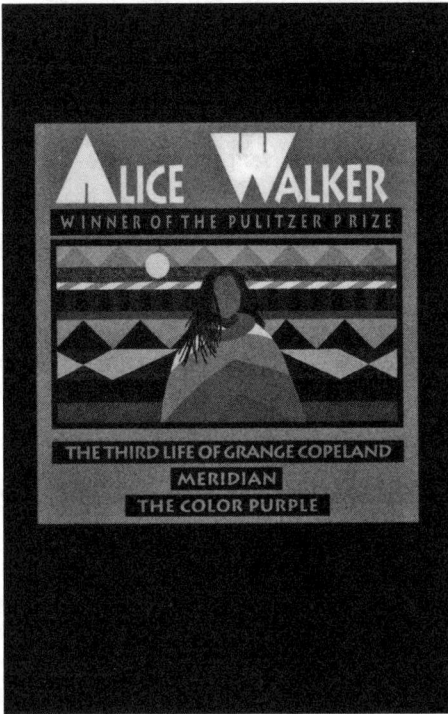

FIGURE I.6 Cover for Alice Walker's novels *The Third Life of Grange Copeland/Meridian/The Color Purple*, 1990.

FIGURE I.7 Jacob Lawrence, *And the Migrants Kept Coming*. 1940–41. Panel 60 from the *Migration Series* by Jacob Lawrence. © 2018 The Jacob and Gwendolyn Knight Lawrence Foundation, Seattle/Artists Rights Society (ARS), New York. Digital image © The Museum of Modern Art/Licensed by SCALA/Art Resource, NY.

and authoritative as well as highly politicized and apolitical. Moreover, Lawrence's *Migration Series*, specifically, speaks not just to the blustering migration I witnessed on the train every morning but also to the new and old migratory circuits of family formation amid mounting class status and movement into cosmopolitan urban cities and predominantly white suburbs.

With its bold and robust use of color and geometric figures, Synthia Saint James's iconic 1992 cover art for *Waiting to Exhale* asserts exuberance and optimism about Black female characters creating family among themselves, undermining Black bridal pathos as they move across geographic and economic spaces, while the book title offers anticipation about the women fulfilling a fairy-tale goal of marriage and children. It is a strategic print and visual grammar of ambivalence that attracts readers to McMillan's work. Authors are not always able to make the final decision about their cover art, but McMillan confirms that she had Saint James's print (*Ensemble*) on her bedroom wall and insisted that it be used as the cover image for *Waiting to Exhale*.[60] The intense hues in *Ensemble* rouse ebullience as the hollow faces encourage readers to insert their faces into the silhouettes, signifying a visual choreography of cultural unison among author, characters, and readers. The eye-catching cover art is also cleverly and intimately tied to the late twentieth-century cultural scene, which confirms McMillan's racial belonging as it expands her readership. The vibrant lime green, dazzling crimson, and electric chartreuse mirror an energetic and lively color-blocking approach and sartorial aesthetic expressed in Black American fashion designer Carl Jones's 1989 clothing brand Cross Colours, as well as Ebony Fashion Fair's highly pigmented makeup and clothing designs.

The cover art encourages a relationship among author, characters, and readers and across class lines, and the book titles and nom de plumes punctuate individualism and racial kinship, including Terry McMillan's *Mama*; Julia A. Boyd's *In the Company of My Sisters: Black Women and Self-Esteem* (1993); Bebe Moore Campbell's *Brothers and Sisters* (1994); Connie Briscoe's *Sisters and Lovers* (1994); Lolita Files's *Scenes from a Sistah* (1997); and the pseudonym Sister Souljah. The use of *mama* (rather than *mother*) and the repetition of *sister* and *sista* reveal an expanding cultural desire for sisterhood, family, and fictive kin that jettisons the traditional configurations of family that the state and Black political nostalgia venerated. They substantiate the assertion that Black romance "does not deny collective identity yet allows black people to see themselves as individuals."[61]

As *The Cosby Show* did during its heyday, McMillan installs work by African American visual artists such as Frank Frazier, Joe Overstreet, and

Harlem Renaissance painter Charles Aston in her characters' homes, underscoring the critical importance of visual culture to the readers and author. The installation of art on both the exterior and the interior of these texts implies that McMillan is establishing herself as an artist rather than a sociologist, thwarting the timeworn conflation of Black fiction with sociology. The cover art as well as the intertextual references to Black visual artists allows readers a form of self-making or a mode of constructing their identity across class divisions and through racialized family formation. Scholars note that economically privileged Black women and men use Black visual art to fashion and articulate their racial identity, history, pride, and unity.[62] Unlike the late twentieth-century upper-middle-class African American women and men who began collecting prints by Black artists, such as the expensive installations on Savannah's wall in *Waiting to Exhale*, working-class and middle-class readers could consume art and reconstruct their identities through the more affordable and portable popular fiction cover art and book jackets.

Still, McMillan's growing cultural imprint did not inspire and edify everyone. In 1990, Leonard Welch, the father of her son, launched a $4.75 million defamation case against her, Penguin USA, and Simon and Schuster, which eventually made its way to the New York Supreme Court. In his twenty-seven-page complaint, Welch alleges that he is identifiable as the main character, Franklin Swift. Novelist Marita Golden called his case an "intolerance of the imagination," fearing that if Welch won, it would effectively silence fiction writers.[63] Welch lost his suit, but it had specific implications for Black women writers and readers. Fiction had become an important late twentieth-century space for Black women to negotiate their subjectivity as the politicization of their private lives intensified, but it also had a long historical trajectory. About nineteenth-century literary history, Hazel Carby explains that Black women authors regarded the novel as essential to the cultural and political project of Black liberation.[64] Thus, Welch's case jeopardizes all writers but also threatens to obliterate one of the few remaining available spaces for Black women writers and readers to participate in and control the narratives about political discourses connected to their lived experience.

McMillan's literary credibility and the visibility of Black women's private lives continues to mutate as McMillan gains more visibility in the orbit of mainstream media. She was feted by the media and "would soon be considered 'popular' rather than literary, and as such, unworthy of scholarly criticism," but McMillan was faced with other kinds of criticism.[65] Politicians and cultural critics sparked contentious debates or "culture wars," which prompted responses to Black cultural production and its representation of intimacy and family. Because of her growing prominence and visibility, McMillan's work was eventually included in these debates, subjected to harsher gendered and racialized critiques, and seemingly made to be a blanket privatized solution that supplants political policy. In 1993, an issue of the *Middle-Atlantic Writers Association Review* included "Images of Black Males in Terry McMillan's *Waiting to Exhale*" but had no colloquia interrogating depictions of Black women in work by male writers in this way.[66] In reference to *Waiting to Exhale* and its film adaptation, *Ebony* magazine's April 1996 issue included a symposium titled "Exhaling and Inhaling: Was the Movie Fair to Black Men and Black Women?" though the magazine had no forums in which they painstakingly scrutinized the depictions of Black women in male-authored texts in the same way.[67]

The criticism directed toward McMillan's work eerily reprises the gendered criticism Walker and many other Black female writers in the previous era faced and also reinvigorates the political burden placed on Black fiction and relationships absent state assistance.[68] This pattern of recurring critiques and the novel's failure to concede to the typical happily-ever-after ending also indicate that there are grave and far-reaching unresolved sex, gender, and race conflicts that have carried over from the Black Power era to the post–Black Power era. These unflagging debates continue to haunt Black cultural cosmologies and are symptomatic of a complex intersectional discord.

I read McMillan's migration from the "literary" to the "popular," with her novels safely tucked under an implicit "apolitical" and "popular" categorization, as a way for her work to mitigate some, though not all, of the "highbrow" attention and disparagement directed toward work by Morrison, Walker, and others. Put another way, the intensified politicization of Black intimacy and marriage in the post–Black Power era inspired McMillan to migrate toward a more supposedly apolitical genre that might hopefully circumvent the celebrated feminist "personal is political" adage. Whereas early mainstream feminists' proclamation of the "personal is political" was, at least in theory, meant to be liberatory by claiming the private sphere as a legitimate realm of political analysis and resistance, Black women were caught in the double bind of a private sphere that had been politicized for deleterious agendas. The reconfiguration of one's intimate relations as a form of political resistance confronts Black women less as an opportunity than as a *demand*—a demand for which they are all-too-often seen as inadequate in some way.

Some critics tend to think of McMillan as a writer from the "wrong side of the tracks" and she has confessed to feeling snubbed by esteemed authors, but she was instrumental in the development of *Breaking Ice: An Anthology of Contemporary African American Fiction* (1990), which was published by Penguin Books and included a preface by John Edgar Wideman.[69] As the editor of *Breaking Ice*, McMillan included fiction by writers such as Alice Walker, Gloria Naylor, Rita Dove, and Ntozake Shange. Just two years later, McMillan was the cover story for the literary magazine *Poets and Writers*. The *New York Times* frequently reviews her work and she was successful in persuading her colleagues to give Charles Johnson's 1990 novel *Middle Passage* the National Book Award.[70] Her short story, "Quilting on the Rebound," is nestled between work by Gloria Naylor and Rita Dove in the first edition of the *Norton Anthology of African American Literature* (1997), further establishing her place within an esteemed and well-respected coterie of poets and fiction writers. The *Norton* includes headnotes that describe McMillan as the "apotheosis of the renaissance in writing by African American women" and maintain that she is a "hilarious" writer whose work "in no way ignores life's difficulties."[71] The headnotes also acknowledge that McMillan has "become something of a celebrity."[72]

Astonishingly, *Norton*'s editors omit McMillan's short story in the subsequent 2004 and 2014 editions. Editors change and reshape anthologies over time, so this omission is not the only revision in the text. The editors added five new contemporary authors and moved prose and poetry by June Jordan and Audre Lorde to a different section in the second edition. The second edition editors write that "limitations of space and prohibitions on copyright" hindered the inclusion of "several authors whose texts are important to the canon and whose level of excellence warrants exclusion," so the cost of McMillan's text could have been prohibitive.[73]

Nevertheless, for scholars and students who are not privy to these various shifts and the behind-the-scenes editorial decisions about what to include in the *Norton*, it may look, at least on the surface, as though McMillan's disappearing act is precipitated by a rising celebrity status that ultimately becomes too gauche for gatekeeepers. Taking notice of her "ornate gold-plated earrings" and "stylish clothes" in their profile entitled "McMillan's Millions," the *New York Times* declared that McMillan "might just be as far as you can get from the traditional image of tweedy novelist."[74] McMillan's fame grew as prominent scholars complained that the Western canon and literary studies were becoming too lax in their scope. The *Norton Anthology of African American Literature* has continued to publish many of the writers that are included in *Breaking Ice*, but "Quilting on the Rebound" was eventually excised from the *Norton*'s second and third editions, summarily terminating what some viewed as McMillan's honeymoon with "high-brow" literary communities.

As such, my examination of McMillan's literary history and migration galvanizes *Veil and Vow*'s migratory ellipsis, bypassing debates about whether McMillan or her contemporaries should or should not be included in "the canon." Like other scholars of African American popular fiction, this project's cartography goes beyond using canonical standards to appraise the "aesthetic standards or merit" of these texts.[75] "The boundaries between conventions of popular and serious black literature have always been permeable"; there is little evidence that these authors aspire to be included in "the canon," and academia's canonization has been, at times, capricious.[76] African American literature, feminist texts, and speculative fiction writers such as Octavia Butler are just a few examples of its mercurial temper. Wary of these faulty taxonomies, Toni Morrison writes with some jest that, "First novels shouldn't be successes—they are supposed to be read by a few. They are not supposed to be profitable—they must be limited. If a first novel 'makes it,' then there is some suspicion about its quality."[77] Morrison's qualms and McMillan's exclusion and (perhaps contested) divorce from the *Norton Anthology* summon a need for manifold canons and invigorate arguments concerning the faulty metrics used to construct anthologies and determine what constitutes a canonical text.[78]

These debates resemble the ways in which McMillan's work is often considered formulaic; popular; and steeped in pathos, lived experience, and sentimental tropes—much like Harriet Jacobs's slave narrative—as well as how we remain wedded to traditional conceptualizations of "the canon" rather than exploring multiple, voluminous canons. Much like the rhythm-and-blues songs interspersed in her novels, McMillan's work is assailed for its sentimentality but also astutely taps into and theorizes lived experience. Through a well-placed vamp or elliptical clause, the sonic and print narratives render the nascent thoughts and insight held by scores of readers and listeners. The fertile capitalist and sociopolitical terrain notwithstanding, McMillan's skillful aesthetic innovation hews its own canonical and theoretical space.

McMillan's interstitial work, much like her Black female protagonists celebrating and critiquing marriage, proves unruly as it challenges and upholds diverse methods of categorization and theorization. McMillan adamantly rejects the "chick-lit" label for her novels, and although McMillan is housed in the romance section of many brick-and-mortar bookstores, dyed-in-the-wool romance readers and writers are ambivalent about her inclusion.[79] McMillan's work aligns with a "post-Moynihan blues," or what

Imani Perry sketches as cultural engagement with Moynihan's specious construct of Black family.[80] While, Mark Anthony Neal locates a "post-soul aesthetic" in McMillan's *Waiting to Exhale*.[81] Neal developed this term, first used by Nelson George, to explore the ways in which contemporary Black popular culture is "consumed with contemporary existential concerns," relies on a "proliferation of black 'meta-identities,' . . . while reanimating 'pre-modern' (African?) concepts of blackness."[82] As I have explained, McMillan's work shifts throughout her career, but much of her writing engages facets of the post-soul aesthetic.

Inspired by McMillan's ambit, I intertwine an examination of print, sonic, and visual culture with political and literary debates in *Veil and Vow*. My interrogation is not monogamously wedded to one disciplinary field; it stages a polygamous community of scholars across varied disciplines as theoretical interlocutors who provide the structural apparatus for the project. This multilingual critical method unearths the ways in which canon formation is messy and volatile and deciphers how McMillan's initial hovering on the precipice of the "literary" and the "popular" helped her take advantage of unresolved epistemological debates about African American literature, what constitutes "the canon," and what stories about Black women's intimate lives would or would not "fit" in academia and established genre categories.

Veil and Vow

I frame each chapter with music lyrics and sonic texts, which collectively operate as *Veil and Vow*'s soundtrack or score. I theorize this coupling as a rhapsodic sonic/print call and response in order to "articulate the imaginative possibilities for blackness . . . and black politics" and to capture the diverse but percussive desires reverberating in African American communities.[83] In order to understand the torque and camber of these helical desires across time and space, I critically examine the "interdisciplinary cultural affiliations that entangle distinct networks and expand the discursive and material reach" of Black cultural production.[84] Using Anita Baker's 1990 rhythm-and-blues song "Fairy Tales" as the sonic interloper, chapter 1 illuminates the ways in which Terry McMillan's novels are caught between doubting and desiring "fairy-tale" notions of romance in order to defy politically entrenched myths about dysfunctional African American families and the "breakdown of the family."

In chapter 2, lyrics by the politically conscious hip-hop group Public Enemy set the tempo for a chorus of novels by Sister Souljah, Omar Tyree, and Eric

Jerome Dickey, which feature tropes of hypergamy or "marrying up." I read this three-part harmony of fictional texts alongside and against the Violent Crime Control and Law Enforcement Act of 1994, which increased funding for prisons and police officers, subsequently intensifying interest in tragic images of disenfranchised African American men in fiction and film. I disentangle how these late twentieth-century representations highlight state violence but also forge a new system of patriarchy that enforces additional modes of policing women. By exploiting the political landscape, these texts compellingly disparage aspirational female protagonists and celebrate disenfranchised male characters in order to champion a model of patriarchal power that upholds male authority but has excised the obligatory role of monetary support.

I knit together two songs, Michael Jackson's 1991 up-tempo pop hit "Black or White" and Me'Shell NdegèOcello's 1993 wounding ballad "Soul on Ice" for chapter 3's countermelody. Read in the shadow of the watershed 1967 *Loving v. Virginia* Supreme Court decision ending the ban on interracial marriage, this chapter turns to the portrait of "marrying out" by examining the contours of Black and white interracial courtship. I maintain that Sandra Kitt's *The Color of Love* (1995) and Eric Jerome Dickey's *Milk in My Coffee* (1998) metaphorically yoke the political insistence that African American people must "support black business" to the directive for African American women and men to "marry black" spouses. As national markets consolidate, the declining practicality of "buying black" resuscitates and amplifies African American intraracial matrimony as a form of political liberation. I elucidate how the resurgent need for heteropatriarchal figures causes African American female protagonists to endure more hurdles in their interracial romance than do African American male protagonists. I also uncover how Black and white interracial romance is subtly proffered as an antidote to racial inequality, while African American intraracial intimacy is saddled with racial politics and unable to bear the luxury of love. Chapter 4 is a deliberate counternarrative to the preceding chapters and critical rupture to representations of traditional family as an elixir for systemic inequality. In this chapter, I use Sweet Honey in the Rock's 1983 song "Testimony" as the armature as I weave together Sapphire's *Push* (1996), Louis Farrakhan's *Torchlight for America* (1993), the 1996 DOMA, and the 1996 PRWORA to unmask and deromanticize the onerous political burden placed on matrimony. This chapter further underscores the fraying edges of romance tropes by illustrating the ways in which touting marriage and heteropatriarchal family as a political responsibility enables violence and abuse.

The penultimate chapter, "Viewer, I Married Him," riffs on Charlotte Brontë's iconic "Reader, I married him" finale in *Jane Eyre* (1847). In this chapter, I bring together my examination of print, sonic, and visual culture to analyze Malcolm D. Lee's 1999 film *The Best Man*; Gina Prince-Bythewood's 2000 film *Love & Basketball*; and corresponding soundtracks, screenplays, and publicity. I turn my attention to film in this chapter because the relationship between film and fiction began intensifying in the late twentieth century. The expanding readership for Black popular romance precipitated the release of several romantic comedies and dramadies with predominantly Black cast members. The characterization of *The Best Man*'s eponymous character as a popular writer is emblematic of the burgeoning relationship between fiction and film.

Visual culture is essential to understanding Black creative expression and *The Best Man* and *Love & Basketball* are some of the most important texts in the African American cultural canon. As my chapter title suggests, I am interested in how the characters in both films negotiate coupling and arrive at matrimony. I unearth the ways in which the films creatively refashion genre conventions as well as how they encode progressive and pernicious messages about the process, shape, and formation of African American love and marriage. *Veil and Vow*'s migratory ambit ends with a Benediction that returns to Terry McMillan and moves forward with a whistle-stop exploration of recent visual, sonic, and print culture. Threaded together, these chapters emphasize the urgency in critically examining representations of courtship and marriage in cultural production, positing that marriage still matters for African American communities.

CHAPTER ONE

Marrying the Movement

Who it is that brings this woman to this man?

This chapter uses "movement" as an interpretive anchor to critically examine the intermittent movement between romanticizing and deromanticizing marriage as well as to parse Black women's fidelity to "the movement," a colloquial term for the civil rights movement and a metonym for Black political nostalgia and activism. Extending this anchor, characters in *Waiting to Exhale* belong to Black Women on the Move, "a support group" for women "willing to . . . do *something* for black folks."[1] This doing "something," McMillan's titular gerund, and the nomadic women on the train are echoes of this movement, and these coiling, peripatetic emblems outline this chapter's course.

The film adaptations of *Disappearing Acts* and *Waiting to Exhale* experienced varying degrees of commercial success, but I examine the original print iterations because they not only are underexplored but are two of the few popular novels that expose the deep tension between romanticizing and deromanticizing heteropatriarchal marriage and the natural and unnatural ways it is coerced. The rejection of the typical fairy-tale marriage finale in *Disappearing Acts* connotes Black women's ambivalence about marriage and reflects the novel's broader political terrain but also highlights a leitmotif of unrequited love between conflicting political ideologies in the domestic sphere. In contrast, *Waiting to Exhale* remembers and deploys a fairy-tale neoliberal version of the civil rights movement that facilitates a relatively conventional denouement. It is an ending that nearly suffocates the Black female characters under the weight of marriage and in the burdensome way it is deployed as a form of political activism and patriarchal vigor.

The themes and motifs in McMillan's work complement a cultural landscape of sonic texts. This link has enabled her novels to have a unique cultural elasticity and broaden her wider readership as well as establish a critical paradigm for her work. Because of its cultural import, music is integral to understanding the rich polyphonic textures of African American fiction.[2] For people of African descent, "music functions as a method of rebellion, revolution, and future visions that disrupt and challenge the manufactured differences used to dismiss, detain, and destroy communities."[3] Daphne Brooks urges readers to consider how the contemporary sonic backdrop informs McMillan's work specifically, as her novels include numerous intertextual references to rhythm-and-blues songs and soul music.[4] Using these premises as points of departure, I structure my analysis of McMillan's work on an exchange between sonic and print culture.

McMillan's texts insist on a multilingual analytical framework, and contemporary rhythm-and-blues singer Anita Baker is a valuable sonic interlocutor and collaborator. In 1990, one year after McMillan published *Disappearing Acts* and two years before she published *Waiting to Exhale*, Anita Baker released *Compositions*, her third platinum-selling album. In "Fairy Tales," her third single from the project, Baker's narrator adeptly scrutinizes the fables her mother read to her as a child, ones in which the stories always concluded with "happy endings."[5] In the fairy-tale "paradise" the narrator envisions, a man would "ride up on his horse" and take her away, a familiar trope repeated in *Cinderella, Rapunzel*, and *Mufaro's Beautiful Daughters*, among other fairy tales highlighting marriage.[6] Daphne Brooks insists that "just as in the case with Terry McMillan's fiction, cultural critics have largely overlooked contemporary rhythm and blues — and particularly Black women's rhythm and blues — in favor of a critical privileging of other forms," such as hip-hop music, which is assumed as "the genre most worthy of cultural critique and political actualization."[7] "Black women's popular desire is thus depoliticized and disregarded," according to Brooks, "for its reflections on domestic and socioeconomic politics and sexual fulfillment."[8]

Black women's popular desires merit cultural critique, and I explore what it means to think about Baker's "Fairy Tales" as a soundtrack for this chapter because the song echoes the narrative torque between romanticizing and deromanticizing marriage with a reverberating movement between the natural and the supernatural. By virtue of their name, fairy tales necessitate a supernatural or divine manifestation, such as a fairy godmother, for their resolution, yet they also seem to be natural in that their goals are common and routinely desired. They are portrayed as "naturally occurring" as universally accessible formations in which women and men organically fall into and fit their (conventional) roles in the romance. "A fairy tale has no toleration for ambiguities. It is abrupt, immediate and often brutal — more tip of the blade than bonny glen."[9] As the guiding sonic text, Baker's song compels an exploration of McMillan's work that interrogates the brutal simplicity and supernatural intervention or "magic potion" in these myths, as noted in the second half of the song.

I read Baker's "magic potion" as the alchemy of a supernatural meritocracy, cohering with the etymology of *merit* as "spiritual credit" and "divine pity," and underscoring the magic required for meritocracy to work.[10] In theorizing McMillan's romanticized and deromanticized tales, the alchemy of meritocracy works alongside a marriageocracy that manifests as the allegorical poison apple, which the song's narrator consumes in the third verse. The poison apple and magic potion bookend the contours of marriageocracy, or the idea that the preservation of marriage merely requires hard work. Like marriageocracy, the magic potion and poison apple both have appealing and dangerous facets, which rely on an alluring exceptionalism when the merit yields success and an unrelenting reproach when it fails to produce a favorable outcome.

These fantastical elements in Baker's "Fairy Tales" expose the unsustainability of these idealistic, moralizing myths and represent the prevaricating desire for marriage in McMillan's work. Baker's "Fairy Tales" and McMillan's novels are poignant in the way that they remix and reprise preceding sonic texts such as Womack and Womack's 1984 hit song "Baby I'm Scared of You," where Linda Womack repeatedly insists that she does not "believe in magic" and does not desire a man "pulling rabbits out of his hat."[11] Recapitulating fairy-tale imagery, she likens herself to "little red riding hood" and her lover as "the fox," while Cecil Womack responds with an offer to "pull flowers" out of his hat and do a "disappearing act."[12] Their call and response pattern highlights the ambivalent desire for magic potions and fairy tales. Collectively, all of these texts speak to the pattern of "placing people of color into western fairy tale frameworks," while unmasking the "erasures that must take place to construct fantasy."[13] I critically examine *Disappearing Acts*, *Waiting to Exhale*, and corresponding sonic texts in order to extrapolate what these erasures make possible and foreclose, unveiling the ways in which these powerful fairy tales are not universally accessible but crescendo into recurring natural and unnatural conflicts for African American female characters.

Unrequited Love and Politics

In *Disappearing Acts*, I locate the rejection of the typical fairy-tale ending and the persistence of Black women's slippery equivocation within a depiction of unrequited political visions. Taking the romance trope of unrequited love depicted in novels such as Edith Wharton's *The House of Mirth* (1905) or Emily Brontë's *Wuthering Heights* (1907), McMillan adapts and transforms it into a trope of unrequited political ideologies that stall the courtship between the principal characters, Franklin Swift and Zora Banks. Their discordant visions and characterizations erect a false dichotomy between warring ideas of gender and race oppression as well as personal responsibility and structural oppression. The unique form of the novel buttresses this bifurcated conflict. Unlike most romance novels, *Disappearing Acts* grants Zora and Franklin with first-person narrated chapters—and the split is nearly equal. Zora is allotted eighteen chapters, and Franklin is allotted eighteen chapters. This antiphonal or call and response narrative arrangement chronicles their harmony and atonal clamor. The novel's structure offers a facade of unmediated reflection but also enunciates the isolation of the characters and the schism in their political unity. Through the depiction of failed shared beliefs, McMillan taps into a deep historical legacy outlining the necessity of Black partnerships for the project of Black liberation. Black intraracial marriage has long been a part of the larger project of nineteenth-century racial uplift, championing the economic security and moral progress available through marriage as a key method of resisting white racism.[14] For African American women and men, wildly disparate political visions for liberation could impede collective racial progress and amount to a relationship in which one partner discounts the other's humanity, creating a deep rift.

By critically examining the political tenor of *Disappearing Acts*, I diverge from claims asserting that McMillan's novels are steeped in apolitical frivolity. Writers and critics have disparaged McMillan's fiction for speaking in "the practiced tongue of white mainstream literature."[15] Critics challenged writers to create enclosed Black worlds that decentered the white gaze but also urged them to explore the hazards of racism in their novels. McMillan and her literary descendants were argued to be "dangerously frivolous because they do not grapple with racial tensions the way African American literature had in the past."[16] McMillan's characters participate in organizations such as Black Women on the Move, but there are other, less explicit textual references to political engagement. The curt assessments of McMillan's work elide nineteenth-century racial uplift methods of using marriage as a form of racial progress, depoliticize Black intimacy, and maintain hard divisions between racial and sexual politics. Of nineteenth-century novels, Claudia Tate contends that formulaic and sentimental female-authored novels granted the "recently emancipated" a space to explore political autonomy at a time when African American civil rights "were constitutionally sanctioned but socially prohibited."[17] Other scholars assert that twentieth-century African American fiction reveals and negotiates dominant society's conception of the home as the locus and origin of African American political problems.[18] As such,

Disappearing Acts warrants a more complex and assiduous analysis that takes serious the unyielding disruption of romance with political strife.

Zora is depicted as a single, middle-class, college-educated junior high school teacher with aspirations of being a professional singer. She is not tethered to one particular musical genre, but McMillan's characterization of Zora as a singer mirrors many contemporary Black women writers, who used the blueswoman as "a symbol of female creativity and autonomy."[19] The novel conveys Zora's creative aspirations and class status through her New York City apartment, with its high ceilings and dedicated spare room for her piano. Franklin appears to be a mismatch for Zora. He has not finished high school, and his small rented room includes two mattresses on the floor and mouse feces atop a pile of sawdust. But Zora is quickly smitten by and sexually attracted to Franklin because he embodies *masculine veneer*, a common cultural trope of Black heterosexual male characters depicted as working class, racially oppressed, and possessing conservative sex and gender politics, but protected by a hermetic seal of striking good looks, a strong work ethic, and political consciousness.

Franklin's veneer forms early in the novel, when he describes himself as a "six-foot-four jet-black handsome" construction worker who exercises at the gym three days a week.[20] Zora also characterizes him in the most attractive terms. She describes his eyes as "black marbles set in almonds. . . . His hair was jet black and wavy. That nose was strong and regal, and beneath it was a thick mustache. His cheeks looked chiseled; his lips succulent. And those shoulders. They were as wide as any linebacker's. His thighs were tight, and his legs went on forever. . . . His arms were the color of black grapes."[21] Typically, the hero in romance novels is "powerful in key ways upheld as masculine ideals within patriarchy: He's tall, big, strong, capable or masterful in various ways, sexually skilled, successful, and often downright dominant."[22] The early placement of such a superfluous and effusive portrait of Franklin falls squarely within the romance tradition.

Coupled with Franklin's striking good looks, Zora admits to being impressed with Franklin's familiarity with her namesake, Zora Neale Hurston. McMillan's Zora puts Hurston's novel *Their Eyes Were Watching God* next to a photograph of her dead mother, hinting that Hurston, as literary foremother, will haunt McMillan's story. Hurston confesses that "when a man keeps beating me to the draw mentally, he begins to get glamorous," and McMillan's Zora feels similarly about Franklin.[23] Franklin is often the winner when he and Zora play Scrabble, and he reads work by James Baldwin; at one point, Zora thinks to herself, "How ironic. He reads more than I do," adding to his veneer.[24] Franklin is, by all accounts, an everyman, or a seemingly perfect amalgamation. He is a skilled manual laborer who is both well-read and street smart. His name affirms his "frank" and plainspoken disposition and works to reject the bourgeois Black masculinity erroneously linked to homosexuality and reputed down-low Black men in the late twentieth century. These so-called complementary characteristics mean to portend a successful relationship and an eventual marriage.

Franklin is sheathed in masculine veneer, while the female characters negotiate Black bridal pathos, or the widespread presumption that Black women desperately covet heteropatriarchal marriage, and makes visible the latent fear and anxiety that "unbridled" Black women want nothing to do with marriage. In the first italicized page of Franklin's first-person narrative, he exclaims that he is "tired of women. Black women in particular," alleging that women begin "hearing wedding bells" and "start thinking about babies" after intercourse, auguring Zora's pregnancy and desire for marriage.[25] Yet when he accuses Pam, his estranged wife, of preparing to marry another man and she denies it, he promptly disparages her for having sex without the protection of marriage. It is a tautological premise that the female characters cannot win, and it foreshadows the racialized gender conflict that emerges in the narrative.

Unlike most romance novels, race and gender oppression are one of the first narrative conflicts to surface in Disappearing Acts, mobilizing fissures in Franklin's and Zora's political imagination. When Zora attempts to assert familiarity with the racism that Franklin experiences, he bluntly rejects her empathy, saying, "You couldn't possibly understand, baby. . . . Because you ain't a black man."[26] Franklin's response forecloses a shared understanding and conflates racism with Black heterosexual manhood, typifying the kind of treatment of race and gender that Gloria T. Hull's All the Women Are White, All the Blacks Are Men, but Some of Us Are Brave: Black Women's Studies (1982) denounced. Published a year before the setting of Disappearing Acts, Hull's edited collection and titular criticism excoriate the ways in which dominant rhetoric about race and gender routinizes the invisibility of Black women's race, gender, and sexual oppression, dissolving it under their educational and economic achievements.

In chapter 7 of Disappearing Acts, Franklin's behavior continues in its circumscribed construction of identity. Using a clichéd image of racial discrimination, the novel depicts him unsuccessfully attempting to hail a cab. After three failed tries, Franklins finally asks Zora to do it, and she is successful. As soon as he enters the taxi and slams the door, Franklin unleashes a tirade that makes the cab ride tense, shouting, "If you big and black in America, that's two strikes against you—did you know that, Zora? They think all black men is killers and robbers and that we gon' cut their throats, then take all their fuckin' money. Ain't that right, sir?"[27] The nervous cab driver silently continues to drive, but Franklin is not finished with his protest; he sees a No Smoking sign in the cab and promptly begins smoking a cigarette to further antagonize the driver.

These scenes put several unrequited matters in motion. Both vignettes narrowly map racial oppression onto heterosexual Black masculinity, rehearsing the race and gender hierarchies of the previous era that I outline in the invocation. By reversing the fairy-tale image of male suitor commandeering the chariot for his damsel in distress and instead putting Franklin in the vulnerable "feminized" position, the scene proffers an ominous clue to the novel's unrequited racialized gender politics. In this way, the novel pronounces the necessity of nuanced understandings of Black female subjectivity that are not smothered by Moynihan's report, mainstream political and cultural polemics, and idealistic fairy-tale renderings. As Gloria Naylor maintains, "Black women have rightfully not depicted themselves as frail damsels given to fainting spells. . . . Our history decreed that if we tried to pull something like a fainting spell, our heads would hit the floor."[28]

Already negotiating her elevated socioeconomic capital against Franklin's disenfranchisement, Zora's chariot-hailing predicament forces her into another position of power. Because of the ways Black women are characterized as "emasculating," it is a position she cannot afford to occupy. These overwrought negotiations are not new ones, though; the state's antidote to slavery's devastation of Black families hinged on patriarchal family, though the "problem of black women's labor made apparent the gender non-conformity of the black community."[29] It is a cyclical tormenting nexus of contradictions that both McMillan's Zora Banks and Janie, Hurston's protagonist from her 1937 novel *Their Eyes Were Watching God*, must confront.

In *Their Eyes Were Watching God*, that nexus presents itself through violence, with Janie as a haunting nineteenth-century silhouette hovering in the plot. Toward the end of Hurston's novel, Janie is financially comfortable, but her handsome beau, Vergible "Tea Cake" Woods, is a less economically stable, working-class man. Their monetary imbalance parallels Franklin and Zora's disparity as Tea Cake's physical attack of Janie echoes the violence Zora faces at the hands of Franklin. These acts of violence against Zora and Janie function as punishment for their transgressive gender norms, but Tea Cake's violence is not mollified in the way that Franklin's assault is in *Disappearing Acts*. Though McMillan carefully isolates and highlights Franklin's experiences of racism, the novel announces Zora's rape quickly and without spectacle, profanity, or shouting. After arriving home late one night, Franklin demands sex from Zora, and she refuses. Zora says, "Oh, so you're going to rape me, is that it?" Franklin's calm response to her is simply, "I guess so," illustrating the ways in which the novel disavows the "typical" romance or fairy-tale contrivance of the suitor protecting the female protagonist from harm.[30] McMillan's unusual decision to include a depiction of rape frustrates the novel's status as "romance" and asserts the importance of discourse about Black women's gendered violence and the high rates of rape and sexual assault they face. Zora and Franklin's hollow exchange during her rape scene, however, signals society's apathetic response to Black women's rape and sexual assault, while the matter-of-fact tone frames it as quotidian.

The austere tone of Zora's rape scene and Franklin's response reveals the ways in which the novel registers racialized gender violence against Black women as routine in courtship, deromanticizing the portrait of marriage. Zora's rape scene comes well after several depictions of Franklin experiencing racism, and a mere question and answer precedes her assault; it is not marked by an explosive display of anger, as is Franklin's cab scene. McMillan's pithy syntax corroborates the lack of outrage about the rape and sexual assault of Black women, specifically crimes committed by husbands, partners, and lovers. As depicted throughout *Disappearing Acts*, these offenses are invisible and all but "disappear" because the criminals are relatives or lovers. In its review of *Disappearing Acts*, the *New York Times* describes Franklin as a "compelling character" who is vexed "by his dealings with the white construction world," but it does not mention Franklin's rape of Zora.[31]

Franklin's destitution and racial victimization magnify his privileged-victim status and also literally and figuratively suffocate Zora's ability to voice her concerns and resist Franklin's assault, as she says, "I didn't say a word. I just lay there, numb as a rag doll."[32] Zora's rebuttal is paradigmatic of what historian Darlene Clark Hine calls the "culture of dissemblance," or a comportment that enables a facade of sincerity but veils Black women's interiority from those in power.[33] The self-imposed silencing allows Black women to reserve a "psychic space" in which they can breathe and live.[34] Franklin's poverty and fruitless job search constantly occupy the privileged spotlight of oppression, magnifying Zora's silence. He is incapable of paying for the meals on their dates; his wife, whom he cannot afford to divorce, lives in low-income housing; and rodent scat litters his studio apartment. When he enters Zora's spacious Brooklyn apartment, he must repeatedly confront her middle-class status.

Zora's employment as a teacher and desire for a singing career characterize her as purportedly having an excess of possible career and economic opportunities, signaling the myth of Black women impervious to racism, sexism, and capitalism. Although the novel details the racism he faces in his job search, Zora's job as a teacher in New York City is a veritable utopia, with no psychic space for anecdotes about a sexist boss or racist coworker. She is presumably an emblem of a fairy-tale neoliberal, meritocratic society but of course is missing the last puzzle piece—a husband. Class conflict is a familiar hurdle in romance novels, but in *Disappearing Acts*, it intensifies the unrequited political ideologies by linking class to race, gender privilege, and victimization in a way that recalls the previous era's debates about race and gender hierarchy.

The text further punctuates Franklin's inculpability through Zora and Franklin's professed love for each other before and after her rape, the minimal consequences he faces, and the power and privilege he assumes thereafter. The next morning, Zora asks for an apology, and Franklin curtly declines her request, discursively summoning the unresolved racialized gender issues of the previous era. His refusal conjures what female writers saw as a failure to acknowledge how their allegedly unfair depictions of Black men point to an epidemic of sexual violence against Black women. Zora's decision to stay with Franklin speaks to the overwhelming power of Black bridal pathos. In contrast, Franklin, feeling no remorse, announces that he needs a break from *her*. The depiction of his abandonment gels with the narrator in Baker's "Fairy Tales," who laments being "alone" and forsaken "in the wilderness."[35] As a literary device, the wilderness often symbolizes an unknowable, undisciplined, and uncontrollable space outside the home. Yet the narrator's grievance in "Fairy Tales" illuminates how Zora's home is a space of familiarity as well as a wilderness. Franklin's disappearance and violence represent an unknowable volatility that is "out" in the wilderness and an ungovernable but familiar crisis at home.

Magic Potions

Franklin's and Zora's unrequited political beliefs extend from false race and gender hierarchies to disputes between growing fairy-tale neoliberal ideologies of "personal responsibility" and arguments exposing the machinations of structural oppression, deepening the political stakes entrenched in the novel. When Zora meets Franklin's family for the first time, she admits to wishing that "black people wouldn't harp so much on the past and stop blaming white folks for everything. . . . We've got more opportunities now than we've ever had before. Some of us are just too lackadaisical."[36] Zora's minimization of race and racism allows the novel and Zora to more closely link to the romance genre, as dominant culture usually downplays racial identity in romance fiction.[37] Zora's invective signifies her divorce from "the movement," or Black political investment in dismantling wide-ranging forms of inequality, and adheres to the hackneyed profile of female characters as an antirevolutionary representation of the past and male characters as a symbol of progressive, radical futurity. In 1968, Eldridge Cleaver infamously declared, "When I embrace a Black woman, I'm embracing slavery," and in 1969, Keorapetse W. Kgositsile's Revolutionary Black Theater deemed Black women "old" and intellectually stunted.[38] As a symbol of regression, Zora embodies the fairy-tale notion that the civil rights movement has established an egalitarian playing field for African American people.

Extending and unsettling this symbolism, Zora acknowledges having had two abortions, which also showcase the fraught political stakes of Black women's reproductive freedom and justice. For some conservative thinkers, her abortions can signify her regressive ideals vis-à-vis her failure to embrace Black motherhood as the conduit for racial futurity. Conversely, Zora's terminations and her repeated misgivings about having a child allude to her mistrust of prevailing fairy tales about the country's political evolution and commitment to Black economic stability and liberation. In 1982, one year before the novel's setting, the country was in one of the worst recessions since the Great Depression, with the Black unemployment rate skyrocketing to above 20 percent. The dissonance between fact and fairy tale is striking.

Following up with more Reagan-era rhetoric, Zora asserts, "If they [parents] instilled more confidence in us, maybe we'd grow up feeling more secure about who we are and what we're capable of doing, that's all."[39] Zora's "magic potion" advice positions her as an exalted neoliberal fairy-tale model of meritocracy and conservatism with retrograde politics. Likewise, Pauline—Franklin's former girlfriend—"at least" attempts to get off welfare and go to secretarial school, disproving the stereotype of the welfare queen exploiting the government and epitomizing the brand of personal responsibility that Zora endorses. Pauline's and Zora's supernatural ideas of "personal responsibility" obscure their vulnerability and affirm hyperbolic perceptions of Black women that dehumanize them as perpetually strong and invariably resilient.

In some ways, Zora's beliefs are not surprising. Much like the fairy tale of the perfect romance, the myth of meritocracy is a romantic, seductive neoliberal fantasy that allows Zora and Pauline to frame their individual hard work, fortitude, and intellectual ingenuity as the sole explanation for their accomplishments. This comforting myth can be an especially appealing mode of thinking for marginalized people whose efforts are grossly underestimated and whose accomplishments are often belittled or disparaged at work and at home. But by ignoring systemic obstacles, state and familial support, and simple luck, among other resources, Zora, with a broad brush, renders swathes of working-class and poor Black people who are not ascending the socioeconomic ladder as indolent and simpleminded.

Presenting Zora and Pauline as models of meritocracy and conservatism, while Franklin seethes about systemic oppression, also links to the widespread flawed idea that Black women are colluding with white men and the state against Black men. During the same year that Viking published McMillan's *Disappearing Acts*, Civilized Publications released Shahrazad Ali's infamous relationship manual *The Blackman's Guide to Understanding the Blackwoman*, which I discuss in the invocation. In it, Ali claims that Black women ignore Black men but are "always ready with an eager appealing smile when a white man, especially one in a suit and tie, tries to make light conversation with her."[40] In tandem with Ali's claims about Black women's obsequious behavior toward white men, Black male scholars and critics alleged that Black women "had it easier because the entire paraphernalia of this country: its educational institutions, its courts, its political structures, have not been aimed at the black woman. It has been aimed at destroying black men as men."[41] Black women's socioeconomic mobility is often dependent on educational institutions, ones that according to some critics are designed to destroy Black men. Zora has a college degree, while Franklin does not, and it is Franklin's son, Miles, who says that Zora "talk like white people."[42]

Through her elocution and socioeconomic status, Zora embodies the racialized and gendered fears of various Black scholars, writers, and cultural leaders who are distressed about the future of Black family formation. Zora vaunts that her white landlord did not bother checking her references because he was impressed that she had "been to college, was a teacher, and was able to bring him back a certified check for fifteen hundred dollars the same day," suggesting that class status can avail her unprecedented forms of power.[43] In his chapter "Educated to Become a White Man," child and family therapist Michael Porter echoes Ali and warns in *The Conspiracy to*

Destroy Black Woman (2001) that "the African American professional woman must be doubly careful not to become a White man" and advises these women to achieve the Kwanzaa principle of Kujichagulia (self-determination) by jumping "out of the patriarchal White male supremacist's vehicle," so that they may have the all-important "successful wife-husband relationship with a man."[44] Academia may derisively label Porter's book, which is published by African American Images, as dilettantish and his transracial claims about Black women absurd, but his citations from bell hooks and Angela Davis alongside census data, cultural references, and distrust of white men and women give his statements an unexpected power and a commonsense legitimacy. Together, these fictional and nonfictional texts evince that Black female characters such as Zora are under suspicion for colluding with white men and the state. Less powerful than white men or systemic barriers, Black women become more accessible and exploitable targets for abuse and domination because of their perceived collusion.

Zora's lecture negotiates the dangers of the bridal veil, symbolized by a coverture or concealment of the tension between and seeming convergence of political nostalgia and neoliberal fairy tale, but the novel intricately represents this tension and convergence. It muddles the dichotomy between personal responsibility and unequal structural forces and the ways they are characteristically racialized and gendered. In some instances, Zora's commitment to personal responsibility is a strategic mode of compelling Franklin to take personal responsibility for his behavior and violence. Presented as a moment of possible requited racial politics, Franklin surprisingly concedes to Zora's incendiary lecture about the importance of family values. In an attempt at explaining his behavior, Franklin claims, "My moms stripped me of my manhood before I was a man," drawing on Moynihan's fallacious claims.[45] Thus, it would seem, Zora is an extension of his mother's emasculation as well as a tool by which he attempts to reclaim it. Unmoved by his rationalization, which is tied to family values, Zora clings to her bootstrap philosophy, forgoing the possibility of shared racial politics. She exclaims, "No one can strip you of anything unless you let them."[46] Zora wrestles with a cyclical racialized gender discord orbiting once again as Franklin's misappropriated anger parallels Black men's feelings of powerlessness against racism and their misdirected anger toward Black women, enacted in Black political organizations operating during the 1960s and 1970s. Madhu Dubey maintains that "black nationalist leaders . . . identified the black woman as an active agent of the black man's social and economic emasculation."[47] Extending this disharmony, other scholars insist that "discussions of Black family breakdown and Black male endangerment in contemporary political discourse are an amplification of 1960s and 1970s Black nationalism's emphasis on the Black male."[48]

Disappearing Acts demonstrates how Black cultural production offers a unique point of entry into debates about the ways in which political ideologies are racialized, gendered, and sexed, as it presents and disrupts the analogue between Zora and Franklin and racial victimization and personal responsibility. In that brief exchange between Zora and Franklin, the novel extends the possibility for political consummation but ultimately denies broad claims of personal responsibility and victimization a future as sustained ideological bedfellows because there are abounding, but unresolved deep-seated issues. At the same time that the text defines racial oppression as Black, male, and heterosexual, it represents personal responsibility and economic success through the figure of the Black heterosexual woman. Zora's commitment to personal responsibility impedes Franklin's access to middle-class identity, as she highlights meritocracy while downplaying racism. In other words, Franklin's access to middle-class identity is predicated on a meritocratic ideology that he believes is patently incompatible with his experiences of racism. Franklin's gendered constructions of "authentic" Blackness as heterosexual, working-class, Black, and male weaken Zora's racial belonging. While Zora adopts a problematic color-blind facade, her indifference to Franklin's experiences of racism challenges his privileged victimhood and undermines his use of misogyny as a tool by which to claim his masculinity and liberation.

Poison Apples

Class position lingers and meanders as a narrative conflict; it is a contested terrain in which an unrequited or mismatched vision of Black political liberation is marshaled in *Disappearing Acts*. Zora seemingly reaches her limit when she discovers that Franklin is a high-school dropout, has two children, and is still married because he cannot afford a divorce. These new facts about Franklin's life undercut the fairy tale of marriageocracy. It is only roughly one-fourth of the way into the novel's plot before Zora discovers these damning pieces of information, which could severely impede their romance and exemplify her poison apple. The premature discovery also suggests that there are perhaps additional narrative conflicts or revelations yet to appear before the novel's climax and falling action. As such, the novel gives Zora an extraordinary amount of conflicts to bear and negotiate early on, especially for an "apolitical romance."

In a pointed statement to Zora, Franklin embraces marriageocracy and arguably diminishes or veils the gravity of her newly discovered information by challenging Zora to reject the idea that "money and status and education . . . counts more than what people feel about each other."[49] In cultural narratives, this choice is constructed as both a magic potion and poison apple for Black women. Whether intentional or not, Franklin's sentimental supplication puts Zora's racial and patriarchal solidarity, financial stability, and sex and gender propriety at risk, as it simultaneously calls her belonging and citizenship into question. In nonfictional and fairy-tale versions of romance, money and social status must not affect love and romantic outcomes. Thus, the ostensible incompatibility of love and capital puts Zora in a bind but leaves Franklin at a clear advantage. Refusing Franklin's maudlin proposal rejects romance conventions and establishes Zora as a gold digger, a woman whose proximity to the image of the politically maligned sex worker is often in name only. Stereotypes about Black women as inherently promiscuous affirm this link and will mitigate Zora's claim to respectability and sexual propriety. Franklin's plea also underscores the "community norm that sees independent black women as somehow failing to support black men" and more broadly capitalizes on the "patriarchal way that racial solidarity has been defined in the black community."[50] Because the reclamation of Black masculinity and patriarchy in the political and popular imaginary undergirds the fight for racial justice, and thus Black women's allegiance to Black patriarchy constitutes racial solidarity and kinship, Zora's response is a delicate gamble of consanguinity and betrayal.

And Pretty Maids All in a Row

Zora's friend group is a revealing mirror to the novel's political stakes and functions as a critique of her and Franklin's unrequited or asymmetrical political ideology and image of sexual liberation. The friend groups in these novels often incorporate characters with diverse socioeconomic class statuses, which represent a kind of Black community and solidarity and thus appeal to a heterogeneous female readership, including buppies and working-class Black readers. The depicted enclaves of Black friend groups and fictive kin may desire marriage, but those same strong networks of real and fictive affinities can also function as a challenge to the "necessity" of marriage as a final goal and enhance multidimensional portraits of Black women's interiority.

Pleasure is central to *Disappearing Acts* and causes notable conflict with men and between women. Zora is flanked by Claudette, her married, upper-middle-class Black friend; Portia, her single, working-class Black friend; and Marie, her queer Black female friend. Marie is a representation of Zora's shared principles with Franklin via homophobia and makes legible the possibilities of Zora's malleable homoerotic desire. Queer Black female sexualities represent "discursive and material terrains where there exists the possibility for the active production of speech, desire, and agency."[51] Hence, in my analysis, I coax a reading that vouchsafes alternative modalities of speech, desire, agency, and political subjectivity.

In first-person narration, Zora describes a nonconsensual encounter in which Marie's "hands had slid underneath my armpits and moved to my breasts."[52] It is a complicated depiction of assault and stereotype. Though not at the hands of Franklin, Zora is a victim of assault again, and this scene is also congruent with rampant late twentieth-century stereotypes about violent and prurient lesbians and queer women. It is through Marie that Zora imagines the possibility of a unified political stance with Franklin, one that designates Marie as sexually "deviant" and therefore hinders racial progress. Audre Lorde asserts that there is "a very real fear that openly women-identified Black women who are no longer dependent upon men for their self-definition may well reorder our whole concept of social relationships."[53] It is a prospect that Franklin fears will erode his power. He is hostile to his sister, believing she has "all the symptoms of a lesbian," and he disapprovingly asks Zora if she is a "feminist" and a lesbian soon after he meets her; thus, Marie becomes the target for his and Zora's shared heterosexist politics and successful relationship.[54]

In just one page and mere moments after Marie's overture, Zora and Franklin's shared heterosexist beliefs are undermined when Zora is not turned off by Marie's proposition but eagerly turned on. She soon begins picturing Franklin and becoming "excited at the mere thought of what" she was going to do to him.[55] Her breasts began "throbbing" at the thought of taking the initiative to awaken Franklin, but also with the nascent memory and imprint of Marie's hands cupping her breasts.[56] It is a doubly significant scene because it unfolds as a "counterparadigmatic narrative" or one "that disassembles, if not ruptures, notions of race/gender/sexual universalism."[57] The text disrupts and unravels established notions of race, gender, and sexuality when Zora is an ethereal figure "floating" on Franklin's body.[58] As much as Zora presents her utter disgust with Marie's intentions, she conjures Marie while she is with Franklin, claiming that Marie "doesn't know what she is missing," which can be decoded as deprivation of Zora's affection rather than Franklin's.[59] The next morning, Franklin, quite bewildered, asks Zora what provoked her uncharacteristic vigor.[60] Zora offers an ego-boosting response to Franklin but omits her encounter with Marie. While offering a striking suture to their shared politics, Marie as an erotic muse also punctures the fragile tie holding it together.

Portia and Claudette, Zora's two other polarizing friends, amplify the unrequited politics between Zora and Franklin. As common tropes in popular culture, Portia and Claudette are arguably the inspiration for *Sex and the City*'s Samantha Jones and Charlotte York and for Maxine Hunter and Regine Hunter on *Living Single*, respectively. Portia counsels Zora to end her relationship with Franklin, while Claudette, using her Black bourgeois respectability to enforce Black bridal pathos, encourages her to stay with him. Portia values sexual and material pleasure and is described as an attractive serial dater, who enjoys shopping and seeks out mates with clear standards of financial stability in mind. Portia embodies some of the disparaging opinions of romance predicated on a patriarchal culture that is "more comfortable with male arousal and satisfaction than its female counterparts."[61] Coupled with that anxiety about sexual pleasure, female characters must reckon with the ways in which "respectability has been a foundation of African American women's survival strategies and self-definition irrespective of class."[62] Consequently, Portia and Zora are subjected to hostile interrogation and hasty advice from the women in their friend group.

Together, both Claudette and Marie scrutinize and counsel Portia because she is the most transgressive character among the women. As an attorney with a husband who is a physician, Claudette represents a perfectly stock version of the middle-class respectability portrayed by Claire and Heathcliff Huxtable on *The Cosby Show*. She attempts to prove Black female respectability in spite of Portia's sexual expression and courtship ethics. Claudette frequently makes comments to Portia, such as, "Women like you give the rest of us a bad reputation," while Marie accuses Portia of auctioning her body "just so she can go on a shopping spree."[63] As a unit, Zora, Portia, Marie, and Claudette create a heterosexual class quartet that is always engaging in a system of checks and balances and evaluating one another's bodies through class, advancement, and sexual propriety.

Portia foreshadows Zora's and Franklin's incongruous political values by calling attention to Zora's body as capital and disregarding Franklin's assumed racial victimization. Portia bluntly concludes that Franklin cannot "afford" Zora, suggests that Zora end her relationship with him, and instructs Zora to find mates with moderate to high financial and social capital, suggesting an effort to undermine the disproportionate accessibility of Black women's bodies. It is a presumably important set of standards for both characters as unmarried Black women, but it is a more critical edict for Portia, who easily elicits more condemnation as a supposed licentious woman and therefore cannot "afford" to give up these benchmarks. Portia suggests that Zora adhere to her checklist, which would result in Zora abandoning Franklin.

Portia and Claudette offer two inharmonious positions that intervene on Zora's and Franklin's attempt at a shared racial politics as well as the novel's tension between conceding or rejecting its position as a romance novel. Zora's initial alignment with Claudette's relationship advice prompts readers to view the plot as sentimental, linking it to popular romance courtship tropes. After discovering that Franklin is a high-school dropout, has two children, and is still married, Zora acquiesces by saying, "I mean we're sort of starting from scratch."[64] On a formal level, Zora's response shapes the novel's employment of romance convention because she endorses popular sentimental tropes of the romance genre that dictate a prioritization of love over education, money, and status. Zora's reply to Franklin and subsequent genre mirroring also attempt to create an equal playing field for Zora and Franklin, supposedly protect Zora from the social pathology tethered to "unwed" and "emasculating" Black women, and solicit a shared political stance with Franklin that prioritizes race over class and gender. Portia disabuses Zora of Claudette's fairy-tale advice by upbraiding Claudette. Portia stresses that she could offer the same kind of myopic advice to Zora if she also "had a live-in housekeeper and was married to a doctor."[65] Of course, Zora has a more precarious middle-class position than does Claudette, which further problematizes her decision to remain with Franklin.

Baker's "Fairy Tales" underscores the plot points of *Disappearing Acts*, while Franklin's narrative strongly reverberates with the tales of contrition in Harold Melvin and the Blue Notes's 1972 song "I Miss You," and Lenny Williams's 1978 song "'Cause I Love You," fortifying the novel's cultural imprint. After countless dramatic conflicts and plot twists, Zora and Franklin have a child, Jeremiah, and before the end of the novel, Franklin has abandoned Zora and Jeremiah, as Baker's narrator predicted. Like the narrators in "I Miss You" and "'Cause I Love You," Franklin returns apologetic and as a changed man, just in time to close the novel, suggesting a détente that bows to the romance tradition.

Even so, the novel's conclusion departs from the tradition by rejecting the finality of a marriage proposal or clear declaration that Franklin and Zora will reestablish their so-called monogamous relationship. Feminist scholar Janet Mason Ellerby argues that McMillan's fiction offers "new options for family," including "arrangements to accommodate both women who divorce and women who choose to create families without husbands."[66] These arrangements in *Disappearing Acts* are not new and are sometimes unavoidable, as African American families have creatively reconstructed family and kinship systems under white supremacy and heteropatriarchy for centuries. The novel's finale signals an adaptability bound to Black women's romantic past and futurity and underpinned by "disappearing" and "waiting." These temporal gerunds offer no finality proffered by fairy tales.

Two years before publishing *Waiting to Exhale*, McMillan writes, "I hope by delivering an exciting and convincing story with a satisfying ending, I can exhale."[67] McMillan's hope pushes readers to consider what constitutes a "satisfying ending" for Zora and Black female characters. The ambiguous ending and depiction of rape demonstrate the ways in which supernatural fairy tales and idealized images of romance and "satisfying endings" are not universally accessible, destabilizing society's fidelity to marriageocracy. Zora remains in limbo at the novel's end, with an ostensible punishment demonstrated by her "failure" to receive a marriage proposal as an unmarried Black mother whom the nation will pathologize and fail to support. Nevertheless, this natural and unnatural ending also functions as indefinite possibility, because Zora is not legally tethered to a violent, abusive suitor. It is a coda that undermines the claim that middle-class identity is a political and romantic refuge for Black women and substantiates the assertion that "degreed black women are deprived and maligned in sexual and reproductive relations."[68]

In contrast, Portia engages in an extramarital affair, has a lengthy sexual résumé, is working class, and exhibits the most economically aggressive courtship ethos throughout the book, but by the end of the novel, she, rather than Zora, is granted a marriage proposal. The novel "rewards" Portia's bold and enterprising courtship ethos and outlines a supposedly unconventional route to marriage, putting our most idealistic ideas about romance, fairy tales, propriety, and the institution of marriage under scrutiny. By denying the typical happy ending to the protagonist, Zora, marked by the marriage proposal, the novel revises the traditional romance novel. But by having Franklin's first-person narration begin and end the novel, as it does, the text's claustrophobic architecture privileges his voice, his experiences, and his control over his and Zora's relationship, rejecting a central romance motif of centering the female protagonist. The struggle of being silenced and unvoiced is one that McMillan evokes again in her third novel, *Waiting to Exhale*, through both title and content.

Waiting to Exhale

Waiting to Exhale is a shift in form and setting from the New York City backdrop and diptych narrative of *Disappearing Acts*. Set in Phoenix, Arizona, *Waiting to Exhale* features four middle-class protagonists—Bernadine Harris, Gloria Matthews, Savannah Jackson, and Robin Stokes—inviting readers into an already established sisterhood in the face of neoliberal-inflected feelings of individualism and isolation, substantiated by the narrator's repeated griev- ance in Anita Baker's "Fairy Tales" about being left unprotected to "stand alone in the cold."[69] Bernadine is a stay-at-home mother with dreams of being a caterer, though her culinary skills work in a divergent way through her catering to her two children and wealthy philandering husband, who is ready to abandon her for a white woman. Gloria owns a beauty salon, is a beautician, and also likes to cook. She is depicted as a single mother who is passive but also overinvests in mothering her eighteen-year-old son. Savannah is unmarried and recently moved from Denver, Colorado, to Phoenix to work for a television station. Her sister and mother constantly pressure her to get married and are unaware that she is dating a married man. Robin, a narrative extension of Portia, is a beautiful insurance underwriter who dates several men throughout the novel and is depicted as the most ma- terialistic and vain character.

Just as McMillan transformed the twentieth-century literary device of un- requited love in *Disappearing Acts*, she mimics Louisa May Alcott's nineteenth- century quartet of female characters in *Little Women* (1868).[70] McMillan notes that Alcott's biography is the first book she read for pleasure and admits that she felt she could relate to Alcott's life.[71] She also names Katherine Anne Porter, Jane Austen, and Virginia Woolf as the writers she found most powerful when she first began writing, solidifying her aesthetic interest in romance, domesticity, and sentimentality.[72]

In *Waiting to Exhale*, McMillan continues to affirm the significance of sonic texts to her fiction and African American literature. In the late twentieth century, African American literary critics and writers theorized the presence of blues literature and themes. Likewise, McMillan, as Daphne Brooks ex- plains, adapts and pioneers a rhythm-and-blues and pop aesthetic sensibil- ity. In *Disappearing Acts*, Zora is depicted as an aspiring singer, and in *Waiting to Exhale*, the protagonists imagine themselves as instruments in a quartet, with Robin identifying as a soprano saxophone, Bernadine as an upright bass, Gloria as a flute, and Savannah as a harp. McMillan includes four female friends in *Disappearing Acts*, but by centering them as protagonists in *Waiting to Exhale*, they conjure the polyphonic female rhythm-and-blues/pop vocal quartets of the late twentieth century, such as Sister Sledge, En Vogue, and Xscape. In *Waiting to Exhale*, the friends do not function as background singers as they do in *Disappearing Acts* but are given the range and psychic space of harmonizing lead vocalists.

Out in the Wilderness | Rewinding and Remixing Critical Responses

Despite its reign on the *New York Times* best-sellers list and successful film adaptation, *Waiting to Exhale* incited several spirited responses from critics, which I broadly trace in the invocation. The New American Library (now owned by Penguin Random House) published the first edition of the novel and has published work by George Orwell and William Faulkner, but some readers were not impressed with this kinship. Writers dismissed the novel because of its "sexual frankness."[73] Others praised it for its universalism: "Her story is not black or feminist. . . . [It] speaks to most women and to the issues surrounding most women, regardless of race."[74] bell hooks declares that it was "not a feminist book and it was not transformed into a feminist film," and she slams McMillan for failing to hire Black women directors and Black women writers for the film's screenplay.[75] Oddly enough, social scientists also weighed in, forcing the book to speak in a language of documentary and public policy. In the authoritatively titled essay "You Can Breathe Now: A Psychological Response to *Waiting to Exhale*," clinical psychologists Richard Majors and Ronald F. Levant claim that the book "depicted black men in a highly prejudicial manner, which reinforces powerful negative stereotypes to the detriment of black men and their relationships with women."[76] Supporting their assertion, Majors and Levant allege that Black men's problems stem from "cultural adaptations to racism" and that their violence toward Black women is caused by their attempt to protect themselves against pain and oppression by adhering to a "tough guy image" or a "dysfunctional compensatory adaptation," an interpretation that dovetails with Franklin's justification for his behavior in *Disappearing Acts*.[77]

Majors and Levant denounce the book's portrayal of Black men because it does not accurately reflect that "African American males were more likely than African American females or European Americans to endorse the importance of the provider role," a claim that runs counter to Black writers who criticized "Dick and Jane" illusions about "perfect" white families and Black feminists who called for a dismantling of the traditional role of bread-winner.[78] Fifteen years before *Waiting to Exhale*, the Combahee River Collective urgently proclaimed, "We have a great deal of criticism and loathing for what men have been socialized to be in this society. . . . But we do not have the misguided notion that it is their maleness, per se—i.e. their biological maleness—that makes them what they are."[79] This statement points to an untenable and dangerous pedestal that has plagued and tormented African American communities.

It is a pedestal that functions as magic potion and poison apple in dominant culture and literary studies. In a circular pattern, these debates replicate the criticism impugning Alice Walker's *The Color Purple*. In their examination of the responses to *The Color Purple*, literary theorists take note of the disparagement condemning Walker's male characters as "impotent" and "stripped of their manhood."[80] Literary critics draw attention to the ways in which the criticism elides Walker's redemption of the male characters at the end of the novel and its tribute to progressive gender equity rather than patriarchal power. Albert's sewing suggests his "acceptance of a less traditional gender comportment [which] going along with his [ultimate] humanization in the text . . . allow[s] him to access the 'spiritual creativity' that has traditionally been assumed the province of black women."[81] The hostile responses of Walker's work patently ignore the ways in which the male characters eventually "transcend traditional notions of gender, leaving room for a multitude of pleasureable possibilities."[82] Scholars conclude that people who denounced *The Color Purple* often "blatantly misrepresented the entire context. . . . They only looked at the first third and disregarded the growth of all of her characters."[83]

Akin to the criticism of *The Color Purple*, critics of *Waiting to Exhale*, as I will explain, ignore the male characters—such as James Wheeler and Marvin King, who materialize as near-perfect suitors for Bernadine and Gloria, establishing their "happily-ever-after" ending. It is a conclusion that yields to several underexamined but aggressive forms of pressure that include, but are not limited to, diminished state support, state-sanctioned surveillance and policing of unmarried Black women, clinical psychology, and literary critics, which meld and blur into an esemplastic landscape. Gloria Naylor posits, "Just as the black woman's body was the battleground for 'proving' the chastity of an entire race, now it is the black women's novels that are held accountable for 'proving' that the Afro-American community contains harmonious and loving couples."[84] As state support weakens and neoliberalism strengthens, there is an additional strain on late twentieth-century Black cultural production to disseminate images of an unrealistically powerful Black patriarchy as they come to embody political meaning, which appears radical on the surface but periodically follows the logic of the state.

The novel's civil rights emblems and allusions extend the historical arc of redefining and overburdening Black women's intimacy as a magic potion political remedy. This redefinition of Black women's writing and romantic choices establishes a narrow cultural and political imagination for what constitutes love and happiness, which often resides in the space of the heterosexual and patriarchal. It coerces women to remain in abusive but "politically important" relationships and diverts attention away from power structures restricting power to those who do not choose "correctly." Although social scientists and other scholars saw the novel as "airing dirty laundry" between Black women and men, the civil rights iconography and political nostalgia suffocate Black women under the feint of "repairing" intraracial conflict and structural inequality.

Defeating the Evil Prince and Slaying Political Dragons

The novel's setting allowed for a more legible and acute politicization of Black women's romantic conflict and success. Arizona refused to observe Dr. Martin Luther King Jr.'s birthday as a national holiday between 1987 and 1992, making it a literary backdrop rife with racialized political contestation. New Hampshire and Utah did not observe King's birthday in 1992, but Arizona was featured most prominently in the news as a regressive political agitator. By placing Bernadine, Gloria, Robin, and Savannah in Arizona, McMillan is better able to traffic in "Civil Rights idealism," which "represents, at its core, . . . [an] affective and ideological potency of a set of ideals in relation to which modern African American political identity has been forged."[85] Sonic texts strengthened the vigor and intensity of these ideals. Public Enemy released a 5:47-minute song in 1991 titled "By the Time I Get to Arizona," with an introductory feature by Sister Souljah, and a controversial video denouncing Arizona's then governor Evan Mecham's decision to rescind the King holiday. Their song is illustrative of the ways in which Arizona was a locus of political and cultural controversy and civil rights iconography when McMillan published *Waiting to Exhale*.

Zora, in *Disappearing Acts*, eventually grows impatient with Franklin's unemployment and feelings of being "stripped of his manhood," but her rage never matches Bernadine's acrimony in *Waiting to Exhale*. Each protagonist has a distinct story line in the novel, but Bernadine, as the novel's bass, stands out among the four women. She is the only woman who has been married, she carries some of the most dramatic scenes in the text, and her story closes the novel. After learning that her husband, John, is divorcing her in order to marry a white woman, Bernadine responds with a vengeful wrath befitting a scorned woman. Gathering John's expensive clothes, she dumps them in his luxury car and sets everything ablaze at once. When the fire department arrives and informs her that it is against the law to burn anything other than trash, Bernadine responds flatly, "It is trash."[86] Not entirely pacified by the inferno she has spurred in front of their house, she assembles his remaining luxury items, including an expensive antique car, and sells them at a garage sale for one dollar. After she has sold everything, she is thrilled and exhibits a smile "a mile wide."[87]

This spectacle eclipses Franklin's tirade in the cab and, as extralegal justice, appears to redress Zora's dissemblance and passive "rag doll" response to Franklin's assault. Bernadine confesses that over the course of their marriage John began to think of himself as "a black clone of Donald Trump," so her retaliation connotes an appeal to neutralize Black male desires for forms of power located within white supremacist heteropatriarchy and thwarts the right-wing promotion of books and print media praising Trump that I discuss in the invocation.[88] Symbolically, Bernadine's fire is also a rich analogy to the novel's setting in Phoenix. A familiar mythological trope, the phoenix, represented by Bernadine, is a large bird rising from the ashes of a fire as a cyclical sign of rebirth and regeneration. The blaze calls forth Arizona's more visible political fires in need of extinguishing.

Romance typically uses "elements of ancient myths and legends" in order to "celebrate female power" and convey "hope for the future."[89] The hopeful symbolism of the supernatural phoenix and Bernadine's rebirth galvanizes her "female power" and future romantic "success" as she closes the novel with the traditional happy ending. As a setting, Phoenix, Arizona, has other, more obvious representations of "women in heat" or women "thirsty" for emotional and sexual gratification, which McMillan alludes to in her talk at the 1992 American Booksellers Association convention, in which she says the "emotional texture" of Black women's lives "feels more like a desert. . . . Our hearts are dry. . . . Our minds are like monsoons."[90] Bernadine is exemplary of McMillan's desire to slake the figurative thirst she describes. Bernadine's divorce attorney is able to secure her a $1 million settlement from John, countering Anita Baker's bleak "Fairy Tales" narrator, who has given up on "fantasy" and is "no longer living life in paradise."[91] Bernadine also begins a promising relationship with James Wheeler, a civil rights attorney who is charged with terminating Arizona's political fires. Her relationship with Wheeler recalls the battles fought during the civil rights movement, mimicking the way *Disappearing Acts* subtly repeats the conflicts raised by the Black feminist and Black Power movements.

Waiting to Exhale traffics in what Erica R. Edwards limns as "hagiographic accounts of the civil rights movement and Black Power era" positioning "Martin Luther King and Malcolm X as moral exemplars and semi-divine martyrs."[92] It is a "public memory," animated by the "seductive draw of charismatic black political leadership as a narrative technology," which is mobilized as a magic potion in the popular imaginary.[93] McMillan weaves smaller emblems of this unique nostalgic memorialization or political mirage into the novel, including the narrator describing Robin perusing a vendor's table with "African crafts: kinte [sic] cloths, . . . T-shirts with Africa on the front, . . . posters of Nelson and Winnie Mandela, Malcolm X and Martin."[94] Wheeler, a bigger emblem, is an embellished avatar for King, representing the fiction of charismatic Black political *and private* leadership, particularly for a renewed and revitalized Bernadine. In concert with Arizona's nonfictional racialized political conflicts, *Waiting to Exhale* choreographs an intentionally presentist depiction of Wheeler's desire to wage a battle to make Arizona honor Dr. Martin Luther King Jr. with a federal holiday and later joining a coalition that would stop "allowing so many liquor stores in the black community."[95] Arizona's proliferation of liquor stores in Black communities and resistance to the King holiday sullies the post–civil rights era racial fairy tale that Zora imagines, but Wheeler, depicted as the romantic hero, functions as an inexhaustible symbol of justice as he restores community coherence, propriety, and justice to Bernadine's life, as well as to Black Americans and American life in the United States more broadly. Through him, Bernadine is on track to being married to "the movement," with Wheeler being placed on the dangerous pedestal that the Combahee River Collective warned against.

If *Disappearing Acts* represents an unresolved constellation of unrequited racial politics, *Waiting to Exhale*, over twenty-eight chapters, illustrates a seamless fusing of requited racial politics. The orbit of Black iconography in the late twentieth century, exemplified by the Malcolm X poster Robin sees, Public Enemy's "By the Time I Get to Arizona," the increase in Black History Month programs and performances across the country, and Stevie Wonder's 1981 "Happy Birthday" song—dedicated to Dr. Martin Luther King Jr. and sung by the women in the novel—provide the cultural topography for which an indulgence in depictions of civil rights–inflected leadership is made possible in *Waiting to Exhale*. Although critics claimed that the novel vilified Black men, it deploys Wheeler to reconstruct the previous era's faith in the so-called far-reaching fairy-tale power of patriarchy in and outside the home, as his political activism and his relationship with Bernadine sutures romantic and political harmony.

No Royal Kiss Can Save Me | No Magic Spell to Spin

Waiting to Exhale offers depictions of compassionate, attractive Black male characters who are also charismatic and able to seduce the novel's Black female characters without much effort, verifying their immeasurable power. When Bernadine first meets Wheeler, she is cagey and disinterested, even hopeful that "he wouldn't start talking to her."[96] After a brief introduction, Bernadine's apprehension wanes and she is quickly dumbstruck by "how good he looked."[97] It is in their very first handshake that Bernadine is "positive she felt some kind of current run from her palm to her arm and straight to her head, and then it permeated her whole body," mimicking the parlance of romance.[98] This portrait of Wheeler diverges from the typical way "romance novels invert the power structure of a patriarchal society because they show women exerting enormous power over men."[99] bell hooks notes that Wheeler is characterized as a "man of integrity who is compassionate, in touch with his feelings, and able to take responsibility for his actions."[100] These enviable traits make Wheeler's poignant role as Bernadine's breath and life possible. He is a fairy-tale incentive to exhale.

Gloria, owner of the Oasis beauty salon, has a relationship to men that proves similar to Bernadine's, as both have conventional opinions about what constitutes "acceptable" Black masculinity. She is in a rage after walking into her son's bedroom and discovering him in a sex act with their female neighbor and exclaims that she would send him to his father if his father "wasn't gay."[101] Gloria's domestic labor as a single parent is particularly arduous because, according to Gloria, Tarik's father's sexuality renders him useless as a form of support and help. Gloria's heterosexist version of fatherhood precludes her from seeking his assistance, thus exacerbating her fatigue and promoting the superwoman myth about Black single mothers.

Wheeler's work on Arizona's opposition to the Martin Luther King Jr. federal holiday resonates in Gloria's life when she meets her prince charming, Marvin King. It is difficult to imagine how McMillan's hostile critics overlooked her flattering characterization of King. Not only does his surname connote imperial monocratic rule and patriarchal power, but his full name is but one letter away from Martin King, alluding to civil rights iconography, again tethering Black women's romance to politics. Just as Bernadine is dumbstruck upon meeting Wheeler, Gloria is addled when she sees Marvin. She decides that he is "definitely good looking up close" and admits that "she forgot what she'd been about to say," marking her unvoiced-ness.[102] Scholars caution that "successful couplings between black men and women" are not always "instances where black women subordinate their desires in order to capitulate to the demands of patriarchy," but the tremendous power consigned to the male characters reveal insecurities about patriarchy as an antidote and expose angst about African American political progress.[103] Though they are benevolent men, King and Wheeler are erringly charged with the monumental task of both stopping and provoking the women's breath.

These men fill a cavernous void in their lives, as Gloria's King becomes a patriarchal palimpsest. When King asks about Tarik's father, David, Gloria fabricates his "disappearance," telling him that he is "in California somewhere."[104] David's absence creates a space for King to replace David and ascend his throne in Gloria's life. Moreover, Gloria's characterization of David as powerless constructs the space for a more potent heteropatriarchal authority and influence common in the romance tradition. Together, Tarik's acceptance into a program for teenagers and imminent departure and David's sexuality and silence provide Gloria with the necessary but tremendous space in which to incorporate King into her life. As King compensates for David, Wheeler, whose white wife has died of breast cancer, is the novel's ameliorative and compensatory figure for Bernadine's John, who has abandoned her for his young, white secretary. The tender, warmhearted but somewhat romanticized happy endings that King and Wheeler provide for Gloria's and Bernadine's story lines echo the fiction of a civil rights–era happy ending that eradicated racism, sexism, and poverty. As fairy-tale prince charming figures, King and Wheeler again are called to do the formidable work of precluding and inducing Gloria's and Bernadine's exhalation.

Gloria's resuscitation is extraordinarily important because, among other ordeals, McMillan characterizes her as on the brink of death, having endured a heart attack. Gloria regularly works twelve- to fourteen-hour days at her salon, has high blood pressure, and is characterized as "overweight," with McMillan naming the sixth chapter "Fat" and her penultimate chapter "The Weight of All Things." Though disabled, Gloria attempts to fulfill the irreconcilable expectations for African American single mothers to financially support their children despite their unequal wages and also be infinitely available and home to satisfy domestic obligations.[105] The "weight" of these burdensome expectations, in addition to other forms of racism, sexism, fatphobia, and ableism, could leave Gloria vulnerable to health problems. In fact, McMillan initially intended to kill Gloria by the end of the novel, rather than just give her a heart attack, but Gloria evades coroner for coronation; she is permitted to live and is attracted to King.[106] Her narrative triage and affair with Marvin troubles the notion that "being black and fat is still unwanted and unacceptable" and that those without "physically fit characteristics remain deviant and inadequate."[107] Gloria is also depicted as a figure of excess and comfort, from her desires for food to her yearnings for sex. As a character who longs for physical intimacy, she is a slight revision to the asexual big mama trope, but she fits it through her relationship to food. When she meets King, she invites him over for dinner with a "modest" menu: "All we're having is leftovers, to tell you the truth. I've got some greens and corn bread over there, some candied yams, a little potato salad, and few slices of ham."[108] Her offer signifies her so-called insatiable appetite but also underscores her culinary brilliance and burgeoning affection for Marvin.

Although she is made to represent excess and disease, Gloria is rewarded with King, a romantic tourniquet or reparative figure for her "broken" heart because she embodies a mosaic of corporeal, literary, sonic, political, and cultural nostalgia. Literary scholar Andrea Elizabeth Shaw argues that the depiction of the fat Black woman in literary and cultural texts defies white standards of beauty privileging thin bodies.[109] As the only fat Black female character, Gloria's alleged excess flesh represents a rejection of white beauty standards exalting skinny bodies, but it is also incompatible with the minimalism, sleek lines, and austerity generically tied to modernity, enabling her link to nostalgia. Just as Zora Neale Hurston influenced McMillan's protagonist in *Disappearing Acts*, Gloria Naylor is a possible influence for McMillan's decision to structure the novel around several Black female protagonists as Naylor does in *The Women of Brewster Place* (1982) and give one protagonist the name Gloria, suggesting an undercurrent of literary nostalgia.

Gloria also recalls the past *glories* of the civil rights era and evokes Enchantment's 1976 elegiac and adulatory hit ballad "Gloria," in which they croon, "Things ain't been the same / since you been away," limning a mood of wistfulness and sentimentality about the past.[110] Zora, in *Disappearing Acts*, signals an antirevolutionary past animated by her bootstrap ideology, while Gloria's variegated representation of the past is mobilized by a romanticized nostalgia. She is the oldest character among the four women, the only one who does not own a compact disc player and still plays "old-fashioned" records on her phonograph. Her friends sing Stevie Wonder's 1980 song "Happy Birthday" to her, and her parents are from Alabama, highlighting sonic and geographic civil rights iconography. Anita Baker's "Fairy Tales" alludes to the "once upon a time" fairy-tale convention in the opening lines of the song, when Baker sings, "I can remember stories / those things my mother said."[111] The song's contemplative narrator summons nostalgia for the past that eventually withers as "reality steps into view."[112] McMillan's characterization of Gloria, nevertheless, deviates from Baker's somber tone and invokes nostalgia for the past that is more hopeful, but obscure.

The novel conveys a complicated uneasiness about the future through its celebration of the past. As an old-fashioned, authoritarian matriarch, Gloria is "emblematic of an 'authentic' black upbringing sometimes known as 'home training,' a style of child rearing that emphasizes morality, common sense, and obedience."[113] She demonstrates her "tough love" commonsense parenting style when she puts her hand on her hip and chastises her son, saying, "Look. I don't know where you're getting this nasty little attitude from, but you better get it corrected. Today."[114] Her wise "authentic" gestural and verbal parenting style is illustrated throughout the novel, and she exhibits a supposedly strong old-fashioned moral compass by deeming herself a sinner for having had premarital sex, giving birth to Tarik outside marriage, and fervently refusing an abortion. Gloria's traditional morals are slightly updated by her financial support of her gay hair stylist with AIDS as well as her defense of him against a homophobic client, though this is complicated by her feelings about Tarik's father. Building on the cultural allusions to Kwanzaa that Porter and Saint James forge, Gloria symbolizes Umoja (unity) as the nucleus of community coherence, who has "always cut and styled and dyed the hair of half the women in her neighborhood," with the novel noting that when women sat in her chair, they "told Gloria all their business."[115] Gloria is constructed as a vessel of community and racial solidarity, transported from a nostalgically intact but undefined bygone era, before legally sanctioned racial integration. Because she is a figure who is able to summon a mélange of nostalgic hallmarks, Gloria is spared death and rewarded with King.

The Fairest of Them All

Savannah and Robin seem to both challenge *Waiting to Exhale*'s obeisance to the romance tradition, as neither close the novel in a monogamous relationship, ostensibly calling forth Linda Brent's unorthodox marriage to freedom in *Incidents in the Life of a Slave Girl*. Robin and Savannah are the only women bestowed with the power and authority of first-person narration, amplifying their story and magnanimity. Robin is committed to helping her family, particularly her father who suffers from Alzheimer's disease, and Savannah supports her mother, whose husband deserted her.

Savannah's and Robin's powerful first-person narration draws attention to the noncommittal male characters in the novel, which critics labeled as "stereotypical," but also highlights Robin's and Savannah's eventual evolution. Savannah finally ends her relationship with her married lover, Kenneth, and in the chapter titled "To Heaven and Back," her vacation fling, Charles, disappoints her, never returning her calls after a passionate weekend together, illustrating Anita Baker's grim romantic "fairy tale" of abandonment, with the song's narrator bemoaning that her suitor "never came to save" her.[116] Savannah's circuitous trip to "heaven" conveys both her excitement about meeting Charles and the so-called supernatural influence of Black men. In her final narrated chapter, after she realizes that Charles is never going to return her calls, Savannah professes that "being lonely has never made [her] feel this damn bad."[117] After Tracy Chapman's 1989 song "This Time" soothes her, she becomes empowered and emphatically decides to enact more stringent standards for romantic suitors.[118] She also finally musters the courage to tell her meddlesome mother to stop giving her relationship advice, calling to mind Baker's narrator's eventual rejection of the unrealistic fairy tales her mother told her before she went to bed.

Robin, depicted as gullible in her romantic relationship throughout most of the novel, concludes the book confident and empowered enough to reject a marriage proposal from a suitor she does not love. She is also pregnant by her married ex-lover, Russell, and is determined to raise her child alone, channeling Baker's narrator, who frets in the opening verse about the failure of fairy tales in revealing that her suitor would "someday . . . say goodbye."[119] Supposedly more self-aware by the end of the novel, both Savannah and Robin declare themselves smarter for having gone through their experiences. Of her fiction, McMillan says, "Everything I write is about empowerment."[120] One book review claims that "although the women are looking for men, the heart of the story is their friendship with each other and their personal growth."[121]

It is not happenstance, however, that the novel's finale offers Robin and Savannah "personal growth" and "empowerment" but denies them the traditional fairy-tale happy ending. They are the only two characters who are in relationships with married men, and their crimes of being mistresses and "sexual deviants" seem to outweigh their laudable qualities and sully their middle-class identities as "conservative sexual behavior is the foundation of the performance of middle-class black womanhood."[122] Robin and Savannah are "punished," according to the romance genre's ideals, with the figurative chokehold of Black bridal pathos, resulting in their being single woman with no prospects for the loving monogamous relationship they desire. About Gloria's and Bernadine's opinions of her, Robin says, "They think I have poor taste in men . . . and they also think I'm a nymphomaniac, which is why they jokingly refer to me as 'the whore.'"[123] In clear contrast, Portia, Zora's close friend in *Disappearing Acts*, engages in an extramarital affair throughout the book, but by the end of the novel she, rather than Zora, accepts a marriage proposal. In this more traditional tale about infidelity and marriage, Savannah's loneliness and status as a single or unmarried Black woman signifies her penance for her adulterous affair with Russell. Inversely, Bernadine is rewarded with an economic form of justice, evinced by her $1 million divorce settlement from her unfaithful husband, accentuating the costly expenses Robin is about to incur from her new role as a single mother.

Savannah and Robin embody fears about the future of Black family formation and Black female subjectivity, but Savannah is spared the more expensive, labor-intensive punishment of single motherhood that Robin is served because Robin must atone for more racialized and gendered "crimes." Her malfeasance includes having hair weave, a breast augmentation, and makeup, which are availing her "too much" social capital, as well as her participation in an extramarital affair, vanity, materialism, and shunning of a "good" Black man who happens to be fat. It is a banality repeated in Black cultural production, in which the "materialistic" and sexually active Black female character is discarded for the pretty but demure and down-to-earth character, who is less sexually aggressive or indifferent about her suitor's class status. Examples of this disposable vixen include Patrice McDowell (Allison Dean) in *Coming to America* (1988), Sharane (A. J. Johnson) in *House Party* (1990), Jacqueline Broyer (Robin Givens) in *Boomerang* (1992), and Brandi Web (Lynn Whitfield) in *A Thin Line between Love and Hate* (1996). Not always but often these disposable characters are dark skinned. The punishment or poison apple for excess and pathological behavior in *Waiting to Exhale* is undeniably more so-called pathology: Robin has to raise a child alone, a fate Gloria as well as the nation has already lamented and fails to adequately support. Robin's surname, Stokes, complements the novel's symbolic play with fire and torridness and insinuates that Robin has stoked or incited her own pathological inferno.

Living up to her characterization as a seductress, Robin was able to attract attention for the book from literary scholars. Of Robin's "vanity," literary scholar Rita B. Dandridge writes that "McMillan's text makes an overt stab . . . at black women for the purpose of behavioral correction and ethnic identification."[124] Dandridge condemns Robin for her "poor" choices and lack of racial pride and insists that Robin's "liberation begins with the right personal choices," reinforcing a fairy-tale neoliberal logic of personal responsibility that Zora defends.[125]

After discovering she is pregnant, Robin announces that she refuses to "hold [Russell] accountable," and like Charles and David, Russell escapes culpability for his actions.[126] The women gleefully profess that they will help and support Robin, which acts as nostalgia for "community as a response" to or replacement for paternal lack and adequate state support.[127] Relieving Russell of his parental duties functions as a form of both discipline and redemption for Robin; the novel suggests that her epiphany about Russell is an indication of her personal growth and a new postfeminist sensibility of "women's empowerment." McMillan's nuanced romanticized and deromanticized narrative centers the romantic lives of unmarried African American women and mothers and the kinship between them as it waivers in reinforcing and challenging "individualism and the heteronormative nuclear family as the means for economic and social security."[128]

Ultimately, Robin and Savannah are penalized for the unbridled freedom and authority first-person narration confers. As patient, long-suffering, and accommodating women, Bernadine and Gloria exemplify marriageocracy and are coronated for their tedious domestic labor, pain, conservative sexual demeanor, and bridled third-person narration, with Wheeler and King as their metaphorical freedom to breathe. Third-person point of view is a typical feature in romance fiction, so McMillan's deliberate use of third-person point of view for Gloria and Bernadine aligns their heartening story lines with the romance genre. "Romance as a genre derives its power and pleasure from the extent to which it operates in the realm of fantasy," and for Gloria and Bernadine, the power and pleasure they are availed necessitates fantastical allusions to the supernatural, exemplified by the phoenix, as well as a great deal of visceral pain and the politicization of their relationships, while the "wanton" women are summarily punished.[129] Gloria and Bernadine are spared in part because "single mothers who make it clear that they want some day to remarry are 'eligible for future legitimacy' and thus granted temporary respect and even admiration."[130] Gloria tells her son, "Don't worry, one day Mommy'll get a husband and you'll have a daddy that lives with us."[131] As single mothers, Gloria and Bernadine are given the deus ex machina fairy tale of a prince charming, while Savannah and Robin are disciplined for their pathology and denied the "privilege" of breathing. The novel's characterization of male partners as "rewards" and censure of single female characters further advocate the importance of marriage as proof of citizenship and escape from social death, echoing Baker's narrator who proclaims that the poison apple is her "destiny to die."[132]

Visions of a Perfect Paradise and Happily Ever After

Without question, African American women deserve the kinds of dynamic representations of female friendship, romance, and pleasure depicted in novels like *Disappearing Acts* and *Waiting to Exhale*. These fictional tales offer extraordinarily powerful portraits of African American life that mainstream culture often discounts and overlooks. These images, nonetheless, are not without complexity. At the end of Baker's "Fairy Tales," the narrator concedes that "reality steps into view," disrupting her "perfect paradise."[133] The song's acknowledgment of "reality" is analogous to McMillan's representation of nuanced, but visceral romantic disharmony.[134]

In varying forms, both *Waiting to Exhale* and *Disappearing Acts* champion strong relationships between women, but also verify the virulent racism, sexism, and homophobia undergirding constructions of marriage for Black women. They make clear that the "airing of intimate antagonisms in literature demonstrates the ways that systemic hierarchy and exploitation 'out there' can be 'internalized in here.'"[135] *Waiting to Exhale* exemplifies a persistent and appealing reduction of a "heterogeneous black freedom struggle to a top down narrative of Great Man Leadership."[136] James Wheeler and Marvin King are representations of "charismatic" leaders, with Wheeler operating in the so-called private and public spheres via his civil rights work and his romantic relationship with Bernadine. *Disappearing Acts* offers less charismatic male leaders but makes Black women's rape visible and unravels new and old forms of racialized, gendered, sexed, and classed ideological discord, which construct and critique marriage as a means of remedying inequality.

Though *Waiting to Exhale* has a pretense of finality, McMillan's profound titular liminal anchor of "waiting" stands as a generative and powerful ambiguity. Because the politicization of marriage by a white supremacist heteropatriarchy has Black women by the neck as an asphyxiating snare, Bernadine's and Gloria's first failed partnerships are an elliptical omen now, even as they have committed themselves to righteous political "Kings." The impossible roles that King and Wheeler must ascend repeat a dangerous unsuccessful pattern and exceed the humanity of the male and female characters, threatening another respiratory collapse. These politicized pedestals also grant the male characters room to cause harm and enact violence that goes ignored and unchecked. Gloria Naylor posits that, "In the writings of Afro-American women, the test of love is what the black woman stays *through*. It is normally only death or desertion that tears her from the man."[137] As the novel evinces, it becomes difficult to rely on fairy tales when their resolution or irresolution is linked to your humanity.

CHAPTER TWO

Marrying Up

With this ring, I thee wed, as a symbol of love
that has neither beginning nor end.

In McMillan's *Disappearing Acts*, Zora Banks navigates the friction and confusion that arise from having an economic misalliance with Franklin Swift. As I demonstrate in chapter 1, Zora's position dovetails with the stereotypical emasculating Black woman that floats across political and popular culture. In this chapter, I shift the analytical focus to the inverse of that construction — that is, what happens when Black female protagonists actively pursue Black male suitors whose economic status trumps theirs. A striking counternarrative to prevailing sentiments about "domineering" Black women, marrying up requires that female protagonists cleave to traditional norms of submission and docility. They are, in a sense, "tamed" by this trope.

It is a partnership that would seem destined for success. The romantic hierarchy of marrying up allows the male suitor to finally assume the enviable role of leader and head of household that is deemed atypical in relationships with Black female characters and allegedly reverses inequality, as politicians claim that the Black matriarchal family causes racial disparities. Novels and cultural texts, including fairy tales, champion this patriarchal route for female characters and romanticize its utility. Charlotte Brontë's *Jane Eyre* (1847) exemplifies the marrying up or hypergamous plot structure, camouflaging the ways in which money and wealth — which are traditionally viewed as sullying the romance ideal — influence the eponymous character's decision to get married. Fairy tales such as Giambattista Basile's *Cinderella*, which Anita Baker's "Fairy Tales" may have been referencing, offers the same kind of marrying up lesson. By confirming male power, the marrying up convention is an ostensibly perfect amalgamation of romance and wealth but bears the pretense that one has no influence on the other.

I analyze the marrying up leitmotif in Sister Souljah's *The Coldest Winter Ever* (1999), Omar Tyree's *Flyy Girl* (1997), and Teri Woods's *True to the Game* (1998) because all three novels center Black female protagonists with a traditional romantic goal of snagging a male breadwinner. The desire for well-heeled men is rewritten for these characters though, with the novels depicting them as esurient gold diggers in distinct, complex ways. Instead of bestowing them with the conventional Cinderella conclusion, this triptych provides them with wealth while denying them love, reroutes their desires to underprivileged men, or transforms their monetized courtship goals into criminalized racial treachery. It would seem, then, that Black female characters are placed in an impossible position of being challenged whether they marry up or marry down.

As I explain in the invocation, the Violent Crime Control and Law Enforcement Act of 1994 exponentially increased funding for prisons and police officers. It subsequently amplified interest in tragic images of disenfranchised African American men in fiction and film and magnified real and perceived notions of Black male scarcity, invigorating harmful cultural ideals. With a more visibly violent prison state and Black bridal pathos, leaders and writers began championing a model of patriarchal power that upholds male authority and sanctions abuse, but has excised the obligatory role of monetary support. The desire for well-heeled men is thus imagined as Black female characters abandoning "good," but disadvantaged Black men, who are centered as victims of white supremacy via unemployment, police brutality, substandard education, poverty, homicide, and the prison industrial complex. For their perceived abandonment of disenfranchised Black men, female protagonists are refused hypergamy and punished with an intractable hostility, communal and racial exile, and even carceral punishment.

These severe penalties come out of what Black feminist theorist E. Frances White calls "African American Nationalism" (indebted to Afrocentric philosophy) and what African American studies scholar Wahneema Lubiano identifies as Black American commonsense nationalism.[1] These ideologies are conceived from cultural nationalist movements of the 1960s but sanction a deeply appealing "oppositional strategy that both counters racism and . . . construct[s] utopian and repressive gender relations."[2] A garbled form of nationalism, Black American commonsense nationalism and African American nationalism encompass a repertoire of supple, multidimensional, and pragmatic tools to combat white supremacy, such as articulating shared values and racial kinship, but fall into a political schema that charts radical and progressive paths to Black political liberation through romanticizing amorphous, nostalgic constructions of Africa as they galvanize Black bridal pathos and masculine veneer.

It is a schema yoked to feminist scholar Anne McClintock's account of nationalism, in which "women are represented as the atavistic and authentic body of national tradition (inert, backward-looking and natural)," and men embody "the progressive agent of national modernity (forward-thrusting, potent and historic).["3] Historians have exposed how the previous era's Black political leaders relentlessly challenged this gendered partition. Florynce "Flo" Kennedy's political work and life story "forces us to recognize the Black Power movement's central role in shaping radical feminism."[4] Conversely, women such as Tarika Lewis, Linda Greene, and Joan Bird coaxed the Black Panther Party's "evolution from a male-dominated group to one of the first Black Power organizations to formally support women's liberation and actively work toward a gender-inclusive organizing structure and ethos."[5]

Nonetheless, many late twentieth-century texts misremember progressive Black nationalist leaders and instead adopt the gender binary that McClintock describes by employing a lax, nostalgic, and narrow memory of the previous era's political strategies. In doing so, they preserve gender roles that reproduce incendiary depictions of Black girls and women, men, and nationalism. These tactics offer a "respite from the oppressive realities of daily life in a hostile environment," but construct a "male-centered definition of the problems confronting the black community" and propose "pseudosolutions that further marginalize and denigrate black women."[6]

With the expansion of neoliberalism and the state's obliteration of prominent Black power and queer feminist organizations in the late twentieth century, these depictions intensified in cultural production, especially fiction. *The Coldest Winter Ever*, *Flyy Girl*, and *True to the Game* are exemplary of the ways in which cultural texts employ a seductive political paradigm that refashions marriage, family formation, and young Black women's bodies into tools of political activism. It is seductive facade because as Robin D. G. Kelley explains, there is a "general conspiracy of silence against the most radical elements of the black freedom movement, . . . and activists that spoke of revolution, socialism, self-determination, armed struggle."[7]

That silencing is coupled with distortion. Nationalist emphasis on self-determination is upended and shifts to a feminized ethos of personal (ir)responsibility and victim blaming, while the radical political attention to structural inequality is used to make male characters sympathetic and atone for intimate partner violence and other criminal activity. Racialized gendered crusades of victim blaming are aggressively waged against Black female characters, while the male characters in *The Coldest Winter Ever*, *Flyy Girl*, and *True to the Game* personify vulnerability in order to deter Black girls and women from seeking the patriarchal power dynamic they have heretofore been punished for failing to capitulate to.

For the sake of space, I do not explore any of the numerous sequels to these novels, but *The Coldest Winter Ever*, *Flyy Girl*, and *True to the Game* are extraordinarily influential in African American culture, and their disparate plot design, when read together, yield the subtle traces of dissonance and uniformity in negotiations of Black sexual economies. By reading these texts anachronistically or out of order, I resist linear analyses and instead signal the circuitous thematic exchange and diffuse impact of these texts on African American culture.

Excavating Crises | Crime and Class Uncoupling

The genre hybridity of *The Coldest Winter Ever*, *Flyy Girl*, and *True to the Game* help facilitate the racialized gendered crusades of victim blaming waged against Black female characters. As I explain in the invocation, references to luxury vehicles, designer handbags, and other lavish items in these novels resemble chick lit's attention to meticulous sartorial staging, but they also riff on street/urban fiction, or what cultural theorist Justin Gifford describes as "quasi-autobiographical" Black crime fiction about pimps, players, sex workers, street hustlers, drug dealers, and political revolutionaries.[8] Quasi-autobiographical Black crime fiction set against "white constructed spaces of containment and surveillance" is generally equivocal about using crime as a "radical stance against systemic white racism" and a "politically ineffectual black bourgeoisie."[9] The poor urban New York City and Philadelphia settings in the novels I examine in this chapter unquestionably register as "white constructed spaces of containment," but the surveillance that Gifford identifies does not simply occur over low-income housing tenements but is also enacted over the Black female characters.

Gifford argues that *The Coldest Winter Ever*, *True to the Game*, and similar novels "challenge misogynist gender dynamics" typical in the Black crime novel because they feature a "female perspective" and have "produced a massive female readership and new literary market."[10] While these female protagonists do embrace the "hustler ethos" that has long defined Black crime fiction, the novels also uphold a dangerous mode of racialized misogyny by insisting that Black women are complicit with the state, a cliché I discussed in chapter 1. Many of the male street hustlers and drug dealers depicted in these novels are hypermasculine heroic outlaws and are wildly suspicious of Black women's collusion with white racism and also envision Black women as imperfect possessions that necessitate investigation, surveillance, and violent discipline. The use of military and law enforcement nomenclature and concepts in these novels, such as *soldier*, *probation*, and *protection*, buoy this high-handed stewardship. This constabulary language is also indicative of a cultural reckoning with the 1994 Violent Crime Control and Law Enforcement Act as it rehearses the link between state and intimate partner violence. Drawing on Gifford, I explore how the competing and complementary discourses from crime and romance fiction sustain Black female criminalization, policing, and surveillance by characters who imagine that Black women and their romantic goals fall under their jurisdiction.

Music, nonfiction, and film substantiate how neoliberalism exacerbated a violent prison industrial complex, unemployment, miseducation, and subpar housing that victimized Black men. Through characters such as *Waiting to Exhale*'s Robin, Savannah, Bernadine, and Gloria, Black women were imagined as successful middle-class college graduates, having established lucrative careers after migrating from urban blight to predominantly white cities, towns, and suburbs. They were rarely broadcast as victims of police brutality or the prison industrial complex, and this dissonance in the popular imaginary — between a feminine Black middle-class and a masculine Black working-class — inflamed conceptualizations of Black women ascending the socioeconomic ladder more quickly than do their male counterparts. N.W.A.'s 1988 song "Fuck the Police"; Jawanza Kunjufu's *Countering the Conspiracy to Destroy Black Boys*, volumes 1–3; *New Jack City* (1991); *Boyz n the Hood* (1991); the LAPD's beating of Rodney King (1991); *Juice* (1992); *Menace II Society* (1993); F. Gary Gray's *Friday* (1995); and Spike Lee's *He Got Game* (1998) — exemplify this masculine urban dystopia.

The characterization of Black female achievement against Black male socioeconomic impotence fostered heightened condemnation of aspirational Black girls and women who were migrating across class categories and leaving "their" Black men behind. Their "abandonment" and socioeconomic accomplishments elicited questions and suspicion about the nature of their success, specifically how they were able to escape racism and sexism, and flourish within capitalism, while social structures decimated Black men. Wahneema Lubiano asserts that cultural narratives about Black middle-class women's "disproportionate overachievement [worked to ensure] the underachievement of the 'black male' in the lower classes."[11]

Black women's alleged socioeconomic success and familial "dominance" often masked high rates of domestic or intimate partner violence, racialized gender wage gaps, in which "black women either make less [than men] for the same work or work twice as hard for the same pay," and deflected attention from the disconcerting number of Black women leading progressive political organizations and serving as elected officials.[12] In a 1994 *New York Times* article titled "Black Women Graduates Outpace Male Counterparts: Income

Disparity Seen as Marriage Threat," a Black male interviewee explains, "It's been easier for black women to go a lot farther than black men. Perhaps there's some unconscious racism—companies can see the female side and then, perhaps, the black."[13] Through this interpretation, Black women's gender is a "privilege" and is prioritized over race—a stratification that counters the work of Black queer feminist organizations, such as the Third World Women's Alliance and the Combahee River Collective, which rejected race and gender hierarchies. Along with the interviewee's justification for Black female success, Black women's achievements are coded as "gifts" and unearned "handouts" because they have been accomplished in the face of racism, sexism, and capitalism.

As Black middle-class women were criticized, poor and working-class Black women were also excoriated in the political and popular imaginary. President Ronald Reagan called for widespread welfare reform by inferring that Black women were using the welfare system to swindle the government. This political legerdemain, coupled with the mistrust of middle-class Black women who were earning more than their husbands, confirmed Black women's monetary threat to private and public displays of patriarchal authority. Reagan's conservative political legacy bled into the 1990s, as President Bill Clinton enacted policies such as the North American Free Trade Agreement (NAFTA) and the Telecommunications Act of 1996, which repealed state regulations and ensured that the "invisible hand" of the market would prevail, while simultaneously suggesting that welfare benefits and, by extension, Black women's bodies require stringent regulation.

Inflating Assets and Sonic Sexual Economies

Sundry forms of sonic culture fomented the surveillance and policing of young Black women's bodies. It is imperative to analyze urban, street, and crime fiction alongside the criticism of Black girls and women in the mainstream media, such as the *New York Times*, but also within a rich Black musical legacy, which vigorously buttressed their power and force. Hip-hop feminist scholars contend that the "massive proliferation of black women's hip-hop novels demands a new set of literary critical frameworks that take into account the hip-hop aesthetic."[14] Not only do authors such as Sister Souljah work in dual roles as hip-hop artist and fiction writer, but urban and street novels are called "hip-hop fiction" and include references to hip-hop songs and fictional hip-hop artists. Danyel Smith—former editor in chief of *Vibe* magazine and *Vibe Vixen* magazine—explains that hip-hop fiction is inspired by the "spirit of hip hop from its earliest Bronx, Harlem, Compton days."[15]

This spirit, which renders urban life through narrative, dynamic plot twists, cultural allusions and iconography, humor, trickster tales, and allegory, can be traced from Donald Goines's Black crime novel *Black Girl Lost* (1973) to Nas's 1996 hip-hop song "Black Girl Lost." Purported conscious hip-hop songs by male artists vaunted material gains and sexual prowess, but disapproved of "lost" Black girls and women who did the same. Female artists took a different perspective but also reprised themes depicted in street literature, confirming the cultural exchange between fiction and hip-hop. With brazen sexual personas and vivid, corporeal lyrics articulating a desire for a rich suitor, rappers Foxy Brown, Trina, and Lil' Kim rose rapidly in fame and status as street literature gained popularity. Song and novel titles further substantiate the harmonious relationship between fiction and music, including Kanye West's 2008 song "Coldest Winter," London-based rapper Ms. Banks's 2018 album *The Coldest Winter Ever*, Grandmaster Flash and the Furious Five's 1988 song "Fly Girl," Queen Latifah's 1991 song "Fly Girl," Ice Cube's 1991 song "True to the Game," and Pimp C's 2015 song "True to the Game."

Reiterating the male characters in the novels I explore in this chapter, male hip-hop artists get more candid about their fears of the gold digger's unscrupulous ploys and surveillance of their money. Though critics have mocked them for supposedly relegating rhythm and blues to a genre of rhythm and "begging," Jodeci opens their song "Feenin'" with a dramatic "Take my money, . . . my house, and my cars" supplication to female lovers, contrasting the qualms about Black women's so-called fiendish economic desires articulated by their hip-hop peers. The narrator in Notorious B.I.G.'s 1997 song "The World Is Filled . . ." fears that women are surveilling him with "eyes" on his "goods." In the same song, artist Too Short warns of "pretty" women who want to love a "rich man." In 2005, Kanye West's song "Gold Digger" spent ten weeks at number one on Billboard's Hot 100 chart, broke the record for the most digital downloads in one week, and amplified cultural panic about the stereotypical Black female strumpet. Before West's hit single, hip-hop group EPMD released a song in 1990 titled "Gold Digger," and in 2004, Ludacris recorded a song with the same name. As a popular trope, the gold digger haunts Black heterosexual relationships and signals a courtship impasse repeatedly staged in hip-hop and Black cultural production.

These hip-hop personas, coupled with the fictional men in the novels, illustrate that Black girls and women are made to embody all the fears and machinations of neoliberalism's violent inequality. With precarious middle-class statuses, these men know and fear that their economic standing can be abruptly toppled by an unreasonable or exorbitant medical bill, family tragedy, or corrupt police officer, tarnishing the fantasy of meritocracy. Those anxieties are mapped onto "unreasonable" heterosexual Black girls and women looking for love and are already imagined to be complicit with the state. In turn, male characters deploy the state's constabulary language to surveil, abuse, and police female characters, reinforcing the link between intimate and state violence as well as a patriarchal nation and patriarchal family. Female characters in all three novels suffer abuse, assault, and surveillance. The male characters recognize the ways in which the state's nomenclature is an effective tool to claim power and absolve responsibility and subsequently co-opt it in their relationships with women.

The suspicion of African American girls and women defrauding men in the "private" spaces of courtship and consummation coalesced with the image of Black women supposedly swindling men in the "public" sphere. The government's racialization of Black "welfare queens" with superfluous expenses makes it easier to massage the image of scammer and trickster or "trick" onto fictional and nonfictional Black working- and middle-class girls and women. Moreover, cultural proclamations about Black female promiscuity and the graphic depiction of their sexual escapades in novels by Souljah, Tyree, and Woods aid in equating female characters with pedestrian depictions of sex workers who slyly attempt to withhold money from their "pimp," a well-known and respected characterization in hip-hop music. The overlapping layers of political and cultural fables about Black female monetary deception as well as vanishing state support make these caricatures more compelling and shape the plot twists of these narratives.

Backtracking before the better-known songs by Too Short, Notorious B.I.G., and Kanye West, I use Public Enemy's 1987 song "Sophisticated Bitch" to set the tempo for this chorus of novels because the song lyrics augur the familiar perception of Black female characters who comingle love, sex, and money. What is more, Sister Souljah's membership in Public Enemy, an important "socially conscious" hip-hop group that rose to fame during the 1980s and 1990s, is concordant with her fictional and political work. S. Craig Watkins calls Public Enemy the "prototype of insurgent style," and as innovators, Public Enemy forged a "new sonic style in the production of rap music, fashioned an image that adroitly mined the racial signs in American culture, and achieved a popular following among a cross section of youth."[16] Public Enemy ingeniously used nostalgic Black Power and black nationalist iconography, including black berets; a red, black, and green color palette; a crescent and star; camouflage fatigues; images of Black men in crosshairs; and clock necklaces tacitly bellowing "It's nation time!" Melding political activism and artistry, Public Enemy admitted they wanted to be identified as the "Black Panthers of Rap."[17]

Their corpus includes incisive songs about the crack epidemic and the failure of the state to support Black communities, but in "Sophisticated Bitch," they attack Black women for being aspirational and underhanded. The narrator vilifies the title character, who "used to steal money out her boyfriend's clothes" but "never got caught," because she symbolizes angst about neoliberalism's violent inequity.[18] A palimpsest of Duke Ellington's 1932 song "Sophisticated Lady," Public Enemy's "Sophisticated Bitch" reveals that even as the independent middle-class Black "lady" became something of a stock character of empowerment in novels by McMillan and others, its gradual metamorphosis into "bitch" and "gold digger" began eliciting distrust and acrimony as it embodied the fears and machinations of the state's subterfuge.

The title character's "sophistication" in Public Enemy's song does not connote her intellectual or cultural depth but instead signifies her rejection of working-class suitors who "talk slang" and highlights her intentions to bilk wealthy, light-skin Black men.[19] The narrator mercilessly impugns the title character as "nasty" and a superficial "ho" because of her desires,[20] illustrating the ways in which Black American commonsense nationalism depends on Black women's marginalization "even as they are represented as vessels, literal bearers, of 'the black people.'"[21] The song's narrator worries that the titular character as a cultural vessel will infect other Black women with a "harmful" courtship ethos that shuns working-class Black men, who have a presumed veneer of "authentic" blackness and radical politics.

Driving the point home about dangerous "sophisticated" bitches, the song crescendos into proposing that the eponymous character be beaten "until she almost died" because of her behavior. The song's title character represents an effort by Black women to "express themselves as desired and desiring subjects," yet they are severely punished because Black women are "fetishized as the very embodiment of excessive or non-normative sexuality."[22] The sophisticated bitch's ambitious spirit and non-normative sexuality draw attention away from the depiction of intimate partner violence as well as structural solutions, while the song implies that asymmetrical relationships between Black middle-class women and Black working-class men will function as resistance to injustice. Lubiano affirms that "even as [black nationalism] functions as resistance to the state on one hand, it reinscribes the state in particular places within its own narratives of resistance. That reinscription most often occurs within Black nationalist narratives of the black family."[23]

Following the logic of the state, "Sophisticated Bitch" magnifies the power of the Black family and evokes how the bridal veil conceals the union of nationalist nostalgia and neoliberalism. The song's lyrics make Black women's racial authenticity and political engagement contingent on their relationship to working-class Black men and expose the high stakes of Black women's romantic choices by using their sexual behavior as a justification for sentencing them to death.

Sister Souljah | Winter Is Coming

Sister Souljah had a quarrel with President Clinton about racial oppression in the early 1990s and was also a member of Public Enemy, but the popularity of her novel *The Coldest Winter Ever* eclipses her fray with Clinton and rivals that of Public Enemy's best-selling singles. A precursor to captivating television programs like *The Wire*, *The Coldest Winter Ever* was Souljah's first fiction novel and dramatically magnified her fame. Walter Mosely calls Souljah the "Emile Zola of the hip-hop generation" and *Essence* magazine and the *New Yorker* have reviewed the novel.[24] First published in hard cover by Atria Books (now owned by Simon and Schuster), *The Coldest Winter Ever* is a cult classic that has sold over one million copies, with twenty editions. *The Coldest Winter Ever* has translations in German and Spanish, and Souljah has published a prequel and a sequel, also national best sellers. *The Coldest Winter Ever*'s popularity is a result of both Sister Souljah's political activism and the novel's riveting plot twists and spellbinding protagonist, Winter Santiaga, a recalcitrant sixteen-year-old girl living in the New York City public housing projects. The novel is a cautionary tale that "reimagines the novel of manners" and modifies the "mafia sagas of Mario Puzo."[25] Winter is unemployed, but her expensive Gucci shoes, Donna Karan dresses, Coach purses, and gold jewelry call to mind the kind of "sophistication" that Public Enemy castigates.[26] Winter's father, Ricky Santiaga, and her mother, Mrs. Santiaga, reject the "norm core" associated with the pretentious yet ostensibly disciplined affluence of suburbia. They adorn their daughter in gold jewelry before she can walk and support regular trips to the salon and shopping mall. Sister Souljah "presents one of the few book-length treatments of hip-hop culture's materialistic bad bitch."[27]

The novel's affectation smacks of the ghetto cliché that celebrities and politicians obtusely denigrated in the late twentieth and early twenty-first centuries. The Santiagas upset commonsense ideas about what poor and working-class Black people should be able to purchase and own as they simultaneously demonstrate how marginal and hybrid cultures understand their lives as ephemeral and not within the context of a 401(k), unsettling dominant constructions of time and space. That understanding proves true. Santiaga's drug empire crumbles, and he is incarcerated; Mrs. Santiaga's eventual drug addiction leads to her death; and Winter winds up homeless, struggling to survive as she clings to her expensive standards of living without formal education or patrimony. Winter's only inheritance is her mother's advice to find a man who "knows how to provide" because "beautiful women are supposed to be taken care of."[28] Scholars point out that, "For the Santiaga women and their counterparts, being a 'bad bitch' entails attracting the sexiest, richest, most powerful men available in the drug game."[29]

Consequently, Winter tries to survive through the gilded cage of hypergamy by seducing her father's protégé and consigliere, Midnight, whom she is genuinely attracted to but also sees as a means toward a comfortable life. As Winter's father's power weakens and she descends into poverty, Midnight becomes financially stable and prepares to escape the projects. Winter's ultimate scheme is to marry up and re-create the power and wealth that Ricky Santiaga established, but she concludes the novel alone and incarcerated. Midnight rejects her; gets married; adopts her two younger sisters, Mercedes and Lexus; and leaves town.

Midnight's attractiveness and power are mechanisms used to strengthen the appeal of the Black commonsense politics of the novel, which render hypergamy unnecessary, immoral, and criminal. Like Franklin in *Disappearing Acts*, Midnight is physically impeccable. His skin is "smooth and perfect. . . . He was tall, . . . perfect. His muscles were defined, his veins stuck out, emphasizing his strengths. . . . To make the package complete, Midnight's kicks were always new and clean."[30] Though he sells illegal drugs and lives in public housing, Midnight frequently visits Columbia University's library and reads Frantz Fanon's *The Wretched of the Earth* (1961), Sun Tzu's *The Art of War* (1974), and Karl Evanzz's *The Judas Factor: The Plot to Kill Malcolm X* (1992). Winter loves that Midnight "always looked like he was thinking deep thoughts and had a lot on his mind."[31] Serving as a figure of patriarchal protection, Midnight rescues Winter's younger sisters from the projects and violently assaults a male character, Slick Kid, because he publicly screens a nude postcoital video of Winter without her permission.

Midnight, like Franklin, is underemployed and street smart, but he demonstrates his intellect through his reading habits, exemplifying masculine veneer and also recapitulating Black American commonsense nationalism's "heroic narratives about powerful male presence."[32] The novel's setting in the New York City public housing projects and Midnight's occupation and proximity to incarceration establish his power and vulnerability and link him to poor and working-class Black communities. Mimicking Franklin, Midnight's "sophisticated" reading interests make him palatable to middle-class Black girls and women, thereby conveniently erasing the need for hypergamy. He is represented as a powerful, handsome, and well-read drug dealer who eventually marries, resigns his position as a drug dealer, and invests his money in a Black community by buying a barbershop, thus establishing his atonement and redemption, as it mobilizes the appeal of a powerful Black male presence embedded in commonsense Black nationalism.

In stark contrast, Winter is portrayed as a wild, unrefined, and licentious static character, who confirms racist and sexist assumptions about Black girls and women earning their success through their bodies because their intellectual skills are purportedly underdeveloped. Of her first "sugar daddy," Winter asserts, "I recognized him immediately as a sucker, somebody I could take for all he had,"[33] resonating with Public Enemy's disdain for the "sucker boy with the attaché."[34] Black girls and women, according to The Coldest Winter Ever, are vain, gluttonous, and lazy, much like Reagan's "welfare queen" duplicitously pilfering money from the nation, and thus are undeserving of the patriarchal marrying up construct in the domestic sphere. Midnight upbraids Winter, exclaiming, "Can't you read? . . . That's what I'm talking about—dumb women! You don't even know what's going on around you. If it ain't on the front page you don't know it. But you know the name of every designer in Bloomingdale's."[35] The novel renders the romantic goals of "sophisticated bitches" like Winter as narcissistic and casts their sociopolitical awareness as deficient against a seemingly barren political landscape and during a Black male courtship recession, symbolized by disenfranchised Black men. Though a mesmerizing character, Winter is an exaggerated version of Zora's characterization as antirevolutionary, while Midnight's tirade is in accord with Zora's praise of "personal responsibility."

Midnight's vitriol toward Winter works in tandem with Souljah's literary technique of self-insertion, as she occupies the position as both author of the novel and antagonist in the story as herself—Sister Souljah, creating a narrative prison for Winter that alludes to the novel's dénouement. Because patriarchy is a sociopolitically endorsed construct, engineered by men and reinforced by neoliberalism and cultural production, the novel must go to extraordinary lengths to discourage its use by female characters. As such,

Souljah enlists herself. Stationed in the plot as a textual "soldier," Sister Souljah forcefully challenges Winter's compelling first-person narration and characterization as a sexy, conniving, materialistic gold digger. Souljah, a moralizing mercenary, takes a thinly veiled shot at Winter in her lecture to a group of Black girls and women in prison, saying, "Women are led to believe that being pretty is enough. And while we rely on that, we forget to strengthen our minds so that we can learn how to think, how to build."[36] Her sententious lessons and the novel's claustrophobic narrative architecture reveal that Winter and the patriarchal call for economic patronage celebrated by Lil' Kim, Foxy Brown, and Trina is persuasive and thus requires aggressive dismantling. Stories like *The Coldest Winter Ever* "not only reinscribe the narratives about black women prevalent in Hip Hop music, but also undermine the hustle of their protagonists."[37] Although narratives adhering to Black common-sense nationalism evangelize patriarchal constructions of family, Midnight, "Sophisticated Bitch," and many other sonic texts disapprove of Black women's patriarchal call for monetary support. They covet the privileges of patriarchy but condemn its accompanying obligation to provide financial security.

To make the disparagement of Winter and her hypergamous goals that much more cogent, Souljah sculpts herself as a kind of "Queen Mother" in the novel. Ethnomusicologist Cheryl L. Keyes outlines the contours of the "Queen Mother" as an "African-centered" female hip-hop icon with "intellectual prowess," exemplified by artists such as Sister Souljah, Queen Latifah, and Isis.[38] Abstract cultural references to "Mother Africa," the Nation of Islam's claim that Black women are "Mothers of Civilization and Queens of the Universe," and the legendary civil rights worker and Black nationalist leader Queen Mother Moore also emboldened the cultural cache of the nurturing, maternal "black queen."[39] Regal progenitors like Queen Latifah became venerated because they are linked to Black aristocracy, affirm maternal values, are held in high esteem, counter notions that Black girls and women are powerless and invisible, and embrace "black female empowerment."[40]

In the novel, Souljah bolsters her Queen Mother status by painting herself as a "radical" political activist fighting for racial equality, amid scenes of a homeless Winter unwilling to take "personal responsibility" for her actions as she schemes to obtain money to buy a pricey Coach purse rather than something "practical." Against Winter's marry up goals, sexual sorcery, and policy to attend school only when she has a "new outfit to show off or some new jewels," Souljah easily ascends the throne as a righteous "Queen."[41] It would be easy to reserve sympathy for Winter as the lone assertive female figure among strong, violent male characters, but instead Souljah presents herself as the "archetype" of Black womanhood and Queen Mother, thus capturing the reader's goodwill.

Under her impressive and dignified maternal avatar of Queen Mother, Souljah unfortunately perpetuates a regressive nationalist configuration of women as the "symbolic bearers of the nation" in order to justify the exacting punishment meted out to Winter and young women emulating her.[42] Souljah draws herself as a chaste, politically conscious, and gifted orator and intellectual, so she represents virtue, hard work, and altruism at first glance, upending sexist portrayals of women as materialistic and regressive, as noted by McClintock. Against Winter's stylized and "artificial" gold-digging aesthetic, Souljah, however, is depicted as static, "natural," and "authentic," all attributes linked to women under nationalism. Winter disparages Souljah for being "too natural" because she does not wear jewelry, her clothes are "mixed and matched" from the clearance rack, she has a portly belly, and—perhaps the most egregious crime—she wears nondescript sneakers as though she grew up in a "Long Island flea-market" town.[43]

Demanding a monastic homogeneity and marshaling an oppressive power hierarchy, Souljah refuses to adorn herself in anything ostentatious, including jewelry, despite it being a common marker of queens and royalty, because she must distance herself from the detestable, vain, and money-grubbing Winter. Souljah's distancing and pseudo-nobility allow her to demote Winter, casting her as her ignoble subject rather than granting her the power and conclusion typically afforded a titular character and first-person narrator. Radical Black feminists made clear their unequivocal rejection of "pedestals" and "queenhood" in the Combahee River Collective statement, and Lil' Kim's "Queen Bee" moniker shrewdly subverts the title's wholesome connotation, but Souljah's Queen Mother status enables her to covertly suggest that all Black girls and women fashion themselves as chaste, dignified, and self-effacing "black queens," not "sophisticated" Black "bitches."

If Winter is the novel's "Sophisticated Bitch," Souljah is its silver-tongued sophist. Souljah subtly establishes her status as Queen Mother and her investment in Afrocentric ideology early in the novel, upholding the post-soul aesthetic emphasis on "reanimating 'premodern' (African) concepts of blackness," but her commitment to Afrocentric philosophy crystallizes in later scenes in order to villainize Winter and her courtship desires.[44] Blaring through the car radio, Souljah claims, "The Ancient African elders believed that what you sow, you reap. If you do something positive, something positive will come back to you. If you consciously do negative things, then negativity will rule your life."[45] Souljah's platitudes coalesce with the way that late twentieth-century "African Americans constructed and reconstructed collective political 'memories' of African culture to form a cohesive structure to shield them from racist ideology and oppression."[46] Souljah attempts to disavow racist narratives about Black pathological behavior by encouraging an Afrocentric-tinged ideology of personal responsibility aimed at Winter, rather than critiquing patriarchal structures that allow men to surveil and abuse girls and women.

Literary scholar Stephanie Dunn insists that Souljah's "reclamation of an African sense of being and thinking is a vital antidote to contemporary black nihilism as well as necessary for African American solidarity, spiritual survival, and social empowerment."[47] Souljah's captivating spiritual nostrums, depiction of Midnight as a Sudanese expatriate, and characterization of Ancient African elders appear "vital" at first glance because Souljah rises as a revered Queen Mother in the text; she fills a void of "righteous" Black political leadership; she makes African culture visible in racist Western contexts; her axioms challenge Black nihilism, as Dunn suggests, and adhere to neoliberal ideologies of personal responsibility; and some of her other commonsense wisdom seems endearing and entirely reasonable. In a 1992 *Jet* magazine article, Souljah explains that her mission is to "unite African youth throughout the world" but that her "strongest message" is for "African Women: to understand who we are; to develop definitions of ourselves that are rooted in our history as opposed to inherited through the American media."[48] Like a good pop song, her sentiment is disarming and vague enough to attract a large audience.

But after replaying it a few more times and subjecting it to a more discerning ear, Souljah's melodic ode to Black communities rings less like a pop tune and more like discordant gospel. The bedrock of Souljah's rationale begins to splinter in a striking moment when Winter betrays the novel's political assumptions about reciprocity. Responding to Souljah's loose karmic tenets about "Ancient African elders" sowing and reaping, Winter mockingly concludes that Africa must have done "some foul shit," leaving readers to contemplate if the legacy of colonial violence in Africa weakens the power that Souljah locates within the law of reciprocity.[49] Dunn avers that "Souljah's strategy of providing the view of her African-centered principles through Winter's ever critical voice is an effective one, setting up the novel's critique of the protagonist's code of life and emphasizing how much love and self-recovery are needed for contemporary Winters," who are navigating contentious sexual economies.[50]

But Winter's interpellation quite rightly raises questions about the "reason" for the transatlantic slave trade and colonialism and the lack of justice for oppressed people, given Souljah's cryptic Afrocentric philosophy of karma. Souljah uses Winter's tragic ending and Midnight's triumphant conclusion of marriage, entrepreneurship, and freedom from incarceration to corroborate the "Ancient African elders," but Winter's unanswered question lingers in the text, fraying Souljah's untenable political placebo.

Souljah dedicates considerable effort marking herself and Winter as foils, but their veiled similarities outline a paradigm for a gendered Du Boisian *double consciousness* of always seeing oneself through bilateral vision, thus challenging her persistent denigration of Winter. Using monikers, the novel attempts to deepen the rift between Winter and Souljah. Instead of using Lisa Williamson, Souljah leans on her public persona, Sister Souljah. Her sobriquet recalls her affiliation with Public Enemy, and *sister* and *souljah*, as alliterative vernacular, conjure a taut racial kinship and militarized loyalty. In line with the cyclical season, the name Winter stands in for an alleged racialized and gendered recurring or pathological deviant behavior. As the book title suggests, Winter's characterization and name, connotative of whiteness, coldness, callousness, and death in Western culture, resonates with Afrocentric philosophy's central belief that Eurocentric culture is merciless and "too materialistic."[51]

The novel also relies on cultural references representing white supremacy as cold, from Gil Scott Heron's 1974 song "Winter in America" to Michael Porter's more explicit characterization in *The Conspiracy to Destroy Black Women*. Porter bluntly argues that "the very nature of Caucasians is cold. This coldness manifests itself in the violent, insensitive, and immoral manner in which Caucasians have encountered other nations for the past 500 years."[52] Using this cultural imprint, Souljah positions herself as a model of morality, while Winter, as an analogue to the materialistic trappings of Eurocentric culture, is colluding with a system that threatens Black political liberation. Underpinning this binary, Souljah brazenly declares that Black girls and women have only two homogeneous choices for womanhood, declaring that "you can be Winter or you can be Sister Souljah."[53] Souljah's flawed diremption also erroneously presumes that the only two political choices available for Black people are romanticizing Africa or idealizing white culture.

As a narrative sentry, Souljah is not only leveraging the literary device of self-insertion in *The Coldest Winter Ever* but also drawing on the literary technique of author surrogate, which allows her to use Winter as a way to express her views and experiences. Souljah wants to "magnify the true and accurate essence of manhood," while Winter claims that a male character has "questionable masculinity" because he enjoys fellatio from men in *The Coldest Winter Ever*.[54] In her autobiography, *No Disrespect* (1994), Souljah admits to purposefully donning a "black, tight, short, and sleeveless" dress in order to persuade a man to sleep with her, while she worked as a social justice advocate.[55] Winter similarly attempts to use her beauty and clothing to ensnare men. Both grow up in New York project tenements, move to middle-class areas, and claim to be hungry for male attention.

Such resemblances between Souljah and Winter thwart an easy separation of the two characters and call attention to the warring sexual and racial identities of Black girls and women, buttressing Hortense Spillers's assertion that the "unsexed black female and the supersexed black female embody the very same vice, cast the very same shadow, since both are an exaggeration of the uses to which sex might be put."[56] Perfunctory silhouettes of the "unsexed" and "supersexed" are consolidated, providing the possibility that Souljah and Winter exist not just as physical adversaries but also as psychic companions. Souljah and Winter are consistently antagonistic yet point to narrative doubling and oppositional constructions of Black women's sexuality, as they resist being dichotomized. Winter's and Souljah's antiphonal sexual identities overlap in Souljah's fiction and nonfiction, and Souljah's authorship and risky inclusion in the novel indicate a deep level of intimacy with Winter's character, underscoring the gendered and racialized "twoness" of Black female characters.

Perhaps it is Souljah's uncomfortable psychic proximity to Winter that compels her to wield the regressive gender ideals embedded in masculine veneer in order to criminalize Winter's marry up goals and sexual "excess." After renting a car that her abusive boyfriend, Bullet, used to transport guns and cocaine, Winter is arrested, and by the novel's finale, she is punished for her sexual experience and monetized romantic goals with a fifteen-year prison sentence. Winter suffers a much greater penance than that of Robin and Savannah in *Waiting to Exhale* because she pursues hypergamy from disenfranchised, but heroic characters such as Midnight. Because he is such an extraordinary character, Souljah published more stories centered on him, including *Midnight: A Gangster Love Story* (2010), *Midnight and the Meaning of Love* (2011), and *A Moment of Silence: Midnight III* (2016). Winter's materialistic mother is made to suffer drug addiction and eventual death. Ricky Santiaga is incarcerated, and his occupation is a clear harbinger of his fate, but his undoing also makes more space for Midnight to become a hero. Bullet, though, is never charged with any crime related to domestic violence or illegal drugs, and readers learn that Winter's best friend, Natalie, is sent to jail a year later.

On the one hand, Winter's and Natalie's carceral downfall and containment are markers of the statistics verifying that young Black women are the fastest-growing population in prison and operates as a fictional supplement to the real-life story of Kemba Smith, a young Black woman sentenced to 24.5 years in federal prison for her participation in her abusive boyfriend's drug trafficking ring. In his iconic 1996 profile of Smith in *Emerge* magazine, Reginald Stuart describes Smith as a straight-A college student, domestic abuse survivor, and "daddy's girl."[57] Souljah's tale evinces that street literature can be "understood as a political tool, used to direct the view to neglected figures and to raise underrepresented topics, like that of mass incarceration" as well as implies that heteropatriarchy can be a prison.[58] Cross-stitching real and fictional tales, Sister Souljah publishes *The Coldest Winter Ever* just three years after Stuart's article and portrays Winter as a "daddy's girl" who is punished with incarceration due to her abusive boyfriend's drug trafficking. These fictional and nonfictional texts showcase the tie binding domestic or intimate partner violence to state violence. Patriarchy restricts and controls Black women's sexuality as Black women's link to the carceral state is choreographed vis-à-vis their relationships to men, as either victims of or threats to patriarchal power.

On the other hand, Natalie's and Winter's fate reveals the magnified penalty for hypergamy. The novel portrays Winter and Natalie as consumed with wealth and status and apathetic to how Black men are made vulnerable through the specter of state violence. Even after Winter has traded her gold chains for a new set of chains, shackled to her airplane seat and traveling to her mother's funeral as a convict, she admits to "checking out the shoes, watches, jewelry, [and] dresses" of the other passengers.[59] For their grotesque materialism and disinterest in a volatile Black patriarchy, Natalie and Winter are ineligible for the "reward" of marriage and are punished with incarceration. Winter, Natalie, and girls like them lose the privilege of deserving patriarchal protection, and contrastingly, Black communities supposedly begin to need protection from them.

Readers and critics appreciated Souljah's punishment, containment, and exile of Black female characters such as Winter and Natalie, who exploited patriarchal characterizations of women who only want "execs with checks," according to "Sophisticated Bitch." One review claims that Souljah "reaps the benefits of Martin Luther King's dream and Malcolm X's fury" and that Souljah justifiably demands that Black girls and women "be more savvy about the ways they interacted with men."[60] Souljah's conservative, gendered spiel of personal responsibility and victim blaming obscures how poverty, racism, domestic or intimate partner violence, rape, sexism, and the prison industrial complex atrophy Black women's lives while it fuels and demonizes specious narratives about Black girls' and women's disproportionate concern with being affluent and attractive. Souljah, like Midnight and Zora, succumb to neoliberal beliefs of meritocracy proselytizing virtue, hard work, and "savvy" thinking as the proper way for Winter and Natalie to achieve socioeconomic success and escape the violence of heteropatriarchy.

Midnight and Winter, as waxing and waning naming mechanisms, are episodic and not suspended in time and space as McMillan's "waiting" and "disappearing" titular gerunds are, though this tetrad conveys anachronistic structures of space time or spacetime and disrupts the linear narratives they describe and exist within. This alternate, pliant spacetime unsettles the way linear narratives and chronologies deploy what literary theorist Michelle Wright calls "hierarchical or vertical means of representation," which map taxonomies privileging inflexible "hierarchy (fathers/sons, leaders/followers)."[61] These texts repeatedly wax and wane on these plumb taxonomies. In harmony, the "absence" encoded in McMillan's titular concept of disappearing and Souljah's characterization of Winter alongside the "presence" represented by McMillan's titular concept of waiting and Souljah's portrait of Midnight, sketch and plot elastic Black subjectivities and ontologies that deemphasize how these linear narratives mimic an unremitting, laborious capitalist spacetime, which tabulate meritocracy, value, productivity, and patriarchal hierarchy.

For Souljah's linear saga, Midnight, representing temporal finality, has become the meritocratic hero by the novel's conclusion and is the taut, chronological precision against Winter's more amorphous, expansive seasonal spacetime. Yet the clock has metaphorically "struck Midnight" for Winter, whose Donna Karan dress has withered to rags and Coach purse has magically become a pumpkin, but Midnight is free, is married, and has amassed enough drug money to adopt, support, and protect Winter's abandoned younger twin sisters, Mercedes and Lexus, whose names uphold the novel's characterization of materialistic Black girls. Midnight expresses romantic interest in Souljah, but she rejects him because of his occupation. Nevertheless, he is redeemed and sustains the value of patriarchy and hardworking Black men, or "Robin Hoods," whose adversaries are another generation of covetous Black girls. Midnight, whom Soujah calls "the heart of The Coldest Winter Ever,"[62] finally "fulfills his appointed role in the new, black grand family narrative."[63]

Fool's Gold | Subterfuge, Affluence, and Self-Fashioning

The young, "lost" Black girl, or "sophisticated bitch" who Public Enemy claims is constantly "turning up her nose" at working-class Black men, is rehearsed in Omar Tyree's *Flyy Girl*, which has a comparable circulation to *The Coldest Winter Ever*, attesting to the familiarity of the "bad bitch" trope.[64] Published in hardcover and paperback by Simon and Schuster (a subsidiary of CBS corporation), *Flyy Girl* is set in Germantown, a Black middle-class suburb of Philadelphia, and begins its story with a six-year-old protagonist, Tracy Ellison. The novel's omniscient narrator recounts Tracy's experiences as she reckons with her parent's separation but also dates rich men and maintains her beauty, social capital, and materialistic lifestyle. Tracy is smitten by Carl, a middle-class college student who helps her "evolve" and change her taste in men and alleged superficiality. By the end of the novel, Tracy has not partnered with Carl but has become a racially conscious first-year college student. At seventeen-years-old, Tracy ends the novel happy to have secured a marriage proposal from her incarcerated boyfriend, Victor Hinson, who has also inspired her grand "transformation." Tracy and Victor's relationship prefaces several popular nonfiction books with related motifs, such as Asha Bandele's *A Prisoner's Wife* (1999), which recounts the courtship and marriage between a middle-class Black woman and a Black man serving a twenty-year-to-life sentence in an upstate New York prison.

A spatial logic constructing fluid boundaries between poor, working-class, and middle-class socioeconomic positions vis-à-vis material realities intensifies Black women's racial treachery in *The Coldest Winter Ever* and *Flyy Girl*. Ricky Santiaga, Winter's father in *The Coldest Winter Ever*, never wears the same shirt twice, and her mother wears expensive Italian leather shoes, but they live in the New York City public housing projects, and Santiaga encourages Winter to attend college and partner with a nice college-educated man outside their neighborhood, establishing close ties between working-class and (precarious) middle-class African American women and men. Tracy's middle-class suburban life in *Flyy Girl* is not protected from the kinds of drug dealers, incarceration, and violence typically associated with Black working-class communities. The heterogeneous class settings highlight the proximity and porous borders between poor, working-class, and middle-class Black girls and women and men and mark the importance of kinship across class lines in Black communities. Circuitous geographies between these communities can generate interclass contact but also reinforce specific racialized gender and class expectations for Black women's courtship and marriage. The novels insinuate that this geographic configuration can put more pressure on Black girls and women to choose their disenfranchised working-class Black male counterparts and construct this coupling as a way for them to prove racial authenticity and enact a mode of philanthropy to less fortunate Black communities.

That pressure is intertwined with Winter's and Tracy's negotiation of "protection" imposed by male characters. Initially, Winter's father and Tracy's father both provide protection for their young daughters, but Winter's father is arrested, and Tracy's father eventually moves out of their home. As "fatherless" characters who are sexually active, unemployed, pretty, and "all pretend" as "Sophisticated Bitch" surmises, male characters see Winter and Tracy as girls in desperate need of protection and thus attempt to challenge and suppress their agency under the auspices of safeguarding them. Literary scholar Farah Jasmine Griffin argues that protection is not fundamentally bad, as a "racist patriarchal society is particularly dangerous for black women."[65] Even so, Griffin advocates for dismantling patriarchy and racism because of the way that patriarchal protection demotes girls and women to the role of possession, restricting their "freedom and mobility."[66]

Instead of dismantling systems that make protection requisite, these texts blur the line between protection and possession as well as adolescence and adulthood. On a shopping trip, Winter selects a mini-skirt, and Midnight angrily demands that she "wear something decent," picking out an Eileen Fisher pantsuit, with the hope that the "right" kind of consumption will safeguard her from objectification and sexual violence, though Black male characters are susceptible to state violence regardless of their appearance.[67] As characters and commonsense ideas infantilize the female characters through protection, they also demand their maturity. *Flyy Girl*'s narrative velocity means that Tracy develops from a six-year-old girl to a seventeen-year-old adolescent over the course of just seventeen chapters, signifying the ways in which Black girls are prematurely forced into adulthood. By the end of the novel, she is unable to vote in an election, but she has the all-important marriage proposal. Winter's adolescent body in the type of pantsuit that is usually marketed to middle-aged white women suggests that the hypersexuality linked to young Black women denies them childhood and adolescence. Black female protagonists are repeatedly disallowed adolescence, play, and whimsy, including through the policing of their bodies, being orphaned, and the ubiquitous goal and push for them to get married in all three novels.

Protection, policing, and surveillance of Black female characters takes center stage in *Flyy Girl* when Carl calls Tracy's gold earrings "big" and "clumsy" and insists she remove all "artificial additives" because she is "already attractive" in his eyes, restricting her appearance to his ideals of beauty.[68] Carl inspires Tracy to learn about Africa, wear a Kente print outfit instead of her typical "sexually suggestive" outfits, and swap her trendy shoes and gold jewelry for plain brown sandals and simple, natural wooden earrings, cultivating a possessive dynamic. Carl's sartorial and intellectual directives attempt to defy white racial domination by invigorating Tracy's racial pride yet necessitate consumption and a bourgeois politics of "natural" Black female beauty sanctioned by Black American commonsense nationalism and African American nationalism. Carl's protective rules function as camouflaged prescriptions of personal responsibility that allegedly counter sexual objectification. They also intend to humble Tracy, unmoor her from typical representations of gold diggers, and prepare her for a relationship with an unpretentious, working-class Black man rather than a wealthy man. This wealthy man, whom Public Enemy calls "the devil at her level," is presumed to have conservative racial politics, which hinder Black political freedom, and reputedly prefers materialistic and ostentatious self-fashioning, of which Tracy must rid herself.[69]

Further evincing the entanglement of these novels and authors, Carl's narrow gauge of radical politics is reminiscent of Souljah's autobiography, *No Disrespect*, in which she recounts how her activist boyfriend assails her appearance, saying, "I like girls with natural hair. I've always wondered why you have that fake extra piece of hair weaved in the back of your head. Does it give you that much more of a sense of security and value?"[70] An ostensible analogue to the "natural" and "organic" food and nutrition movements, which are opposed to "artificial additives," the enforcing of "natural" jewelry, hair, and other forms of self-fashioning in both texts is deceptively powerful. Urging Black women to appreciate their "natural" beauty and hair rarely includes the "natural" hair on their legs, armpits, or pelvis, but it masquerades as a way to strengthen racial pride and protect them from society's construction of Black women as hypersexual, which will supposedly distance them from the reach of rich Black men and sustain masculine veneer.

Carl's principles of "enlightenment" for Tracy, much like colonizing missionary work converting the "uncivilized," are presumed routes to social consciousness and refinement, but they morph into registering Black female characters as possessions to be controlled via demands that their bodies trumpet political ideology. Black women have historically "incorporated dress into their activist strategies," but these recommendations for adornment are predicated on a male gaze and deliberately work to reduce the social capital made available to Sister Souljah and Tracy.[71] Just as Public Enemy's red, black, and green palette is a cultural signifier for Black nationalism, Tracy's new "preference" for Kente cloth, brown sandals, and wooden earrings indicates her new "radical" politics but also prepares her for marrying down.

Cohering with the overstated political significance of Tracy's "natural" wooden earrings and Souljah's "artificial" hair, Angela Davis says that being "remembered as a hairdo . . . is humiliating."[72] The complexity of Black political history is distilled into a bulbous silhouette of tight curls, according to Davis, aligning with the ways in which radical racial politics are equated with skirt length, earring size, and hair texture for Black female characters in these novels. This equation also ignores the ways in which Black women are penalized and punished for their natural hair. The patriarchal protection built into the marrying up convention routinizes this surveillance and sexist appraisal of Winter and Tracy, but the hypercritical policing of Black women's hair and adornment is antithetical to the Black Panther Party's caution that "cultural pride" . . . "did not guarantee liberation."[73] Tyree's and Souljah's feckless prescription for liberation includes "natural" hair, longer skirt lengths, wooden earrings, and Kente cloth, exemplifying how Black Power emphasis on dismantling systemic inequity is erroneously discarded for a cultural nationalist ideology primarily aimed at surveilling and policing Black female characters.

The novel's racialized gender politics and "protection" of Black female characters becomes even more alarming as Tracy "matures" and "evolves" in her thinking. In the last quarter of the novel, after returning home from an African cultural festival, Tracy tells her mother, Patti, that a poor "appetite" causes menstruation. As Patti cheers her on, Tracy continues. Worrying that a racist health-care industry has withheld crucial information from Black communities, Tracy recommends that Black communities reexamine how "Africans mastered . . . vegetarian and fruit diets thousands of years ago."[74] Although Patti is a registered dietician, she praises and encourages Tracy in her lecture about "natural" food and amenorrhea. Tracy's hypothesis has become influential in twenty-first-century popular culture. Self-proclaimed health experts and activists rehearse it on popular blogs and vlogs, though it is a myth that is rarely traced back to popular fiction or the early 1990s. My close reading is a call to direct more attention to the serpentine ways this kind of pseudoscientific message migrates, flourishes, and becomes common sense across time and space.

Tracy's unique conspiracy theory may be intriguing and become common sense because it occupies an advantageous place in the novel and among key characters. Inserting Tracy's rant in advance of her highly coveted marriage proposal implies that Tracy is "on the right track," and its location toward the novel's finale, a space where protagonists often make critical epiphanies, positions it as a meaningful revelation. The novel's middle-class setting and Tracy's parents' middle-class careers—her father is a pharmacist and her mother, a dietician—also imparts integrity and thwarts ideas about well-read, middle-class people discounting these premises as nonsensical. Patti's approval, as a mother and a dietician, especially consigns validity to Tracy's words.

Tracy's "alternative medicine" replaces neoliberal sinkholes of state support and rides the coattails of reasonable truths as her cultural allusions and iconography further cement the legitimacy of her words. Her homogeneous, positive invocation of "Africans" conveys her honorable intentions to rally racial pride, approximating Souljah's use of "Ancient African elders" in *The Coldest Winter Ever*. Tracy's rhetoric is tempting because it struggles to fill a gap in a deteriorating health-care system and works toward "protecting" girls and women from a racist medical industry and forms of environmental racism that result in precocious or early-onset puberty. It also aspires to fill a void in a faulty education system that falls short in educating students about reproductive health and nutrition.

Playing in the shadow of the swelling organic food and "natural" hair movement, Tracy's new convictions exploit burgeoning fears about climate change and seek to protect girls and women from food recalls, contaminated food, and food poisoning. It is also a theory that pretends to shield Black girls and women from widespread misogynistic views of their bodies as "unclean" in secular and religious culture and from racist and sexist assessments of Black women's so-called inherent impurity. Kristina Graaff insists that street literature depends on the "reader's emotional and mental 'cleansing'" to provide the novel's "moral instruction."[75] As such, Tracy's manifesto has the countenance of moralizing patriarchal protection and radical political action. Immediately after Tracy's speech, Patti proudly says that Tracy is going to be like "Angela Davis and Assata Shakur . . . another Sojourner Truth."[76]

Tracy's "radical" beliefs, like most conspiracies, are propelled from a shard of truth but end with elaborate subterfuge. The state-supported promises about a neoliberal ethic of personal responsibility buried in her theory have a high physical and psychic cost. These magic potion assurances lead people to indict themselves for a perceived inability to improve their health status and foster devastating stigmatized psychological problems, especially for populations without access to mental-health professionals. Her proposed strict diet of fruits and vegetables could trigger untold health problems, particularly for people with low iron or anemia, and it does not consider some of the most vulnerable populations, who have no access to the amount of fresh vegetables and fruits that would make the diet sustainable. It implies that fresh vegetables and fruits are invulnerable to food recalls and contamination.

Eliminating menstruation also hints at a cultural neurosis about prepubescent people. *The Coldest Winter Ever* and *Flyy Girl* put mature Eileen Fischer attire and adult responsibilities and circumstances of marriage and incarceration onto their fledgling protagonists, but the rising appeal of eradicating menstruation also reveals a contradictory cultural fixation on "clean" prepubescent Black girls. Cultural texts encourage Black women and girls to be maternal and dissuade them from seeking birth control and abortions in order to strengthen Black communities, as the infamous billboard declaring that the "most dangerous place for an African American is in the womb" attempted to do.[77] As they encourage maternity, some of the hidden disinformation that I have unearthed in these cultural texts also potentially inhibit healthy pregnancy and childbirth.

Tracy wrestles with these inconsistent appeals, and because of her class status and willingness to change in accordance with racist and sexist rules governing nutrition, self-fashioning, and comportment, she is eventually "compensated" with a marriage proposal, transforming her hypergamy into a Public Enemy–approved racial uplift and cultural nationalism. Although Tracy acquiesces to his wardrobe guidelines, Carl ends their relationship, but as the novel closes, her desires are rerouted to a more disenfranchised Black male character, Victor Hinson, an inmate at Philadelphia's Holmesburg Prison. Obeying Public Enemy's counsel, Tracy has rejected all the "sucker(s)" with "attaché(s)."[78]

Further exposing the intimacy between dismantling racism and yielding to conservative gender politics under the bridal veil, Victor writes from prison that "white people have a lot of pitfalls set up" and admits that he has been increasingly influenced by the conservative teachings of the Nation of Islam and Minister Louis Farrakhan.[79] He proudly declares that he has changed his name from Victor Hinson, or "the slave," to Qadeer Muhammad, "the man."[80] The novel's racialized gender politics becomes more palpable when Tracy finally receives her proposal from Qadeer, who wants a "correct family," with three children from seventeen-year-old Tracy.[81] Her exuberant sobs signify that she no longer desires a wealthy suitor; she has been persuaded to want Qadeer, affirming the importance of saving disenfranchised poor and working-class Black men through marriage. Qadeer also requests that Tracy send a "big naked" picture of herself to him as he closes his letter, establishing marriage—through his proposal—as the only appropriate space for Black female sexual expression.[82]

Tracy is just a seventeen-year-old first-year college student, but the narrator exclaims that her "desire [for marriage] had been fulfilled." In prose characteristic of the romance tradition, the narrator announces that Tracy begins "dreaming of Victor, Qadeer, black, strong and righteous, as the moon shone and the wind blew, adding to her birthday joy."[83] The shining moon in Tracy's phantasmagoria evokes Midnight from *The Coldest Winter Ever*, binding him and Qadeer as kindred figures whose nocturnal imagery consign auspicious characteristics of strength and righteousness to blackness, a literary symbol usually linked to depravity in Western culture. Both novels insert a racial counterdiscourse challenging whiteness, light, and, not to mention, Winter, as connotative of truth and virtue, leaning on commonsense Black nationalism. Tracy's humbling and capitulation to Qadeer abnegates hypergamy, highlights vulnerable Black men, and endorses the novel's portrayal of unmarried sexually active Black female characters as immoral.

Romantic Reconnaissance | Probation, Marriage Proposals, and Catastrophe

Like *Flyy Girl*, Teri Woods's *True to the Game* has helped build a mass audience for stories featuring Black female protagonists. *True to the Game* is published by Teri Woods Publishing and its popularity has led to two sequels, including *True to the Game II* (2007) and *True to the Game III* (2008), as well as a 2017 film adaption starring Vivica A. Fox. Gena, the seventeen-year-old protagonist, is one of the few Black female characters in urban fiction to end with considerable wealth *and* a marriage proposal, minus carceral punishment. She does not have Winter's acumen, but Gena is patently clear about her attraction to men who wear flashy jewelry, which for her was "meant to represent wealth."[84] Her attraction to affluence leads her to a relationship with Quadir Richards, a twenty-five-year-old drug-dealing millionaire whom she falls in love with.

I examine *True to the Game* because Gena's journey ends with her negotiating the circumstances surrounding Quadir's murder, making this novel a unique counterpoint to *The Coldest Winter Ever* and *Flyy Girl*. Unlike Qadeer, his homophonic counterpart in *Flyy Girl*, Quadir does not initiate a serious relationship with Gena from prison. Male characters also do not badger Gena about wearing Kente cloth or wooden jewelry, but Quadir's dramatic murder emphasizes the motif of endangered Black men that Tyree's *Flyy Girl* and Souljah's *The Coldest Winter Ever* rehearse. While Gena is rewarded with money in *True to the Game* and ends the novel as an independent single woman, her penalty for seeking hypergamy is not only a revocation of the marriage proposal she desired but also experiencing violent trauma.

Woods bookends the novel with tragedy, both confirming the high stakes of marrying up for Black female characters and illuminating racialized gender violence. Gena meets Quadir in the first chapter, but the depiction of Gena's boyfriend, Jamal, assaulting her also comes early in the novel. Gena lives alone, and in the second chapter, Jamal launches a stake out by sitting in front of Gena's apartment and awaiting her return. He strikes Gena when she returns home and admits she has been with Samirah, a friend he has prohibited her from seeing because she is a "gold digging bitch."[85] Like the narrator in "Sophisticated Bitch," Jamal fears that Samirah's economic aspirations are contagious and that Gena will "catch" them. After slapping her, Jamal picks Gena up, charges at her again, and threatens to kill her as Gena's neighbor watches from their apartment window. As the neighbor surveils, they refuse to call the police perhaps because they support this form of violence or because they recognize that Black communities are also under the state's surveillance and susceptible to its violence. This deafening silence and hypervisible intimate partner violence insinuates that heteropatriarchy is not simply a rankling system but a lethal construct that keeps women imprisoned.

This scene revives important discussions about Black girls and women and domestic or intimate partner violence among Woods's predominantly Black working- and middle-class female readership and tempers the sharp one-dimensional characterization of Gena as a vixen, but in doing so, it also marshals praise for Quadir as a figure of salvation. Deviating from *True to the Game*, *The Coldest Winter Ever* introduces Winter as arrogant about her rich family. In contrast, Gena describes her life growing up in the Philadelphia projects as "rough" and Jamal as abusive, "controlling," and "possessive."[86] Gena's upbringing and Jamal's violence generate sympathy for Gena as a character looking for a rich man, but that sympathy also bolsters the favorable depiction of Quadir as her prince charming à la Cinderella. Gena ends the chapter by describing her abuse and desperate need for solutions, with the omniscient narrator's heavy-handed question asking, "How could she break away from him?"[87]

Compressing Gena's psychic space and solitude, the novel moves quickly in its enthusiasm for Quadir's role as Gena's savior from Jamal in the aptly titled third chapter, "Recovery," cohering with the contours of masculine veneer and cultural norms about men as protectors.[88] Though Quadir does not force Gena into wooden earrings and even agrees to celebrate Christmas with her despite his Islamic beliefs, he is deeply invested in the kind of policing and surveillance that appear in *The Coldest Winter Ever* and *Flyy Girl* and are also deployed by police officers and law enforcement. Disguised as a romantic test to see if Gena's love is true, and evoking the novel's title, Quadir's suspicion of Gena compels him to research her past sexual activity to verify her conformity to conventional sex and gender roles. According to the romance tradition, women who do not heed conventional gender and sex norms "fail in traditional feminine areas of influence such as domesticity, motherhood, and love relationships."[89] Quadir's reconnaissance, or background check, will determine if Gena's past sexual history makes her eligible for a love relationship with him. Still, his research is not sufficient; he announces that she is on "probation."[90] Quadir co-opts law enforcement language and establishes his power. In doing so, he polices and criminalizes Gena's sexuality as Midnight polices Winter's behavior in *The Coldest Winter Ever*.

Quadir begins surveilling Gena during her probationary period by running a series of tests, including sending a wealthy decoy to test her fidelity, as practiced on salacious tabloid talk shows.[91] Gena passes Qadir's gratuitous examinations and "succeeds" in domesticity and hypergamy. She is awarded keys to Quadir's apartment and happily accepts his marriage proposal, indexing the features of marriageocracy for female characters who desire marriage as simple hard work through "probation" and a series of exams. Along with validating a lopsided marriageocracy, Quadir's evaluations, rewards, and penalties showcase how romance tropes veil the criminalization and policing of Black girls and women and reinforce conservative sex and gender rules repeated by the narrator in "Sophisticated Bitch," who derides cavalier female characters who "never kept a name" and "never seen a face" of the men they slept with.

Echoing Midnight, Quadir's masculine veneer helps deflect from his excessive surveillance of Black women's sexuality and their financially inflected romantic goals. When he first meets Gena, he has "kilos of cocaine in his trunk," but the narrator attempts to curb stereotypical judgments of Black men by clarifying that Quadir is an "intellectual."[92] He went to college to study dentistry, but graduated with a bachelor's degree in psychology.[93] Quadir is forced into illegal drug distribution because his aging father has no retirement fund, mirroring Midnight's "Robin Hood" characterization and solidifying a Black male redemption and vulnerability that eclipses their gender privilege.

Skin color, as a veneer, is used to affirm their "authentic" Black masculinity. In her assessment of Quadir, Gena counts his dark skin as an advantage, or "plus," following the old adage "the blacker the berry, the sweeter the fruit."[94] Midnight, Qadeer, and Quadir are all dark skinned, substantiating dark skin as a marker of "true" blackness and channeling Public Enemy's tribute to men who are "true and black" and suspicion of men who are "light" and "alright."[95] Through their respective freedom and tragic death, Midnight and Quadir expose the consequences of poverty and other systemic obstacles, but their dark skin and hard-luck Horatio Alger stories excuse their sexist behavior, provide redemption, and elevate reader sympathy.

Spanning five pages, Quadir's dramatic and heartrending demise overshadows his misogyny and the "reward" of Gena's impending wealth. The portrayal of Gena and Quadir enjoying their riches and the company of friends at a party suggests that Gena will happily close the novel with love and wealth. But Woods sends a message to her Black female readership when the fairy-tale dream of a wealth and love finale is violently revoked in the text. Assailants enter the party and abruptly disturb the revelry with a volley of bullets. In his last act of chivalry, Quadir throws Gena's body to the ground, protecting her from gunfire but leaving himself exposed to it.

Typically, a character's murder signals his life as a cautionary tale, which is mobilized in this instance as a warning against illegally selling drugs in Black communities, but the depiction of Quadir's assassination also renders him a martyr for strong Black men as figures of protection. The novel's tragic ending—through Quadir's histrionic death—forecloses Gena's opportunity for marriage and underscores Black male characters as heroes through patriarchal protection, while paradoxically exacerbating "black nationalist anxiety over racial virility" by magnifying their vulnerability.[96] Gena resolves, "There would never be another love like Quadir's. . . . If she could give the money back, she would in the wink of an eye."[97] Her last, elegiac wish to exchange capital for Quadir demonstrates the impossible concomitance of wealth and marriage for Black female characters.

Because of the historically common patriarchal practice of attaching monetary value to girls and women through dowries, fear of the gold digger is not solely an issue with Black women or the late twentieth century. Still, the heightened anxiety about Black women's courtship goals is a symptom of a "fetishization of the black family" that imbues the nuclear family with an impossible political power and challenges racist tropes about dysfunctional Black families, as Black girls and women who desire hypergamy obstruct the route to a revised form of Black patriarchal family that has excised economic patronage.[98] The paranoia about avaricious Black female characters is burdened by a political theater portraying Black women obtaining social and economic gains while inordinately high numbers of Black men are being incarcerated. Black male failure, scarcity, and "racial virility" thereby make it all the more important to weed out parasitic, uneducated, and culturally unaware Black girls, such as Winter, from Black communities, which in the 1990s were especially interested in tightening its racial borders in the face of neoliberalism and dwindling formal, prominent Black political organizations.

As a result, self-appointed and self-inserted leaders such as Sister Souljah supplant the Black Power emphasis on institutional responsibility with personal (ir)responsibility in a post–Black Power era, which includes broadly recharacterizing Black female sexual agency, street-smart education, and rising socioeconomic position as immoral and dangerous sexual behavior, miseducation, and unmerited class position that undermines Black unity and manhood. As a counternarrative to Black male socioeconomic failure, Black hypermasculinity and conservative Black womanhood, as wedded complementary ideals, ineptly redress race and gender inequity, intimate partner and state violence, and heterosexist paradigms for what constitutes protection and family.

CHAPTER THREE

Marrying Black

> Do you promise
> to love, honor, cherish and protect her,
> forsaking all others and holding on to her evermore?

As I discuss in the invocation, African American people have historically sought African American spouses in order to build families and middle-class communities that could serve as a sanctuary from racial terror, defying the ubiquitous presence of violence and death that doggedly menaces African American life and racial futurity. The criminalization of interracial marriage made this tacit "marry black" covenant a straightforward decision for some but not for all. Boxer Jack Johnson, for example, was known for parading his expensive clothes, jewelry, cars, and white girlfriends and wives in front of white men "at a time when southern blacks were assaulted or killed for no better reason than that they had begun to achieve some material success."[1] Others deliberately chose an African American spouse and used marriage as a way to combat antiblackness, including challenging racist myths about Black sexual deviancy and immorality. The contours of African American marriage have changed over time, but it is critical to note that for "middle-class or aspiring middle-class African American couples, marital relationships were interwoven with both public and private pressures."[2]

Marrying Black was not unlike the political tactic of "buying black," or purchasing goods from Black-owned businesses, as these enterprises could also aid in building families and middle-class communities. It is a vision that is brilliantly represented in Eddie Murphy's 1989 film *Harlem Nights* and through the jaunty Boom Boom Room nightclub in his 1998 film *Life*. Before the 1921 Tulsa Race Massacre, Tulsa's thriving "Black Wall Street" in the city's Greenwood neighborhood exemplified how the buy-Black strategy could strengthen families and communities and serve as a respite from racial terror. The "Don't Buy Where You Can't Work" campaigns of the 1930s advocated a boycott of white businesses that refused to hire African Americans; thus, Black-owned businesses became a haven from the racism and sexism African Americans experienced in white-owned establishments. The Black nationalist business model was a powerful response to white businesses that enacted Jim Crow laws. White business owners treated African American people as second-class citizens; disseminated racist advertisements, like the American Tobacco Company's "Nigger Hair" tobacco; or simply ignored Black consumers.[3] Moreover, Black customers "were forbidden use of dressing rooms and restrooms, were prohibited from trying on and returning clothes, and could be arbitrarily refused entrance or service at any moment."[4]

African Americans continued to see the Black nationalist business movement as a viable strategy in the mid-twentieth century despite its capitalistic aims and the looming fear that shop owners would be subjected to violence by their white neighbors, who would also destroy the establishments they had worked so hard to build. In his 1955 "Speech on the 'Buy Black' Campaign," Carlos Cooks—a prominent member of Marcus Garvey's Universal Negro Improvement Association—urged Black Americans to "transfer the commerce, business life and body politic of the alien parasite to its rightful owner, the Black communities."[5] Rehearsing a familiar Black nationalist assessment of racial integration as exploitative rather than a sign of liberation, Cooks insisted that a Black nationalist business model would help resist white supremacy by increasing economic power, effectively ridding Black communities of "unemployment, poverty, crime and alien exploitation."[6]

Building on this tangled historical tableau of romance and business, I critically examine the political tension shaping cross-racial desire in Sandra Kitt's *The Color of Love* (1995) and Eric Jerome Dickey's *Milk in My Coffee* (1998), unmasking the ways in which the cultural injunction to "marry black" takes the discursive shape of the Black nationalist call to "buy black" in the late twentieth century, while the enthusiasm for Black–white interracial relationships follows the logic of neoliberal deregulation of the market, signaling an unregulated romance "market." This network captures the kinship between African American people negotiating public space through business and navigating the private sphere via courtship. Jordan, the African American male protagonist in *Milk in My Coffee*, and Leah, the African American female protagonist in *The Color of Love*, are offered little to no opportunities for sexual or romantic indulgences in their intraracial relationships, seemingly asphyxiated by the regulation and political weight bound up with African American intimacy. I demonstrate how and why marriageocracy fails in fictional representations of African American intraracial relationships but somehow successfully supports "unregulated" Black–white interracial partnerships, shepherding them to "happy endings" with marriage proposals.

The Civil Rights Act of 1964, a growing Black middle-class, and the neoliberal push to deregulate the market made buying Black nearly unsustainable in the mid- to late twentieth and early twenty-first centuries. The Civil

Rights Act desegregated schools and public spaces and criminalized employment discrimination, prompting John H. Johnson to publish *The Negro Handbook* (1966), a manual for white business owners that outlined marketing and advertising strategies Johnson claimed would help attract African American consumers. Some white business owners with generational wealth from slavery were often able to provide more amenities to their consumers than African American entrepreneurs could, debilitating the buy-Black strategy.

The difficulty of buying Black heightened when President Ronald Reagan, heavily influenced by free-market proponent Milton Friedman, gifted tax breaks to large corporations and refused to implement the 1890 Sherman Antitrust Act, a regulatory policy put in place to stifle monopolies and stimulate competition. Local mom-and-pop stores and Black-owned banks could no longer compete with the monopolizing big-box retailers and massive financial institutions sprouting in suburbs and big cities. As a result, buying Black began losing its viability as a political strategy. Verifying the practical difficulties of buying Black in the twenty-first century, Maggie Anderson, an African American middle-class woman from Oak Park, Illinois, launched the Empowerment Experiment in 2009, in which she and her husband, John Anderson, patronized Black businesses for an entire year, marking a fourteen-mile drive to a Black-owned, full-service grocery store as one of their most substantial obstacles.[7] Buying Black became a luxury and privilege for those who had extra time, energy, and financial resources.

Though it appeared that African Americans had more consumer options, some were disenchanted with the failed promises of racial integration and began longing for Black Power nationalist approaches to achieving justice. Racial integration, deregulation, and a burgeoning African American middle-class in the late twentieth century dampened Carlos Cooks's economic manifesto for Black liberation, so African Americans began exploring political alternatives, both new and old. The nostalgia for the Black Power movement magnified, exemplified by Black Panther iconography and the rising fame of artists such as Public Enemy, X-Clan, and Queen Latifah. Losing its hold on the nationalist impetus to buy Black, part of the nostalgia for the Black Power movement began circulating and settling within the realm of romance, intimacy, and marriage, demonstrated by my analysis of Public Enemy's song "Sophisticated Bitch" in chapter 2.

Because Black intimacy had long been a tool exploited by the nation, as I explain in the invocation—from the Freedmen's Bureau regulation of marriage to the 1996 Welfare Reform Act—as well as harnessed by Black communities as a mode of challenging structural oppression, Black family formation became an easy focal point for political engagement. The marry-Black covenant began to more prominently take the discursive shape of the buy-Black protocol as compelling forms of nostalgia for Black Power nationalism grew and saddled African American intimacy with an unromantic burden.

Demonstrating the divergence between a Black Power nationalist nostalgia and neoliberal logics billowing under the metaphorical bridal veil, the marry-Black directive was ostensibly in tension with the nation's "progressive" political trajectory. The perceived need to secure and maintain African American heterosexual families was incongruous with desegregated employment, schools, and public spaces, along with the government's attempt to desegregate or "deregulate" romance and marriage just a few decades earlier. The 1967 Loving v. Virginia Supreme Court case would end "the nation's three-hundred-year history of laws prohibiting marriage across the color line."[8] Loving v. Virginia also purportedly modernized and opened up the "market," permitting heterosexual, Black–white marriages without penalty, and many African Americans took advantage of this political victory. Black cultural production was at the forefront of representing the perils and possibilities of this triumph, as characters navigated the move from Black intraracial intimacy to a Black–white interracial relationship.

Inspired by these discordant sentiments, I knit together two songs—Michael Jackson's 1991 up-tempo pop hit "Black or White" and Me'Shell NdegèOcello's 1993 wounding ballad "Soul on Ice"—for this chapter's soundtrack. Lauding a color-blind romance ethic in the refrain, "Black or White" echoes the rising veneration of love that seems to disregard racial categories and inhibitions. Jackson's narrator, proclaiming that it does not "matter if you are black or white," substantiated the idea that cross-racial desire was now in vogue and confirmed that love, with its attendant connotations of apolitical bliss, reverberated with so-called enlightened and modern, postracial society.[9] Two years later, NdegèOcello released the sonic antithesis to Jackson's refrain. The "recuperative rhythms and negotiated nationalisms" in "Soul on Ice" upended the fantasy of a postracial society and hailed Eldridge Cleaver's 1968 book of the same name.[10] Speaking back to Cleaver's Soul on Ice, which claimed that raping white women was a viable path to Black liberation, NdegèOcello's elegiac lyrics mourn the decline of Black intraracial relationships and disparage Black men for abandoning Black women and fantasizing about "virginal white beauty."[11] NdegèOcello and Jackson capture two popular but disjointed late twentieth-century moods. Their songs contemplate the implications of Black–white heterosexual romance during a moment of red-, black-, and green-tinged Black Power nostalgia, expressing inharmonious tunes of celebration and lamentation.

Marry Black Covenant

Penguin Books published the first edition of *The Color of Love*, which begins by depicting Leah, the protagonist, navigating a less than fulfilling relationship with Allen, her Black love interest. The arguments between Leah and Allen increase in intensity and number as Jason, a white New York City police officer, expresses interest in Leah. She is hesitant about embarking on a relationship with Jason until she discovers that Allen and her sister, Gail, have been engaged in a clandestine relationship. Not only does she suffer heartache from Allen's infidelity and Gail's betrayal, but she is haunted by the memory of a sexual assault by her coworker, drawing attention to her vulnerability and Jason's impending "rescue." Later, Jason comforts Leah after his coworker assaults her and performs the ultimate act of chivalry by protecting her from an assailant's bullet. By the end of the novel, Jason offers a sentimental marriage proposal from his hospital bed, and Leah accepts.

Confirming her acquiescence to the marry-Black covenant, Leah justifies her decision to stay with Allen at the beginning of the novel by citing her lack of "choices."[12] Even after Gail asks Leah if she loves Allen "that much," Leah emphasizes the unnecessary indulgence of love and romance, declaring, "Love isn't the point."[13] Leah's dismissal of love in her relationship with Allen, her Black boyfriend, and her desire for love in her relationship with Jason, her inevitable white suitor, suggests that she is bound by scarcity, the marry-Black code, and old-fashioned ideas about love, as dating or marrying merely for love is a fairly modern concept. Leah admits that Allen "was comfortable to be with . . . and black."[14] Her comfort, scoff at love, and pause before citing Allen's racial identity, marked by ellipsis, hints at Leah's halfhearted concession to an implicit marry-Black pledge, and her resignation suggests that the marry-Black code coerces men and women into lifeless obligatory commitments. Reiterating Leah and Allen's lifeless romance, Gail mockingly calls Allen "the suit," and Leah describes him as "stiff and pompous."[15] As "the suit," Allen's disembodied sartorial veneer reflects his lifeless affectation and reshapes the fleshly human desires linked to love and romance into a mannequin shrouded in the racialized political guise of which Leah must bear.

The high political stakes of Black intraracial intimacy are further augmented when Leah recounts her past relationships. Among them, she describes her college boyfriend, Ron, as an "angry" Black graduate student studying political science who was "verbose and eloquent about the historical injustices done to Blacks in America, and spent a lot of time feeling cheated and vengeful."[16] Fitting the stereotype of the Black revolutionary, Ron is the emblem of the political weight trussed to African American partnerships. Leah summarizes their intimacy as "quick and angry as Ron himself," with love and romance a luxury she is unable to afford in their relationship.[17] His rejection of nonviolence and her resistance to his views are catalysts for his decision to terminate their relationship, according to Leah. With disparate political ideologies galvanizing Ron's decision to dissolve his and Leah's bond, rather than the typical romance conflict of long distance or mismatched age, the novel anchors Black intraracial intimacy to an inflated political valence.

Ron's rejection of nonviolence subtly alludes to the previous era's Black Power nationalism, but the referent is more legible after Leah launches her postgraduate career. When her white coworker, Mike Berger, sexually assaults her, she punches him in the face and yells, "You try that again and you're going to wish you never heard the words Black Power!"[18] Leah once denounced Ron's embrace of violence, but the attempted rape she experiences in college compels her to be more aggressive in this scene. It is a conflict that gives Leah an opportunity to demonstrate her political consciousness by acknowledging and condemning the history of white male rape and assault of Black women before she begins her relationship with Jason. She violently reacts and summons "Black Power" in her response to Mike's assault because she must impugn the cultural presumption that Black women are enamored by or colluding with white men, which I discuss in the preceding chapters. Still, using "Black Power" against her racist and sexist coworker illustrates nostalgia for the Black Power movement and suggests that Leah has no other political movement to call on and use as a defense against Mike. Leah's threatening words are audacious but punctuate how Leah and Black female characters must be a political instrument animated by nationalist nostalgia, since state apparatuses have dismantled radical organizations and collectives.

Dutton Adult Hardcover published the first edition of Eric Jerome Dickey's *Milk in My Coffee* and had also published work by Ayn Rand and other well-known writers. Set in New York City during the late twentieth century, *Milk in My Coffee* chronicles the burgeoning romance between Jordan, the Black male protagonist, and Kimberly, his female love interest, who passes as white for most of the novel.[19] At the start of the novel, Jordan is dating J'nette, a young Black woman, but after several quarrels, he ends his relationship with her and begins one with Kimberly. Jordan begins learning how to negotiate an interracial relationship within his Black community of friends and family, but the narrative conflict is organized around several additional complications. J'nette tells Jordan she is pregnant with their child but later claims that Jordan's friend, Solomon, raped her and is the child's biological father. After Jordan has fallen in love with Kimberly, he is disappointed to discover that she is "part black" because it spoils his idealized visions of Black and white interracial intimacy.[20] Jordan is also unaware that Kimberly is legally married to a Black man, who refuses to grant her a divorce. In a seemingly never-ending trail of plot twists, Kimberly finds her estranged husband, but he is killed, allowing Jordan and Kimberly to prepare for matrimony by the end of the novel.

African American people were attracted to the buy-Black political strategy because it disturbed white supremacy, and analogously, Jordan's attraction to J'nette is based on her negotiation of systemic oppression. Of J'nette, Jordan says that her "arrogance at work turned me on. . . . She dressed striking and professional at work, and radical and hip hop when she got off. That turned me on too. Instead of being a slave to the system, she mastered two worlds."[21] Jordan's attraction to J'nette is sparked and fueled by her resistance to white racism and deployment of a Du Boisan double consciousness, conjuring the way African American people historically used romantic partnership as a shield against antiblackness.

The novel's setting and political iconography signify that Jordan feels politically bound to J'nette as well as portend his interracial relationship with Kimberly. Dickey stages J'nette and Jordan's first meeting at Jordan's workplace, a computer software company described as "political."[22] Their first meeting and attraction in the politically charged terrain of their work environment illustrate the heightened politicization of Black intimacy. Instead of framed images of family members or pets, Jordan has photographs of Malcolm X and Dr. Martin Luther King Jr. in his office, dramatizing it as a political space that has nurtured his attraction to J'nette's resistance to white supremacy. These images also foreshadow Jordan's turn away from the nostalgic Black Power nationalist politics generically linked to the image of Malcolm X and Black intraracial partnership and pivot toward the desegregation goals commonly tied to narratives about King that might affirm Jordan's impending interracial love. In fact, as Jordan's attraction to Kimberly develops, Jordan imagines the photograph of Malcolm X "panting fire and frowning down" on him because of his growing attraction to Kimberly.[23] Malcolm X, according to Jordan's phantasmagoria, has placed Black intraracial relationships on the front line for redressing racial injustice.

Jordan and J'nette indicate that just as African American partnership is called on to mitigate the force and intensity of structural inequality, these relationships are also incredibly vulnerable to race and gender oppression. There is a suspicious recharacterization of J'nette soon after Jordan meets Kimberly; J'nette's impressive mastery of "two worlds" transforms into a problem that plagues her relationship with Jordan. The text begins constructing J'nette's "radical" and "hip-hop" personality as alleged pathological sexual excess and insolence, corroborating Black bridal pathos. When J'nette arrives at Jordan's house for a late-night rendezvous, Jordan notes that J'nette has recently cut her hair, and he is annoyed that she has strewn her boxer shorts and military boots across his tidy apartment, hinting at her domestic incompetence, queerness, and emasculating militancy. Jordan remarks that J'nette makes him feel as though he is "making love to a commanding officer," signifying a stiff sexual comportment that coincides with the passionless rendering of Allen as "the suit."[24] Just as Leah calls Ron "angry," Jordan bizarrely describes J'nette's genitalia as "angry."[25] Though Jordan believes that he appreciates J'nette's confidence, in truth, he resents it. As an "officer" wearing military boots and boxer shorts, J'nette represents a so-called masculine authoritarian who supplants Jordan's patriarchal dominance. He is further wounded because J'nette has an insatiable sexual appetite that he is unable to fulfill, amplifying her as "emasculating" while also telegraphing her licentiousness. J'nette boldly says, "You don't one-hundred percent satisfy *all* my needs."[26] The novel leans on a timeworn racist and sexist caricature of African American women to build a layered critique of J'nette's improper sexual excess and nonconformity.

Serendipity and the Invisible Hand of the Romance Market

Black–white interracial relationships, akin to the invisible hand of the market, occur organically, and Black characters "freely" choose their white partners without the so-called suffocating regulatory edicts of the marry-Black covenant. Both stories rely on serendipitous situations to cultivate interracial desire and presume that the invisible hand of the romance market will sustain it. Neither Jordan nor Leah is single and looking for a mate; instead, both are in failing Black relationships when they meet Kimberly and Jason by happenstance. Jordan unsuccessfully attempts to hail a taxi cab for thirty minutes, and Kimberly happens to be in the taxi cab that finally stops for him. Leah meets Allen at an art opening, but happens upon Jason wandering outside her home, though he does not live in her neighborhood. Kimberly and Jason are readily available as "rebound" lovers who help spark serendipitous interracial intimacy, but they must take the first step in fostering relationships with Jordan and Leah. Upon meeting Jordan in the taxi cab, Kimberly invites him to her apartment, and Jason asks Leah out for coffee. Journalist Jill Nelson contends that Black men construct a fairy-tale version of love that obscures their agency in choosing a white partner, which holds true for Jordan and Leah, who are hesitant about interracial courtship and do not initiate it.[27] Nelson argues that the "more cautious" Black men "insist that it's not that they consciously 'chose' a white woman, they 'just fell in love.'"[28] They conveniently cloak themselves in an adolescent fantasy of love as a state independent of history, politics, and cultural conditioning that they inadvertently "'fall' into, like a sinkhole."[29]

The trope of tumbling into a Black–white interracial relationship is repeated in popular romance novels. Beverly, a Black female character in Connie Briscoe's 1994 novel *Sisters and Lovers: A Novel* (published by Rupert Murdoch's HarperCollins Publishers) substantiates that Black intraracial courtship must be disintegrating before characters are able to consider interracial courtship or "fall" for a white partner. Beverly hesitantly agrees to go on a date with a Black male coworker but is appalled when he hastily proposes that they take their wine to his "king-sized brass bed," where they can "have each other for dessert," all before the wait staff produces the bill.[30] Although she is disgusted with her coworker's proposition, she agrees to go on a blind date with another Black man, who, as she is finishing her meal of chicken wings, announces that he wishes "she would do him like [she] do them wing bones."[31] His sexual innuendo is enough to make her leave before the bill is paid and consider ending her quest to find a mate. Predictably, Beverly's pessimism about Black men grows, but she does not deliberately search for a white male partner; it is only after she is in a car accident with a white male motorist, literally crashing into him, that she seriously considers a white man—the motorist—further signaling her interracial courtship as accidental. *Sisters and Lovers* does not end with a burgeoning interracial romantic affair, but Beverly, Leah, and Jordan's "fall" into love evinces how romantic love is disingenuously represented as "organic rather than utilitarian."[32] Black–white interracial intimacy legitimizes itself as "true" love by emerging as an unstructured, natural union.

Asymmetrical Stakes

Leah and Jordan face disproportionate obstacles in their "organic" interracial relationships, exposing the complex historical terrain they navigate. This imbalance hinges on myopic constructions of power relegating the work of racism and oppression to white male characters. When Jason first reveals that he is a police officer who works with troubled Black youth, Leah admits that she is "thinking about a lot of young Black men killed senselessly by the police. White police."[33] Leah's uneasiness alludes to the acquittal of the white male officers of the Los Angeles Police Department on trial for the videotaped beating of Rodney King, which occurred only three years prior to 1995, the year *The Color of Love* was published. Jordan admits in *Milk in My Coffee* that he was raised to believe "the White man always had a secret agenda."[34] Jordan's beliefs overlap with Michael Jackson's characterization of racism in "Black or White," in which Jackson's narrator proclaims he "ain't scared of your brother" and "ain't scared of no sheets," referencing Ku Klux Klan's white male members.[35] Overemphasizing white male racism justifies the asymmetry between the resistance Jordan faces for his interracial partnership and the burden placed on Leah as she navigates her interracial desire for Jason.

The Color of Love overwhelms Leah with incidents of sexual violence in order to tarnish Black solidarity and the marry-Black covenant, and maintain support for cross-racial desire. Because Black intimacy is overloaded with political objectives, the novel's depiction of Black intimacy and kinship as well as interactions with Black strangers are continually disrupted by dysfunction and violence, compelling Black characters to consider and maintain relationships with white partners as it attempts to win over its predominantly Black female readership. Leah is the victim of an attempted rape in a stairwell by an unnamed Black male character, and the memory interrupts her evening slumber as a reoccurring nightmare and haunts her when she sees a stairwell and as she travels the streets of New York City. Leah admits she "remained a prisoner" to the violence, and her relationship with Allen exacerbates her trauma.[36] She confronts him about his forceful insistence on sex: "You didn't ask, you took. And you took as if you had the right to."[37] The sexual violence Leah faces at the hands of named and unnamed Black male characters and her sister's duplicity leaves her with few allies and sullies the romantic notions of Black community, kinship, and solidarity that mobilize the marry-Black covenant. These incidents atone for Leah's relationship with a white male police officer, and because of the epidemic level of sexual violence against Black women, these depictions cogently justify criticism of the marry-Black covenant.

In *Milk in My Coffee*, Dickey depicts sexual violence against J'nette although it is Jordan who has the (seemingly) white partner. Jordan's hindrances are unequal to Leah's distress, because emphases on white male racism "reify long-standing images of white women either as passive creatures without agency or as moral women who . . . hold fast to the core of American belief of 'color blindness.'"[38] Historians dismiss these misleading images and contend that historically white women have not been "passive bystanders" of white supremacy, but have acted as "co-conspirators."[39] Jordan is not subjected to the kind of violence Leah suffers, but he believes that his victimization is egregious and that his relationship with J'nette is unsalvageable because she is the source of his emasculation and discontent, precipitating his desire for Kimberly.

The sexual violence perpetrated against J'nette is a way to punish her for her race and gender transgressions, emphasize a pathological Black familial dysfunction, and reaffirm support for Jordan's interracial romance. J'nette calls Kimberly a "bitch," and other marginal Black female characters scowl at Jordan and Kimberly, suggesting that the depiction of sexual violence against J'nette is retribution for Black women's refusal to be "colorblind" and their uncomfortable criticism of white female fetishization.[40] In the last quarter of the novel, Jordan learns that Solomon, his "friend who's closer than a brother," is the father of J'nette's child as well as the person J'nette accuses of rape.[41] The details unravel when Zoe (Solomon's girlfriend and J'nette's friend) confronts J'nette in an explosive scene with Solomon and Jordan present, asking pointedly, "Did you come on to him?" putting J'nette on trial rather than Solomon and raising doubts about her accusations.[42] Zoe's accusation suggests that J'nette, as an alleged emasculating figure, does not fit the supposed profile of a rape victim. Jordan has already ended his relationship with J'nette by the time this scene erupts, but Solomon's violation, folded into the context of his and Jordan's fraternal relationship and Solomon's romantic relationship with Zoe (a friend to both J'nette and Jordan), punctures the cultural devotion to Black family and kinship, converting the positive implications of racial solidarity to a violent racial insularity. The novel boldly and repeatedly vilifies Black racial solidarity because the stakes of marrying Black are high and because the power and persistence of white supremacy relentlessly corrodes idealized visions of romantic success between white and Black protagonists. Solomon's violence and fraternal treachery, in the last quarter of the novel, is a last-ditch effort to coax readers who grasp the high political stakes of marrying Black and are still ambivalent about cross-racial desire, to accept Jordan and Kimberly's relationship.

Leah's trauma and feelings of isolation denote Black women's asymmetrical pain and spoil fantasies of Black racial solidarity, often defined by an unconditional allegiance to Black men, but also establish approval for Leah's future romantic choices. Her assailant flees without arrest or prosecution, but the text establishes Jason as the compensatory figure for her unnamed attacker. As a police officer, Jason represents a form of protection and justice that Leah seems to desperately need. The novel deifies Jason as Leah's "prince charming" and "white savior" when Jason's white coworker, Spano, sees Leah in their precinct office alone, assumes she is a sex worker who has escaped detainment, assaults her, and calls her a "nigger whore."[43] This incident threatens to weaken the possibility of romantic success between Leah and Jason, as it portrays law enforcement as excessively violent and recalls the "legacy of Black women's sexual abuse by white men" and Black women's subsequent efforts to negotiate "freedom *from* White men, not the freedom to choose White men as lovers and friends."[44] Jason alleviates the threat when he swoops in and quickly whisks Leah away, making him an endearing figure of security. Later in the novel, Jason takes a bullet for Leah when a Black man holds Leah hostage at gunpoint, signifying Black women's uneven burden of violence and bolstering Jason's commitment to protecting Leah.

Leah rejects Michael Jackson's color-blind "it's not about races" lyrics, and Jason recognizes that he is white and assures Leah that he is not racist, but his actions are at odds with his promise, evincing additional stress for Leah.[45] Immediately after Spano insults and humiliates Leah, Jason protects and "comforts" her, but his succor includes driving her home and initiating their first sexual encounter. Jason's seduction suggests that he is aroused by his ability to protect Leah as well as Spano's emotional and physical abuse of her, conjuring slavery's legacy of eroticizing Black women's exploitation and debasement, which NdegèOcello alludes to when she sings "Masters in the slave house again."[46] Read together, Spano's and Jason's response to Leah evoke the ways in which dominant society is repulsed by Black women's autonomy and aroused by their denigration.

In another scene, Jason's fearlessness is a romantic cover for his resistance to Leah's display of sovereignty. He invites Leah to accompany him to a hockey game, and she declines. He responds, "I'm trained not to take 'no' for an answer."[47] Jason's romanticized persistence is compatible with Leah's desire to feel shielded from danger, but his answer recalls Leah's victimization in alarming ways. His response calls forth the violence Leah experienced with her attempted rapist; her ex-boyfriend, Allen; Spano; and her white male colleague, Mike, but Leah laughs at his response and accepts his invitation. Jason's so-called incapability of accepting "no" adumbrates more pain for Leah, but it does not elicit her censure because Jason is overdetermined as an organic figure of rescue and marriageocracy.

The presumption of white women's powerlessness and antiracist beliefs allow Jordan and Kimberly to whimsically transgress gender norms in a way that Leah and J'nette are not permitted. Kimberly asks for Jordan's hand in marriage at the end of *Milk in My Coffee*, but Leah is barred from such capricious play with gender and romance tropes (consider the warning that J'nette's gender play issues to African American women). Jason's proposal, as he recovers from the bullet he shielded Leah from, animates and familiarizes conservative norms about patriarchy, family, and gender. Obeying the romance tradition, Jason declares, "I want to marry you" on his hospital bed, and Leah accepts his proposal while sobbing.[48] Leah negotiates how the emasculating stereotype clings to African American women and the ways in which suspicion of promiscuity always hovers over African American female victims of sexual violence, so she must rigidly abide by sentimental tropes and traditional gender constructions. These lopsided scenarios dovetail with the assertion that Black men become suitable partners for white women when they "achieve educational and economic success," which "lighten" and "masculinize" them, whereas Black women's success fosters characterizations of them as "sub-feminine" and "castrating."[49] It follows the historical legacy of "sociologists, psychiatrists, and the male literi" characterizing Black women as "castrating" and "unfeminine" in the 1960s.[50] Leah succumbs to conventional gender scripts, as these norms are presumed to offset her success and exaggerations of Black female castration, sub-femininity, and promiscuity.

Calculating the Cost of Freedom

Despite the long history of white sexual exploitation of Black women and men, Black protagonists in *Milk in My Coffee* and *The Color of Love* inscribe appealing myths about white partners, insinuating Black intraracial partnerships purported incompatibility with romance and the exceptional ability of white partners to precipitate love and passion, ultimately humanizing Black characters. Jordan's sexual vignettes with Kimberly could not be more different than his encounters with J'nette, his Black love interest; he describes Kimberly's body as "soft," "hot," and even emitting a "glow,"[51] paralleling

NdegèOcello's sketch of white women as "snow white passion."[52] Kimberly does not interrogate Jordan when she calls him and J'nette answers his phone or when she sees them in a cab together the next day, characterizing her as the easygoing and understanding girlfriend, resonating with Jackson's notion of interracial intimacy as a "miracle."[53] Kimberly waits and confronts Jordan in a modest tone and manner over a glass of wine at his home. In contrast, when J'nette discovers that Jordan has begun dating someone else after they have broken up, she shreds photographs of Jordan and Kimberly, screams at him, and closes the evening threatening him with a knife. The stereotype of the violent and unreasonable "black bitch" helps bolster the case for the Black male's attraction to the undemanding and allegedly more submissive, rational, and civilized white woman.

The novel imbues Kimberly with political ideals of racial freedom—the freedom for Black men to choose whom to love—one that elides how this construction is contingent on collapsing Black subjectivity with bondage, containment, and overregulation. In the original version of the controversial "Black or White" music video, Jackson walks down a staircase as a black panther,[54] gesturing to Black Panther Party leader Eldridge Cleaver, who famously declared, "When I put my arms around a white woman, well, I'm hugging freedom. The white man forbade me to have the white woman on pain of death. . . . I will not be *free* until the day I can have a white woman in my bed."[55] Jordan reprises Cleaver's conflation of white womanhood and freedom when he meets Kimberly, confessing, "I'd never met any woman who was so *free*."[56] Later, when Kimberly talks of traveling to California, Jordan exclaims, "You sure are a *free* spirit."[57]

In their conflation of white womanhood with freedom, Cleaver and Jordan are the imagined subjects of NdegèOcello's lyrics upbraiding her "brothers attempt to defy the white man's law and his system of values."[58] As Kimberly embodies enlightenment and freedom throughout most of the novel, her estranged husband with Black heritage, Peter, symbolizes bondage through his refusal to give her a divorce and the restrictive gender roles he instituted when they were together, such as forbidding Kimberly from working outside the home. Likewise, Jordan's Black ex-girlfriend, J'nette, signifies containment through her military attire, characterization as a "commanding officer," and announcement that she is pregnant with Jordan's child.

The starry-eyed fairy-tale depictions of white partners in *Milk in My Coffee* and *The Color of Love* correspond to the quixotic representation of white businesses. During Leah's love scene with Jason, she begins crying because she is "stunned" by Jason's "consideration and awareness" in contrast to

Allen's sexual violence.[59] The narrator observes that Leah felt a "profound sense of relief," and her "body rejoiced" with Jason.[60] The supposed added "benefits" of Black–white interracial relationships mirror John H. Johnson's claim that Black consumers who have "turned with increasing alacrity to white establishments" are offered "extra services, luxury atmosphere, and a degree of glamour for the same dollar" that they might have spent at a Black-owned business.[61] Comparatively, in discussing her Empowerment Experiment, Maggie Anderson discusses the feelings that some have about Black-owned businesses being inferior to shops owned by white people.[62] This concern about the inadequacies of Black businesses and idealization of the luxuries offered by white-owned businesses resembles the depiction of Black–white interracial intimacy in both novels.

Deregulating Romance and Finance

The idealization of white partners is brought to the fore when *Milk in My Coffee* attempts to intervene and reconcile the historical legacy of white female fetishization against Black Power leaders professing that "Black is beautiful!" In the beginning of the novel, Jordan expresses his hesitation about dating Kimberly, claiming, "If she was a sista I'd be asking for her phone number, offering a dinner date later in the week. If she looked like me."[63] With this claim, Jordan not only implies that an instinctual, regulated racial bond drives Black male attraction to Black women but also that Black women's "natural" desirability puts an end to the need for the Black Power movement's "Black is beautiful" politics. In other words, there is no longer a need to affirm Black female beauty against dominant beauty standards because Black women, or "sistas," are offered dinner dates *just because* they are Black, challenging contemporary reports alleging that Black women are among the most undesirable people on dating applications.

Jordan attempts to establish his appreciation for Black female beauty by overexplaining his attraction to Black women, though in the most vacuous terms. When listening to popular singer Rachelle Ferrell in Kimberly's apartment, Jordan says he loves Ferrell's "strong, black-woman look, . . . her full lips, the arousing way her mouth moved when she hit all those sexy notes as she crooned."[64] He goes on to say, "Part of the reason I was attracted to J'nette was because she has that same look. Ain't nothing like a strong black woman. Nothing."[65] His tribute to "strong" Black women, including J'nette, challenges white womanhood as exemplary of beauty and desirability and African American women as unlovable. Jordan attempts to prove that African American men undoubtedly love African American women and that the postracial battle for a more inclusive definition of beauty has thus been won.

Jordan uses consumption as another way to muffle the voices of dispirited Black women and as a way to dry the "tears of coal-colored children crying for acceptance," as NdegèOcello impassionedly sings in "Soul on Ice."[66] When Kimberly first invites Jordan to her apartment, she uses the opportunity to sell her artwork to Jordan as a ruse for expressing her attraction to him, substantiating how competition, the market, and romantic desire occupy contiguous spaces. Silently, Jordan thinks Kimberly's work is good but that she does not have a "patent on talent; there were a million and one places in Harlem to buy Black art. Black art created with the hands and eyes and hearts of Black people. Not made from our blood, sweat, and tears."[67] Supporting Black businesses inhibits what Jordan limns as the exploitation of Black labor in the art industry. He affirms that the Black art available in Harlem is likely equal to the quality of Kimberly's art, easing the fear that white businesses offer luxuries that Black businesses cannot, as described in Johnson's *Negro Handbook*.

In a clever shift, Jordan's language begins assuaging cultural anxiety that interracial partnership will stymie efforts to preserve and enrich Black creative expression. Tallying up his consumer choices for Black art to "a million and one places," Jordan disingenuously highlights ideas of Black cultural excess and conservative understandings of a free-market advantage, while dismantling the implicit argument that his affair with Kimberly will thwart the preservation and cultivation of Black cultural forms. Much like the case for affirming Black female beauty, it would seem as though the battle for maintaining and developing Black cultural expression is already won. It is also important to note that Jordan does not account for how Harlem, as a supposedly Black segregated urban space, is relatively small in comparison to the options available for purchasing art by white artists across the nation and world.

Jordan expresses his fondness for art by Black artists and Black female beauty but also pits Black women against white women in an effort to defend his romantic goals. Jordan attends a party, declaring that he was prepared for Black women's bad attitudes when he walked in with Kimberly, "but the way she looked . . . her wavy hair hanging over her shoulders and down her back, not a damn thing could be said, especially by the women sporting fake locks."[68] According to Jordan, Black is not as beautiful as it once was when Kimberly walks into a room full of Black women. Deepening the hostility, Jordan praises Kimberly's derriere and concludes that there is a Black woman "in Harlem with an ironing-board *butt*, crying every hour on the hour, trying to figure out who stole her portion of the ancestry."[69] His excessive scrutiny of Kimberly's body and hair confirms the assertion by Black feminists that the "tactic many black men use . . . is to reduce the conflicts between white women and black women to a 'tug-o'-war' for the black penis."[70]

Alongside pitting Black and white female characters against one another, Jordan presumes that Black women's so-called racial inauthenticity makes their criticism of white women's cultural appropriation hypocritical. At the outset, Jordan is uncomfortable when he sees Kimberly's hair in cornrow braids and is initially in agreement about what Black female characters see as an offensive white appropriation of Black culture, but then he recapitulates Michael Jackson's rhythmic appeal for "impartiality" when he sings, "I'd rather hear both sides of the tale."[71] Jordan asserts: "Every time a white woman sported something ethnic, I'd heard the sista's . . . back-handed compliments and . . . negative comments on everything from hairstyles to Kente outfits to . . . the Moonwalk, groaning and wondering if African Americans would ever have anything that the other races didn't steal, imitate, or try to duplicate. . . . Yep. Sistas would rage about white women ripping their fashions off, all while [they] . . . were draped in Levi's and Anne Klein."[72] Jordan reframes white appropriation as a supposed equal, unregulated transfer of culture between the two races, avoiding how Black women are unevenly penalized for their hair and attire in public and private spaces. He alleges that a deregulated clothing industry has benefited Black and white women's consumption equally, so Black women's complaints about white appropriation are "irrational." Jordan's flimsy contention dismisses Black women as angry hypocrites and stokes the political fires between Black women and white women, absolving Black male characters of their glorification of white women. His crusade contests what Malcolm X identifies as a problematic Black male reverence for white women and reassigns the issue to "irrational" and "bitter" Black female characters in order to curtail obstacles to cross-racial desire.

The Racial Coquette and Reconstructed Tragic Mulatta

The novel uses Kimberly as another way to resolve the disharmony between the fetishization of white women and the claim that Black is beautiful, along with the alleged political chasm that Jordan imagines between the image of Malcolm X and that of Dr. Martin Luther King Jr. on his office desk, and the interstice between "Soul on Ice" and "Black or White." As a refashioned tragic mulatta, Kimberly is a figure of mediation, and her tragedy of being teased by her paternal African American family and abused by her estranged Black husband shapes much of her story, but she is not given a fatalistic ending as dictated by the trope. Kimberly is what I call a "racial coquette," who glibly flirts with the color line. She refers to herself as a "mulatta," maintaining that she has an Irish, German mother and a "mulatto" father, who is "black, Indian, *and* white."[73] She is enraged when her estranged husband, Peter, calls her "black," and she refuses to give a straightforward answer when people ask about her racial identity,[74] insinuating that she, like Jackson's "Black or White" postracial narrator, is not going to "spend" her "life being a color."[75] Moreover, she augurs, through her moniker and embodiment, the voluptuous, Black-tinged exoticism and fetishization of another Kimberly popular in early twenty-first century reality-television culture, who also glibly flirts with the color line.

Kimberly's nimble prevarication sharpens the novel's construction of her as a mediating figure and reconstructed tragic mulatta. When Jordan finally discovers that Kimberly is "part black," his fantasy of liberation is ruptured. He eulogizes his freedom, glumly concluding that he is "not as *free*" as he thought.[76] Jordan backpedals on his presumptions of freedom but reveals how Kimberly reigned as a conduit of his pseudo-liberation before her racial undoing. His resolution buoys NdegèOcello's lyrics warning Black men that they "can't run from" themselves because the idea of white women as emblems of freedom is "just an illusion."[77]

As much as Jordan is wounded by Kimberly's lie of omission, he mends quickly because she, fortunately, is not bequeathed with the plain, insipid blackness of J'nette or other "regular" Black American women. She placates Jordan's "frowning" image of Malcolm X and the cultural nationalism tied to "Black is beautiful!" by boasting visits to Accra, Takoradi, and Cape Coast; painting representations of African families, rituals, and ceremonies on her canvases; wearing cornrow braids; and possessing an ample "black" posterior. Conversely, her claims that doctors identified her as "Caucasian" on her birth certificate, despite her "mulatto" father; her account that she was "given a white culture"; and her insistence that when she completed job applications and checked "black" or "Negro," "they always changed it . . . without asking" jibe with the fetishization of white women and appease the dream of integration propelled by nostalgic, watered-down renderings of Dr. Martin Luther King Jr.[78] Her racial identity is an upshot of a modern, desegregated, multiracial nation, but it also illustrates how the "associated shortage of desirable men in the marriage market" gives some Black men an unspoken advantage, but has placed a "premium on having lighter skin" for Black women.[79]

Color Theory and Interracial Investments

The purported modern, desegregated, multiracial nation comes with other inconspicuous costs. The depiction of Leah, an assistant art director, and Jason, a police officer, coincides with an uneven class dynamic often found in literary and popular culture representations of Black–white interracial intimacy. These portrayals frequently include white partners with a lower-paying job or less prestigious career than their Black lovers. Flipper, the Black male protagonist in Spike Lee's *Jungle Fever* (1991), is an architect, and his white lover is his secretary. Marron (Whitney Houston) in *The Bodyguard* (1992) is a famous and wealthy singer, while her white boyfriend, Frank Farmer, is a bodyguard. Kenya McQueen in *Something New* (2006) is a Black female accountant, and her white boyfriend, Brian Kelly, is a landscaper. In Dickey's text, Jordan has a stable position as a computer programmer, and Kimberly is a freelance artist.

Racial identity is an albatross that penalizes and rewards Black and white characters based on their class position. Ralph Richard Banks claims, "Black women marry down more frequently than any other group of women . . . the high incidence of African American marry-down relationships may contribute to racial disparities in divorce rates. African Americans divorce so frequently in part because the educational and cultural gap between spouses renders them incompatible as mates."[80] His claims are at odds with the representation of successful Black–white interracial partnership in fiction and film, where middle-class African Americans regularly choose and share commonalities with blue-collar white partners or white love interests who do not have the well-respected, middle-class careers that their Black partners have. African American middle-class partners appear more attractive in a dating pool, especially by those with lower-paying jobs and less prestigious careers, as their class may counterbalance their stigmatized racial identity.

For those white characters with a maligned social or class status, white privilege is the compensation, presumably creating a more equal relationship with middle-class Black partners. For her ethnographic book-length study *Interracial Marriages between Black Women and White Men* (2008), Cheryl Judice interviewed African American women, who contend that society treats them better because they are married to white men.[81] One respondent confesses that "having a white husband sometimes protects [me] from other forms of white racism," and another woman admits that "there have been times when [I] have gotten better treatment or service because [my] spouse is white."[82] As much as these responses expose the power of white privilege, they also lay bare the vulnerabilities of Black intraracial partnerships. Nonetheless, it would seem that African American male and female characters are unable to "afford" a white partner until they have achieved middle-class status. Because matrimony is a path to "white privilege, a nonwhite partner must earn this opportunity through extraordinary effort. Only the most talented and deserving nonwhite can win the affection of even an average white person. Because race matters, upward mobility through marriage is limited to the privileged few and leaves the color line largely intact."[83]

Imprint of Interracial Intimacy

Kimberly and Jordan exemplify what Celia R. Daileader calls "Othellophilia," or the cultural obsession with depictions of Black male–white female courtship, with *Guess Who's Coming to Dinner* (1967), *Jungle Fever* (1991), and *Love Field* (1992) serving as just a few examples.[84] While Black–white interracial relationships do not constitute the only kind of cross-racial partnership, and some claim that the "black-white dichotomy . . . has exhausted all valuable social inquiry," NdegèOcello and Jackson, along with *The Color of Love* and *Milk in My Coffee*, indicate that these representations deserve more interrogation.[85] My analysis demonstrates how they offer a multifaceted commentary on late twentieth-century perceptions of racial passing and interracial intimacy. A modified version of Carlos Cooks's buy-Black ethic hovers over both novels as Leah and Jordan negotiate the marry-Black covenant away. At the same time, Kitt's and Dickey's market-driven fiction must preserve a "buying black" ethic, or an intraracial transaction between Black authors and a predominantly Black readership, while depicting emotionally satisfying interracial relationships. One way to do this, albeit counterintuitive, is to mobilize Black stereotypes in order to construct unbearable Black relationships, while depicting protagonists falling for, not deliberately choosing, "irresistible" white partners. The exaggerated passion between white and Black partners and eventual marriage proposals in *The Color of Love* and *Milk in My Coffee* verify the sexual and romantic ennui and the failed marriageocracy tethered to Black relationships. Amplified political claims invested in Black courtship compel Leah and Jordan to choose and even glorify white romantic partners without fully disclosing the complicated racial politics and stereotypes implicated in interracial sex.

My close reading pinpoints the social forces shaping intimacy in *The Color of Love* and *Milk in My Coffee*. Both texts make a common assumption that white partners who are able to love Black men and women cannot be racist—a specious logic that extends to men in heterosexual relationships, who therefore supposedly cannot be sexist. Rachel F. Moran points out that love is constructed as an "irrational impulse," but it "transcend[s] the individual," so we must "confront the ways in which race has distorted social boundaries rather than retreat into the easy and unreflective innocence of romantic individualism."[86] Confronting these social boundaries unearths the splintering bedrock of these relationships. By the end of the novel, Leah has traded one form of violent patriarchy, Allen, for another, Jason. Both Leah and Jordan surrender to a stereotypical white savior, with Jason constructed as salvation from a so-called dangerous Black community, while Kimberly operates as a "respite" from the overpoliticization of Black subjectivity. As the novel enacts these "common sense" affirmations, it proffers sexual freedom as a peace offering to readers, obliquely suggesting that Black intraracial intimacy is bound by political agendas that supposedly leave passion dormant.

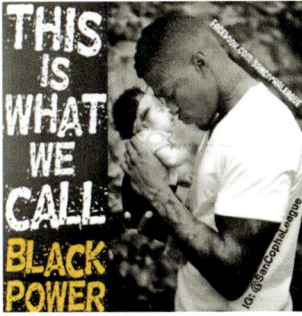

FIGURE 1.1 "This Is What We Call Black Power." Image from the SanCopha League Facebook page. Established in 2012, the SanCopha League is a nonprofit organization based in New Jersey.

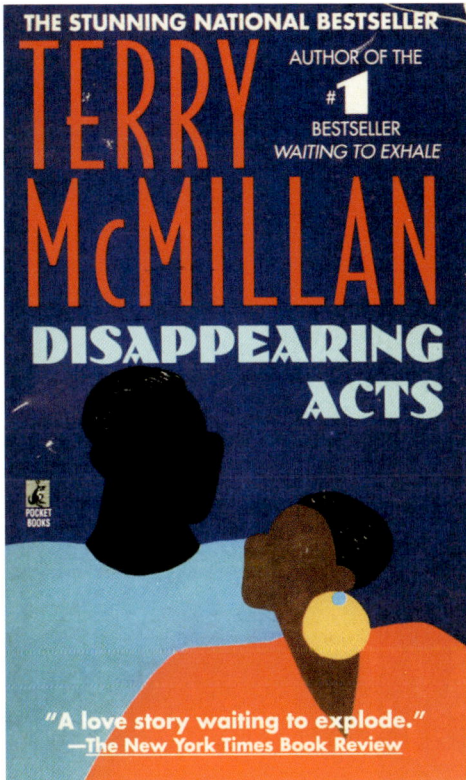

FIGURE 1.2 Cover for Terry McMillan's novel *Disappearing Acts*, 1989.

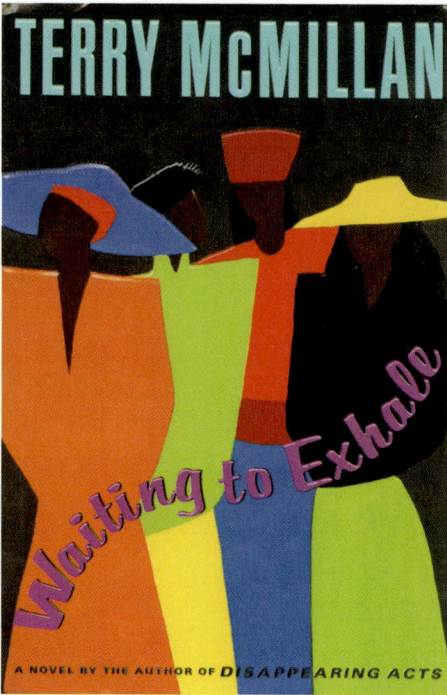

FIGURE I.3 Cover for Terry McMillan's novel *Waiting to Exhale*. Viking hard cover edition, 1992. Cover image, *Ensemble*, by Synthia Saint James.

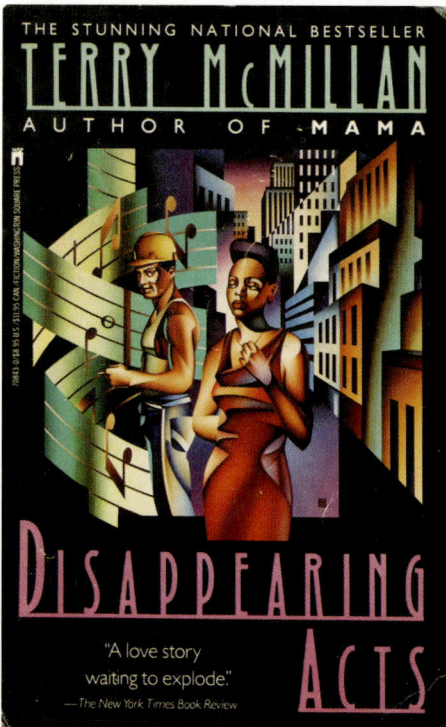

FIGURE I.4 Cover for Terry McMillan's novel *Disappearing Acts*, 1991.

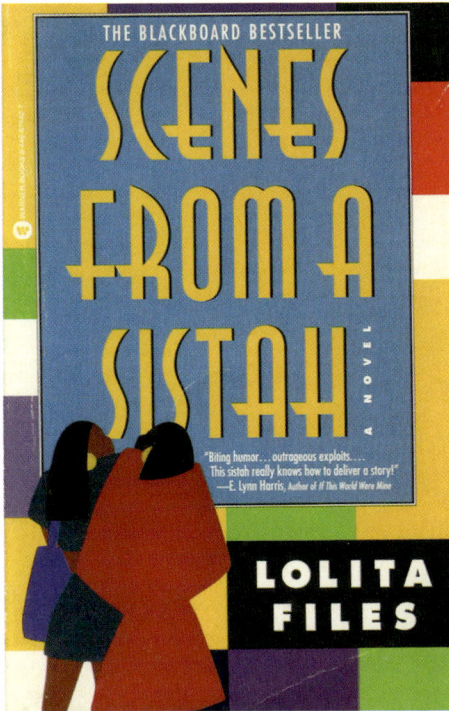

FIGURE 1.5 Cover for Lolita Files's novel *Scenes from a Sistah*, 1998.

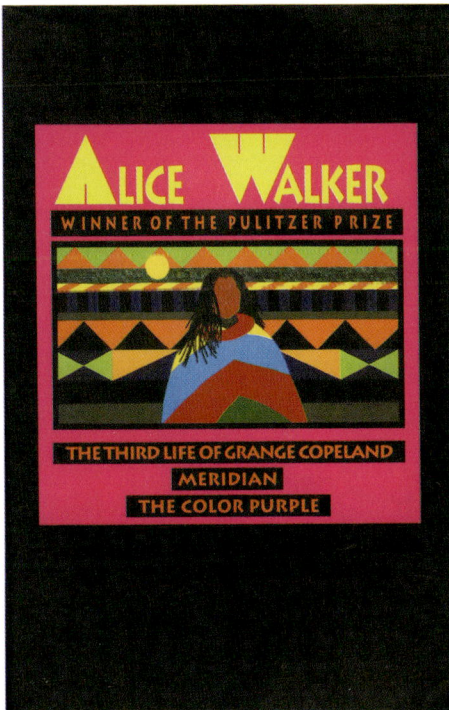

FIGURE 1.6 Cover for Alice Walker's novels *The Third Life of Grange Copeland/Meridian/The Color Purple*, 1990.

FIGURE I.7 Jacob Lawrence, *And the Migrants Kept Coming*. 1940–41. Panel 60 from
the *Migration Series* by Jacob Lawrence. © 2018 The Jacob and Gwendolyn Knight
Lawrence Foundation, Seattle/Artists Rights Society (ARS), New York. Digital image
© The Museum of Modern Art/Licensed by SCALA/Art Resource, NY.

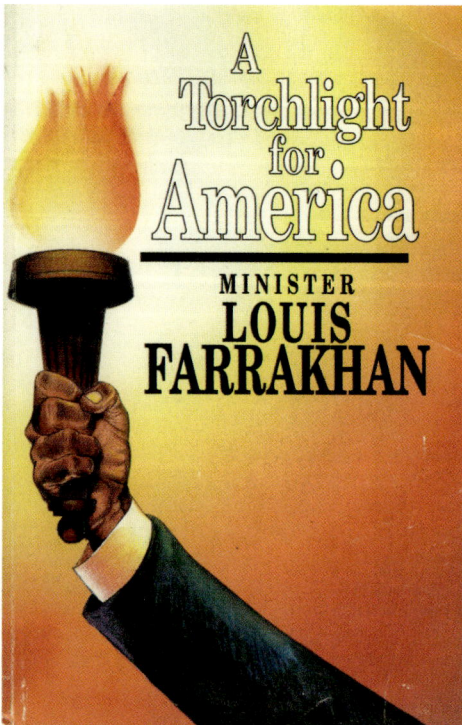

FIGURE 4.1 Cover for Louis
Farrakhan's *A Torchlight for
America*, 1993.

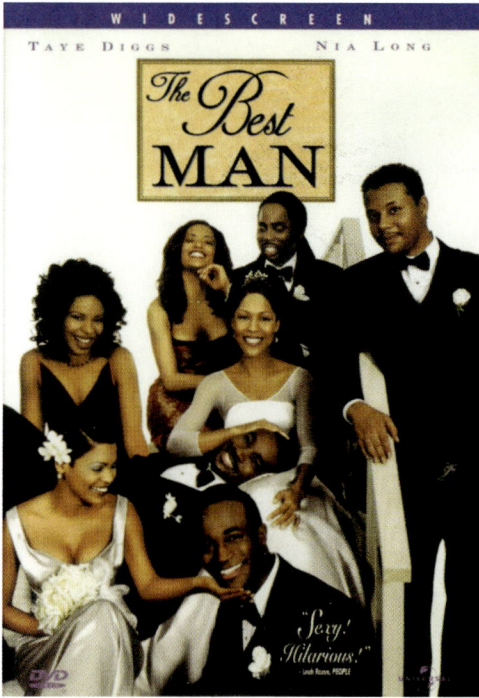

FIGURE 5.1 *The Best Man*. DVD. Directed by Malcolm D. Lee. 40 Acres and a Mule Filmworks. Universal Pictures, 1999.

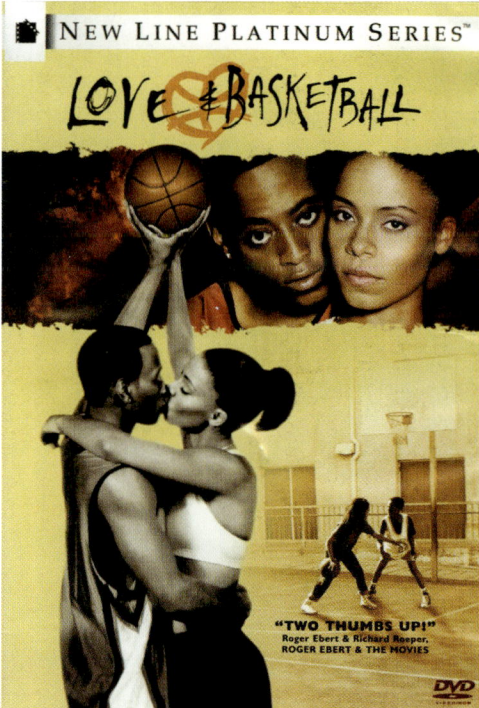

FIGURE 5.2 *Love & Basketball*. DVD. Directed by Gina Prince-Bythewood. 40 Acres and a Mule Filmworks. New Line Cinema, 2000.

FIGURE 5.3 Mia lets her hair down as she approaches Harper. *The Best Man*. DVD. Directed by Malcolm D. Lee. 40 Acres and a Mule Filmworks. Universal Pictures, 1999.

FIGURE 5.4 Monica exhibits confidence on the basketball court. *Love & Basketball*. DVD. Directed by Gina Prince-Bythewood. 40 Acres and a Mule Filmworks. New Line Cinema, 2000.

FIGURE 5.5 Young Monica looks affectionately at the bloody wound, or "kiss," on her cheek. *Love & Basketball*. DVD. Directed by Gina Prince-Bythewood. 40 Acres and a Mule Filmworks. New Line Cinema, 2000.

FIGURE 5.6 Young Monica in a patch of flowers after Quincy pushes her. *Love & Basketball*. DVD. Directed by Gina Prince-Bythewood. 40 Acres and a Mule Filmworks. New Line Cinema, 2000.

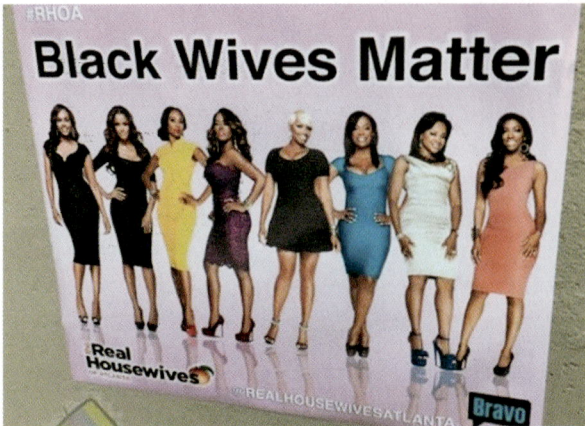

FIGURE B.1
Black Wives
Matter poster.
January 2015.

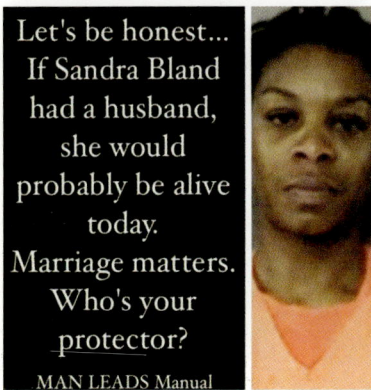

Let's be honest...
If Sandra Bland
had a husband,
she would
probably be alive
today.
Marriage matters.
Who's your
protector?
MAN LEADS Manual

FIGURE B.2 A 2015 meme exploiting Sandra Bland's death, disseminated by Ro Élori Cutno, author of *Man Leads . . . : Woman Follows, Everyone Wins*. Self-published, CreateSpace, 2013.

CHAPTER FOUR

Monstrous Marriage

If any of you can show just cause
why they may not lawfully be married,
speak now; or else for ever hold your peace.

In her pioneering 1978 essay "Toward a Black Feminist Criticism," Barbara Smith declares that the literary world does not know that "Black women writers and Black lesbian writers exist."[1] The existence of Black women writers — by which Smith means Black *heterosexual* women writers — did come to be known in the late twentieth century, although the constrictions of the literary world in a post–Black Power moment shaped how and for what these writers were known. Novels about Black female heterosexual protagonists, such as Terry McMillan's *Waiting to Exhale*, eclipsed fiction by Black lesbian writers centering Black lesbian characters. In her 2005 retrospective, "But Some of Us Are Brave Lesbians: The Absence of Black Lesbian Fiction," Jewelle Gomez points out that the representation of Black lesbian lives still occupies an "inordinately small space in the world of literature," with Black lesbian invisibility constituting an "epidemic."[2]

Fiction by Gomez, Catherine E. McKinley, and Lisa C. Moore, among others, depict Black lesbian protagonists, but Gomez's words still ring true for fiction: there are few places were Black lesbian lives are made to matter in the late twentieth and early twenty-first centuries.[3] As print, visual, sonic, and political culture proliferated around the "wife" and "bride" in the late twentieth and early twenty-first centuries, patriarchy, heterosexuality, and marriage were mobilized through literature as the status quo for African American women. This discursive terrain exacerbated the invisibility of Black lesbian protagonists and writers, and, in tandem, their continued obfuscation bolstered attention to representations of heteronormative courtship and marriage as indispensable.

As such, this chapter is a critical rupture to timeworn representations of traditional family as a balm for systemic inequality. By turning my attention to Sapphire's *Push* and its political and cultural topography, I further underscore the fraying edges of romance tropes and illustrate the ways in which touting marriage and patriarchal family as a political responsibility enables violence and abuse. Authored by Black lesbian writer Sapphire, *Push* features a Black queer character and exposes how emphasis on heteropatriarchy produces horrid consequences. Set in 1987 and told from the point of view of sixteen-year-old Claireece Precious Jones, *Push*, through epistles and prose, details Precious's experiences living in Harlem with her mother, Mary. Precious's father, Carl Kenwood Jones, is an inconsistent presence in her life, but both he and Mary sexually abuse Precious. She eventually reveals that she has two children as a result of her father's rape, which is juxtaposed against her fantasies of being "pretty" and living an idyllic life married to her white male math teacher. Her school suspends her, and she begins attending Each One Teach One, an alternative school for girls, where her Black lesbian teacher, Ms. Blue Rain, teaches her how to read and write. Her progress does not signal a traditional happily-ever-after ending; by the novel's finale, Precious learns she is HIV positive, but she has developed a stronger sense of self-love and formed an alternative queer family with her Each One Teach One cohort.

The romance genre saturated so much of late twentieth-century Black fiction and culture that its heteronormative plot structure was exalted and even used to evaluate Precious's horrific story. When Sapphire's agent auctioned off a half-completed version of *Push*, a potential editor asked if Precious "was going to lose weight and find a boyfriend" by the end of the novel.[4] The potential editor's query, an evaluation laden with romanticized delusions about the protagonist and society, reflects a cultural desire for Black fiction of any kind—especially texts with female protagonists—to adhere to a conventional romance plot structure. Precious's story, filled with graphic details about seemingly insurmountable obstacles of incest, poverty, and illiteracy, is somehow not complicated enough to dissuade readers from demanding a "satisfying" finale. It may also be the case that Precious's story is so abhorrent that it requires such an ending. Nevertheless, the desire for a neat, comfortable postracial and postfeminist conclusion reflects the kinds of societal demands placed on fiction by Black authors and how the public assesses Black cultural production. Sapphire points to the absurdity of such demands, creating space for Black queer characters and an alternative to heteropatriarchy.

What some see as the book title's implicit promise of hope despite the novel's gratuitous representation of violence, trauma, and structural hindrances also functions to overturn our most romantic notions about family and heteropatriarchy. Most of the cover art for *Push* prominently displays the title in black on a red background, without any figurative representation. The simple title and austere cover art draw the reader's focus to the book title, evoking its polysemic connotations, including the definition to strive despite impediments, the Black cultural acronym for *PUSH*—that is, "**pray until something happens**"—and Jesse Jackson's Rainbow PUSH [People United to Serve Humanity] Coalition. Dovetailing with the potential editor's query, all three connotations foster a pretense of hope for Precious's Sisyphean story. But instead of conceding to the multiple subtexts promoting resilience and the cultural demand that Precious lose weight and find a boyfriend (and one who might be an appropriate father figure for her children at that), Sapphire saddles Precious with additional obstacles in the second half of the novel, thwarting the optimism embedded in the title.

As the frame for this chapter, Sweet Honey in the Rock's 1983 song "Testimony" redirects attention away from pushing for a particular outcome and instead foregrounds the jagged process, impediments to, and progress of witnessing throughout *Push*. The novel conjures the song's lyrics, group collaboration, genre, and vocal composition. As the nation celebrates personal responsibility and individualism, the music industry has moved in a similar direction by cultivating solo performers rather than highlighting vocal groups and collectives. This is especially true for female groups. Even if cultural gatekeepers support the development of a female singing group, an artist eventually emerges from the group to pursue a solo career and earns an amount of success and wealth that is disproportionate to that of her vocal collaborators.

Diverging from this pattern, Sweet Honey in the Rock's four female vocalists resemble the cooperation and alliances between the women at Each One Teach One.[5] This symphonic collaborative ethos supplants the sociopolitical expectation that individual hard work can defeat immense structural hindrances. The song's unadorned a cappella arrangement punctuates the crisp precision of the song's vocal harmony and mirrors the Life Story project. Placed at the end of the novel following Precious's first-person narration, the Life Story project comprises a bricolage of candid, unembellished memoirs penned by the Each One Teach One students. Sapphire's use of prose, poetry, epistles, and life stories, along with the blues and hip-hop aesthetics that scholars have unearthed throughout *Push*, complement the ways in which Sweet Honey in the Rock conceived a new genre of music out of poetry, spirituals, blues, and jazz. Finally, Sweet Honey in the Rock's song lyrics and title, with its connotation of justice, legitimize the power of individual and communal witnessing just as Precious and her chorus of classmates are encouraged to give witness to their abuse and survival, which speaks back to legislation attempting to render them invisible.

Similar to McMillan's work, *Push* attracted the attention of elite literary critics and popular consumers alike, straddling high-brow acclaim and the middle-brow stigma of commercial success. Originally published in hard cover by Knopf and appraised as "affecting and impassioned" by the *New York Times*, *Push* quickly solidified its status as an esteemed literary text.[6] More than ten years after its publication, the novel captured the attention of celebrities and Hollywood directors. Oprah Winfrey enthusiastically financed its film adaptation, *Precious* (2009), which Lee Daniels, producer of *Monster's Ball* (2001), directed. Comedian and actress Mo'Nique starred as Mary Lee Johnston, Precious's mother, and eventually won an Academy Award for Best Supporting Actress, while Gabourey Sidibe played the title role of Precious, receiving a nomination for the Academy Award for Best Actress. Not only had a text written by a Black lesbian author and providing a representation of Black lesbian life become visible in some literary circles, but it had enjoyed some of the popular success of Black romance novels.

Lee Daniels's *Precious* amplified the visibility of Sapphire's story, but it failed to capture the novel's sharp critique of a heteropatriarchal post–Black Power era nationalist nostalgia. The film adaptation erases two key figures in *Push*—Malcolm X and Louis Farrakhan—whom Sapphire uses in the novel to indict faulty forms of post–Black Power era nationalist nostalgia and expose the racist and misogynist underpinnings of calls for a "return" to the heteropatriarchal family in the 1990s. The loose, reconstructed memory of nationalist strategies began operating on fictions that reduced the struggle for Black liberation to "a top-down narrative of Great Man leadership," creating "a gendered hierarchy of political value that grants uninterrogated power to normative masculinity."[7] The "epistemological violence" of the "Great Man leadership" that Farrakhan and Malcolm X came to symbolize obscures Black family formations and Black characters existing outside heteropatriarchy.[8]

Although Precious narrates her story more than two decades after Malcolm X's assassination, her relationship with him parallels late twentieth-century nationalist nostalgia: she wears an *X* sweatshirt to school; reveals that Arnold Adoff's children's book, *Malcolm X* (1970) is on her bookshelf; and equates the letter *X* with her "main man Malcolm" when practicing phonetics in her school journal.[9] In the film *Precious*, the title character never wears a Malcolm X sweatshirt, but the *X* emblazoned on Precious's chest as she moves through the world of the novel both signifies a routinized abstract political ideology and marks Precious's body as a patriarchal target and a site to be conquered. The film's eponymous character also never references Adoff's book, nor does the film insert the book into its visual landscape. In the novel, though, Precious is proud to own a copy of Adoff's sixty-four-page children's book sketching Malcolm's life, which is the only reference she has for learning about Malcolm's complicated politics.

Malcolm had become the "redemptive black patriarch" whose image had been "sanitized and diluted, or at least sufficiently jumbled, as to be safe for mass consumption" in late twentieth-century cultural texts.[10] Angela Davis contends that Malcolm was used to "exalt abstract masculinist notions of political activism, with little to no reference to . . . revolutionary politics as strategies and tactics of organizing."[11] References to Malcolm X appear in several of the novels I examine in this project as I have indicated in the preceding chapters. In *Push*, this shorthand hypervisibility of masculine political action signal the fictitious "Great Man leadership" used to usurp heterogeneous political action and more egalitarian forms of authority, such as Ms. Blue Rain and the Each One Teach One classroom.[12] For Precious, Malcolm is both a dead, incorporeal image and a resurrected sacred icon made familiar by her alliterative proclamation that he is her "main man," suggesting kinship or a romantic relationship. By inserting Malcolm into the novel as Precious's "main man," as well as through self-fashioning practices and literacy exercises, Sapphire draws our attention to how this masculinist exaltation is learned, romanticized, and routinized.

A critique of heteropatriarchal nationalist nostalgia is also encoded in the novel's representation of Malcolm X's successor, Louis Farrakhan. As I mention in chapter 2, Farrakhan appears in Omar Tyree's *Flyy Girl*, but he is referenced seventeen times in *Push*. Throughout the novel, Precious rehearses her disgust for illegal drug use and white people because Farrakhan is "against Crack addicts and crackers."[13] Precious reveres Farrakhan, declaring, "First thing I see when I wake up is picture of Farrakhan's face on my wall. I love him"—words she never utters in the film adaptation.[14] For Precious, Farrakhan is an off-key portrait of "godlike and warlike," which Sweet Honey in the Rock sing about in "Testimony."[15] Whereas Malcolm X exists for Precious as memory and icon, Precious installs Farrakhan's likeness on her wall, mimicking behavior befitting a teenage crush and rousing an imagined possibility of romance and kinship. Though she eventually mounts a picture of Harriet Tubman and Alice Walker on the wall next to Farrakhan's image, and her library grows with books by other Black authors, Farrakhan's authority is a powerful fixture in the text.

Through Precious's love for Farrakhan, Sapphire underscores how Farrakhan's celebrity, charisma, and beguiling personality veil his oppressive ideological platform. His attractive artifice is strengthened by robust conservative legislation, and its ability to obscure and muffle progressive grassroots political organizations, such as the Audre Lorde Project, created a pretense of indifference in leftist communities. Barbara Smith feared that the "increasing power of a well-organized right wing" was making activism arduous and that the fear of homophobic violence deterred potential activists, which also buoyed the misconception of Black political apathy.[16] Smith writes that "it is very difficult and sometimes impossible to organize around Black lesbian issues, such as homophobic violence, child custody, and right-wing initiatives, when you do not want people to know who you are."[17]

Emblematic of masculine veneer, Farrakhan steps up and successfully exploits these fears as well as the collapse of beloved political organizations such as the Black Panther Party. A new self-appointed father, Farrakhan nurtures a late twentieth-century nationalist nostalgia that advocates Black patriarchal family and uses conservative gender politics to police Black women's bodies. Henry Louis Gates Jr. acknowledges that Farrakhan fills the "void left by Malcolm" and that Farrakhan "owes much to a vacuum of radical black leadership."[18] Confirming Farrakhan's opportune use of a Black political chasm, Eldridge Cleaver explains, "With Malcolm not being present, where was the best clone you could find? Farrakhan gravitated to the top of the heap."[19] *Push*'s critique of generic forms of post–Black Power era nationalist nostalgia hinges on proliferating iconography that reflected a public crisis of Black masculinity, and thereby Black political leadership, in the 1990s.

As an image of political leadership and celebrity on Precious's bedroom wall, Farrakhan's poster-worthy polished veneer conjures his own wistful and enthralling past as a calypso singer, where he was aptly known as "the Charmer." Sweet Honey in the Rock's warning that "you may fall prey to the jaded jewel" captures Precious's fascination with Farrakhan's charming affectation.[20] The son of Caribbean immigrants, Farrakhan had made a successful career singing calypso songs, such as "Brown Skin Gal" and "Ugly Woman," in which he advises men to marry an ugly woman because she will consistently cook, and a pretty woman will make her husband "look small," while an ugly woman "wouldn't disregard her husband at all / By exhibiting herself to Peter and Paul."[21] After joining the Nation of Islam, Farrakhan abandoned his singing career as a result of an ultimatum from then leader Elijah Muhammad, which called on Nation of Islam members to choose secular or religious music. Farrakhan ascended through the organization's ranks, first under Malcolm X's leadership and then under the direct tutelage of Elijah Muhammad, and continues to function as a "Great Man leader" and father figure for African American communities.

Girls and young women, like Precious, are attracted to "Great Man leadership" and the Nation of Islam for complicated reasons. Although Farrakhan and the Nation of Islam operate under a myopic political agenda, the Nation of Islam has a national and international reputation as a religion that successfully "reforms" formerly incarcerated Black men; establishes AIDS clinics; and rids housing projects of drug dealers, reinforcing its smoke screen of radical politics. Ula Y. Taylor explains that women are inspired by the Nation of Islam's "direct opposition to white supremacy" and that the Nation of Islam's "lethal critiques of white power emboldened members to support and trust its leadership."[22] Women also believe themselves to be joining "an organization that had promised their men would take responsibility" and be dependable breadwinners and faithful husbands.[23]

Invigorating the image of the responsible and dependable Black male breadwinner, the Nation of Islam's student enrollment guidelines boast, "The original man is the Asiatic Black Man; The Maker; the Owner; the Cream of the planet Earth — (Father of Civilization), God of the Universe."[24] Precious's decision to decorate her room with Farrakhan's face reflects the captivating nature of the radical "godlike" and "warlike" political platform her unjust life seems to demand, absent any other voices. While their reasons for joining the Nation of Islam are complex, Black women's participation can come with a high price. Platforms and organizations such as the Nation of Islam can act as a "bulwark against racism" but can operate simultaneously as a "masculinist, homophobic, and conservative narrative of black political history and identity."[25]

Disarming Discourse | Torchlights and Locked Doors

In 1993, F C N Publishing Company in Chicago, which also publishes the *Final Call* newspaper, released Farrakhan's book *A Torchlight for America*, and its enduring popularity is one of the best representations of his rising influence in the 1990s, when Sapphire published *Push*. *A Torchlight for America* attracted a wide readership, and though Farrakhan has penned numerous books, *Torchlight* is his only book available on Amazon, evincing its influence (*Torchlight* is also available on Amazon.co.uk). Farrakhan shrewdly published *A Torchlight for America* after two noteworthy and controversial events in 1992 marshaled nationalist nostalgia for Black political leadership: Spike Lee released his biographical drama film *Malcolm X*, and the Los Angeles police officers charged with Rodney King's beating were acquitted. Lee's film reignited new interest in Malcolm's life and politics, while the injustice of the Rodney King verdict confirmed a consistently unfair justice system through public spectacle. These events suggested that African American communities urgently needed stronger leadership, and popular and political culture subsequently began to generically reconstruct the memory of the Black Power era as a patriarchal but antiracist political project.

Sapphire implicates Farrakhan's gender politics, relatively unchanged from those he harmoniously rendered in his calypso songs, as the inescapable and grotesque backdrop of Precious's life. His inflammatory premises and dogma are clearly delineated in *Torchlight*, especially in the "Toward Eliminating Rape and Molestation" section, a portion most concomitant with Precious's experiences of violence. In it, Farrakhan offers an ostensibly innocuous statement, writing, "Rape and child molestation are not only crimes against the individual, they are truly crimes against the society and nations."[26] In the following sentence, Farrakhan passively claims, "The people must be taught properly and given guidance for conducting themselves among their fellow man."[27] This simple sentence structure, without multiple clauses, resemble the sentences in *Push*. While Precious's syntax conveys her burgeoning literacy, Farrakhan's unpretentious sentences suggest transparency and forthrightness.

His clean, simple clauses bolster trust between reader and author but cleverly erase and obscure culpability. The impotent verbs and refusal to identify who exactly should teach "the people" demonstrates the most telling erasure. Farrakhan's passive language fails to indict a person or group for "teaching" or socializing men to believe they have the right to rape and molest women. This duplicitous rhetorical neglect preserves his innocence as well as his heteropatriarchal claims that the "black man is God," which work to uphold the idea that men should have unchecked power over women. It suggests, on the one hand, that Black men exist as corporeal supernatural omnipotence but, on the other hand, figure as slippery apparitions when convenient. These opposing configurations mirror the conflicting and concordant messages expressed through *Torchlight*'s cover art and content, and the fictional representation of patriarchy in *Push*.

Though the book title suggests it will liberate through insight and wisdom, Farrakhan's prose showcases the bewildering "doors and doors of locks" cited in "Testimony." The book's front cover depicts an ostensibly male hand gripping a torch, evoking Frédéric-Auguste Bartholdi's Statue of Liberty—a

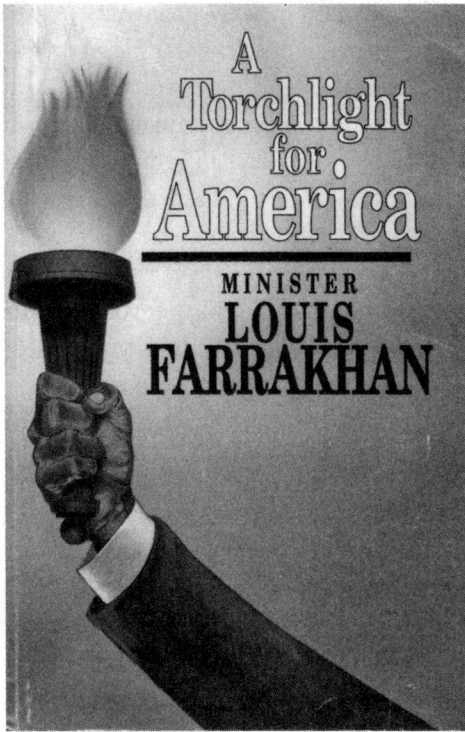

FIGURE 4.1 Cover for Louis Farrakhan's *A Torchlight for America*, 1993.

neoclassical sculpture of a robed female figure signifying freedom (see figure 4.1). The book's title and masculine flame of liberty recapitulate nationalist nostalgia and enshrine the unsustainable belief that Black liberation must be channeled through the nation and through heterosexual Black manhood. Nevertheless, the erasure of the body in the cover image is at odds with the textual aggrandizement of the body in *A Torchlight for America*, exemplified by chapter 4's "Have a Dress Code" and chapter 7's "Knowledge and Valuing Our Bodies Properly." Farrakhan's passive syntax abnegating his presence and culpability in promoting violent forms of power is also a corollary to the cover art and its image of a suit-clad arm absent a body. Likewise, the various fathers in *Push*—Malcolm X, the slain father of the Black nationalist movement; Precious's biological father, Carl Kenwood Jones; and Louis Farrakhan, the father of post–Black Power nostalgia—are simultaneously present and absent as memories, monuments, symbols, signifiers, and objects of Precious's imagination.

As Farrakhan imagines Black men as conflicting configurations, his "Toward Eliminating Rape and Molestation" section is lucid in its blame of women for the violence meted out against them by men. "Women must help to reestablish their own value by never giving themselves to any man unless there is love and commitment," Farrakhan writes, using covert strong-arm tactics to fault women for their victimization.[28] His reprimand is also in sync with marriageocracy; according to him, women can avoid patriarchal violence and "earn" a marriage proposal by working hard to exhibit the "proper" morals. Farrakhan asks, "Why is it that a woman who is exceedingly beautiful must model filth and indecency? . . . Why is it that if she is a singer we end up seeing more of her bosom than hearing her voice?"[29] His victim-blaming emphasis on beautiful women's need for modesty and disregard for the wardrobe choices of average-looking or "plain" women in *Torchlight* foreshadow his twenty-first-century views on the sartorial habits of "beautiful" Black female celebrities and also reflect the constancy of his gender politics over time.

In a September 2015 interview, Farrakhan, in his role as national father and leader, trusses child abuse to the figure of the immodest Black woman. In his advice to Jay-Z, he says:

> I hope you'll take it in the spirit that I give it, out of love for you and honor for your greatness and honor for the love and beauty and greatness of your wife. I would love to see our women clothed, demonstrating the gift of their talent. The gift of their form should be seen by those who are worthy. You got an unworthy dog looking at something beautiful that he wants to paw at but can never have. Do you know what that does to a man, when he can see you and can't have you? Then he wants to go home and attack a child.[30]

Farrakhan addresses Jay-Z as a husband and therefore a leader, offering (unsolicited) spiritual mentoring as he had often done for rappers who sought him out. In the underbelly of his thin, disarming compliment rests a dangerous logic. He chastises "beautiful" Black women for exhibiting themselves to "Peter and Paul," using their supposed immodesty to justify patriarchal violence against children. By characterizing men as animals who lack self-control and become agitated by their inability to "have" "unclothed" women, Farrakhan justifies sexual violence against women as well as children.

Contradictory and misogynistic, Farrakhan's firebrand theories allege that Black men are weak and powerless individuals who do not have the ability to control themselves but also vaunt that they are the Original Man and God. Farrakhan's reasoning about supernatural Black men acts as a template for

Precious, who believes her father's violence is a result of his inability to recognize himself as the "Original Man"—she exclaims that Carl rapes, beats, and has a child by her because he "has forgot he is the Original Man!"[31] Farrakhan's masculine symbols of omnipotence and sexual vulnerability compel African American women to blame themselves and suffer through abuse in order to protect African American men. As hegemonic scripts require, Precious also extends her justification for her father's violence to how society has defined her as "ugly."[32] She insists that if she were a "sexy girl" or a "girl like Janet Jackson" and not "fat, dark skin, short hair," she would be protected from sexual violence.[33] According to Precious, if Carl knew he was the "Original Man" and if she were not "ugly"—reprising the calypso song—and instead had the beauty and purity that Farrakhan celebrates, Carl would not have raped her.

I Got Three Names | Precious, Mary, and Ms. Rain

Sapphire challenges the slippery apparitions and corporeal omnipotence of Black heterosexual masculinity magnified in *A Torchlight for America*, undermining nationalist nostalgia and patriarchal family through a deliberate process of naming. Sapphire's most obvious use of naming as a resistive practice is through the titular character's moniker. Precious shouts, "Everybody call me Precious. I got three names—Claireece Precious Jones," noting that only people she hates call her "Claireece."[34] Precious's preference for her middle name undermines the way in which society renders her life valueless, and her bold declaration functions as a self-affirmation of her full self, one that is in accord with Sweet Honey in the Rock's acknowledgment of one's "spirit" reclaimed through a lived "life."[35]

Precious is fighting against the way her name operates as an analogue to the patriarchal construction of women as precious "gifts" because, as Farrakhan insists, they are "created to provide heaven, consolation, comfort, peace, and quiet of mind to their mate."[36] Precious's name denotes a fragility requiring protection, and her preference to be called by her middle name rather than her first name, Claireece, alludes to a Black nationalist paradigm that encourages men to serve "as the leaders of the family and the community" and for women to agree to that leadership "in exchange for the benefits of femininity: protection and security."[37] Unfortunately, Carl's "protection" of Precious is replaced with monstrous abuse, demonstrating how the overemphasis on heteropatriarchy cultivates a fertile ground for violence and transforms protection into a grotesque form of power.

The chastity that Farrakhan demands of Black women is also embedded in Mary's name, signifying the biblical figure of Jesus's virginal mother. Sapphire critiques Farrakhan's nationalist construction of virtuous women by depicting Mary as a sexual abuser who blindly follows Carl's leadership. Precious reveals that Mary not only knows that Carl rapes her but that "she bring him to me," indicating that Mary brings Carl to Precious's bedroom so that he can rape her.[38] Mary is considered "perhaps the most fiendish literary mother in fiction."[39] Her sexual abuse and role as accomplice makes the Black nationalist importance on women's purity, symbolized by Mary's name, farcical.

Corroborating Ms. Rain's role in helping Precious as a sexual abuse victim, Ms. Rain's surname is a loose acronym for the Rape, Abuse, and Incest National Network (RAINN), but it also links to Farrakhan's assertions about rape and lesbian identity. In *A Torchlight for America*, Farrakhan claims that "after a woman is raped or molested, . . . she could lose all faith in men and become a lesbian," which Farrakhan implies is a failure of the Black family, typifying Black bridal pathos.[40] Encoding a rape advocacy group in Ms. Rain's name and characterization calls forth Farrakhan's erroneous assumption and fear that Black women like Ms. Rain turn to queer forms of love only because of rape and molestation by men. She and her Each One Teach One classroom peel back Farrakhan's masculine veneer and unsettle the spurious political and familial heteropatriarchal leadership he represents.

Ms. Rain's name has another, more subtle tie to reinforcing *Push*'s challenge to nationalist nostalgia. Precious admits to being mesmerized by Farrakhan's teachings as well as the beliefs disseminated by the Five Percent Nation, or Allah's "Five Percenters," a quasi-Muslim group started by a Nation of Islam dissenter.[41] When Precious and her classmates are discussing Celie, a Black lesbian character in Alice Walker's *The Color Purple* (1982), Precious desperately wants to "tell the class what Five Percenters 'n Farrakhan got to say about butches," another declaration excised from the film.[42] Ms. Rain's surname, a homophone of "reign," is an inconspicuous tether to Precious's allegiance to Nation of Islam and Five Percent Nation ideology. Coinciding with my analysis of Sister Souljah in chapter 3, the Nation of Islam often uses perilous heteronormative symbolism to construct Black women as reigning "Queens" and "warriors" and Five Percent Nation rhetoric frequently speaks of women as "Earths" awaiting the "seeds (children) of male fertilization."[43] These naming practices underscore the importance of reproduction and insinuate that Black women are granted honor and reign as monarchs and powerful cosmic figures until some infraction—ranging from immodest dress to homosexuality—forces them to abdicate their throne.

Precious's adoration for Farrakhan, and Sapphire's condemnation of the patriarchal nationalist nostalgia he represents, is magnified when Precious gives birth and names her second son Abdul Jamal Louis Jones. Carl is Precious's biological father and her son's biological father and thus could have been used as a namesake, but he is also a purposely underdeveloped character and an equivocally horrendous patriarchal figure. Declaring her inspiration for naming her second son, Precious announces that "Louis [is] for Farrakhan," heralding Farrakhan as a surrogate patriarch, usurping Carl's role.[44] Thus, Farrakhan serves as a proxy for Carl and a charming, hypocritical placeholder for abusive and absentee Black fathers.

In Danger and Delusion | Black Families Out of Order

To reckon with the turmoil of declining job prospects and income for working-class African American men, coupled with African American women purportedly ascending the socioeconomic ladder, public discourse turned to nostalgia, which provided "a safer, more placid past" and fostered a menacing "historical amnesia."[45] Male politicians and religious leaders alike, across race, decried the birth control pill, premarital sex, extramarital sex, divorce, childcare facilities, and women working outside the home. Although Farrakhan indicted Black families specifically, his narrative about the family was not unlike that of any number of conservative leaders in the post–Black Power era. He alleges: "The traditional nuclear family is an endangered species. . . . Women are working more than men, so the women are providing for their children and even for the men, bringing home the money. Black men sitting home, lookin' at soap operas, [and] she's talking with the man's voice. God's order has been turned around. Whenever the natural order of God is violated, there are serious consequences."[46] Labeling the traditional nuclear family "endangered" reveals a nostalgia that recalls an undefined era in which Black patriarchal families were the norm, failing to account for how African American communities have innovatively created unconventional family and kinship systems for centuries. In characterizing women's work outside the home as a new phenomenon, Farrakhan forgets how Black women have historically had to work outside the home.

Politicians used this amnesia and naturalization of the patriarchal family, along with a deceptive nostalgia about the function and structure of white families, as an antidote to Black poverty and oppression. Farrakhan's popular belief that Black men need to reclaim their rightful position as head of the household is congruent with George W. Bush's 2001 Fatherhood Initiatives, which allocated funding "for projects designed to promote marriage, promote successful parenting and the involvement of fathers in the lives of their children, and help fathers improve their economic status by providing job-related services to them."[47] As Bush promoted heteropatriarchal family, financial support for low-income housing decreased from $50 million in 1977 to less than $9 million in 1988.[48] The reduced financial support for low-income housing echoes the ways in which institutions and social services neglect and fail Precious in *Push*. The institution of marriage is not a form of salvation; Precious's school suspends her; her caseworker, Ms. Weiss, suspects she is a leech who wants the state to take "care of her forever"; and hospital nurses tell her she is "not special."[49] *Push* foreshadows the increasingly intertwined relationship between Black nationalist discourse and violent government legislation and negligence in the late twentieth and early twenty-first centuries. These platitudes and policies almost uniformly focused on sustaining the nuclear family rather than on addressing healthcare inequality, the minimum wage, the school-to-prison pipeline, the gender pay gap, and other structural disparities.

If the 1990s nurtured a nostalgic turn toward the nuclear family, it was also an era during which the dysfunction of the American nuclear family was prominently on display, creating a national dissonance that prefigured the stringent, heteropatriarchal policies of the latter half of the decade and into the twenty-first century. Rising attention to father–daughter incest, in particular, thrust child sexual abuse into the national spotlight through fictional accounts, tabloid talk-show confessionals, and other public discourse. Oprah Winfrey identified herself as an incest survivor, and critically acclaimed fiction—such as Jane Smiley's *A Thousand Acres* (1991) and E. Annie Proulx's *The Shipping News* (1993)—included themes of incest. The escalating attention to incest stories led some to question the validity of abuse claims and some scholars to frame father–daughter incest as the "zenith of child sexual panic in the 1980s and 1990s."[50] Despite accusations of panic and exaggeration, incest stories continued to find a growing national platform, including on *Donahue*, *The Sally Jesse Raphael Show*, and *The Oprah Winfrey Show*.

Whether intentional or not, *Push* capitalized on the late twentieth century's attention to incest and child sexual abuse, but it did so toward liberatory ends. Sapphire inserts Farrakhan in *Push* because he articulates and fuels a heteropatriarchal dominance that enables sexual child abuse.

In one of his public speeches, Farrakhan scolds, "You don't let that man be involved with the changin[g] of that girl. What the hell—that's what you for. Change that damn diaper! Clean that dirty behind. And, tell the man go 'bout his business. . . . [He] don't need to be wiping no vagina!"[51] Not only do such claims attack Black women for their inability to carry out their "natural" gender roles, but they also traffic in racist caricatures of Black men as uncontrollable animals, verify the larger stereotype of the emasculating Black woman, and shift attention away from the behavior of incestuous pedophilia, hebephilia, and ephebophilia. Black female breadwinners are characterized as assuming a masculine posture, which works to condemn Black motherhood and justify incest.

Push suggests a link between Farrakhan's dogged insistence on heteropatriarchy and the public discourse surrounding father–daughter incest. Scholars in the 1980s and 1990s proposed various theories of culpability for father–daughter incest, and the popular "collusion by the mother" theory condemned mothers as purposeful and unwitting accomplices in a variety of ways. Mothers were thought to directly aid their children's fathers in the abuse and were characterized as being implicitly responsible for their children's abuse by abdicating their "natural" domestic and sexual "duties."[52] African American women were presumably gaining socioeconomic success and therefore not purportedly "taking care of home," which supposedly compelled men to abuse children. Men allegedly turned to abusing children to restore the heteronormative masculine power stripped away by women's "emasculating" economic achievements. Again, public discourse cast Black women's new socioeconomic mobility and refusal to acquiesce to patriarchal demands as the cause of societal dysfunction perpetrated by men and proposed it as a reason for father–daughter incest.[53]

Push was certainly not the first novel by a Black woman writer to take on the theme of incest within the Black family, but the depiction of Carl's rape of Precious worked to dismantle the rising glorification of patriarchal power fueled by federal policy, nationalist nostalgia, and political figures such as Louis Farrakhan. Sapphire disrupts nationalist nostalgia, exposing the monstrous consequences of unchecked and excess heteropatriarchal dominance. The novel argues that an idealized Black patriarchy, imagined to be "impotent" in a post–Black Power era, had nowhere to go but within the family, where it menaced rather than protected its most vulnerable members. The expanded emphasis on nationalism in the 1980s and 1990s, through iconography, reconstructed memory, and nostalgia, breeds the kind of power and sexual violence rendered in Push.

Marriage as Monstrosity

The sociopolitical and cultural events of the 1990s flicker and glint as shadowy antagonistic figures in *Push*. Words such as "top surgery," "bottom surgery," "polyamory," and "transphobia" appeared in print for the first time during the 1990s and the word "genderqueer" appeared in print for the first time in 1995, and trans woman and trans man first appeared in print in 1996, offering a window into some of the bubbling fears about traditional gender norms emerging across the country.[54] Sapphire also published *Push* between two momentous political pillars: in 1995, Farrakhan launched his Million Man March; and in 1996, Clinton passed the Personal Responsibility and Work Opportunity Reconciliation Act (PRWORA) and the Defense of Marriage Act (DOMA). At the Million Man March, Farrakhan rehashed his incendiary remarks urging Black men to protect Black women and accept responsibility as the family head. As I discuss in the invocation, the PRWORA drastically reduced the number of welfare recipients and upheld misleading conceptualizations of "personal responsibility" for some of the poorest people in the nation. Not only did the PRWORA reinscribe racist and sexist clichés about Black "welfare queens," but it also claimed that "marriage is the foundation of a successful society," declaring it as a political responsibility.[55] In the same year Clinton passed the PRWORA, the DOMA criminalized same-sex marriage, implicitly strengthening heteropatriarchy. *Push* is an important dissenting voice among these dubious claims.

Inasmuch as family is a synecdoche for the nation, the Jones family destabilizes these illusory claims and reflects the nation's endemic dysfunction. As Carl rapes Precious, he declares, "I'm gonna marry you," and in his premature utterance, he collapses rape and marriage through name and act.[56] His simultaneous violence against and promise of marriage to Precious most strongly suggests a contaminated, incoherent patriarchal family and a defiled nation. Carl's pledge to marry Precious is a tool used to sanction his incestuous rape but also identifies marriage as a site that can be used to legitimize patriarchal power and violence. Countering the potential editor's query, the sole "marriage proposal" Precious receives in the novel is from her father as he rapes her. His macabre declaration in the context of sexual violence not only mocks Farrakhan's nationalist claim that the family is the epitome of "natural order" but also weakens legislative appeals for "order" within the family. Carl's violence and Precious's fantasy of being married to her white math teacher make a mockery of the nation's definition of marriage, and the idea that a patriarchal family can replace social services and fix the nation's mounting disparities is rendered absurd.

Carl and Mary further represent the failure of Farrakhan's form of heteropatriarchy and America's duty to protect its most precious and vulnerable citizens. Though a homophone of "marry," Mary and Carl never wed, but Carl and Mary have been together since Mary was sixteen years old and conceived Precious "out of wedlock," a detail that plays with and perverts her immaculate namesake and her supernatural childbirth. Sapphire does not situate Precious's "illegitimate" birth as the cause of the violence against her. Mary refers to Carl as her husband, but she tells Precious that she and Carl were never married and that Carl has two children with "purty light-skin woman."[57] Sapphire points to the excess and incoherence of a romanticized Black patriarchy as two families—one light and seemingly normative, and one dark and dysfunctional—comprise the horrors of an unchecked patriarchy. It is a disconcerting incoherence echoed in "Testimony," when Sweet Honey in the Rock couple dissonant visions of "godlike" and "warlike" with "madlike and sadlike" in their first verse.[58]

Unraveling Reconstructed Memories

While Carl signifies an excessive patriarchy, Mary's insufficient testimony spurns the comfort of a generic, sentimental past undergirding warped forms of nationalist nostalgia. The novel builds nail-biting anticipation for the moment when Mary will contextualize her relationship with Carl and the sexual abuse Precious faces and, as a result, confirms how nostalgia functions as an important leitmotif. Carl is an inconsistent presence in the novel, so Mary has to answer questions about Precious's abuse. Still, it is not until the novel's finale that Mary is subjected to a forceful interrogation about Precious's sexual abuse, signaling the protracted desire in the novel for a clearer understanding of Precious's trauma.

Sapphire's slow, suspenseful walk with Mary toward the novel's uncomfortable and uncooperative dénouement echoes Sweet Honey in the Rock singing "no matter how slow I walk / there are traces, empty spaces" in "Testimony."[59] Ms. Weiss, Precious's social worker, brusquely asserts, "I think you'd better explain just what happened in that home."[60] Despite Ms. Weiss's hunger for answers, in her account to Ms. Weiss and Precious, Mary renders past events as present, misstates events, and blurs episodes of time, demonstrating the frailty and precariousness of nostalgia. She begins by fondly recalling memories of Precious as a baby, describing how she had a "Pink n' white baby carriage, little pink bootie socks, dresses; everything I put on her pink."[61] Mary's memories of taking Precious out in her carriage "wheeling in the air" are disrupted when she recalls the murder of her neighbor's child during the summer, the season she also says marks Precious's birth.[62] Embarrassed and frustrated, Precious interrupts Mary, reminding her that she was born in November, not the summer, and Mary quickly revises her story, exclaiming, "Yeah yeah thas right. My little Scorpio chile," leaving yet another empty space for Precious and the readers.[63]

In her optimistic account of their life, Mary also attempts to subtly undercut Precious's claims of abuse, though she renders both her memory and the project of nostalgia as mendacious, claiming, "Scorpio's crafty. I ain' sayin' they lie, jus you cain't always trust 'em."[64] Not only are we unable to "trust" Mary's competence as a mother or her nostalgic rendering of the past, but the larger work of nostalgia in the text is abated. Mary's equivocation is doubly unnerving because it forecloses space and opportunity for the reader's solace. When Ms. Weiss asks Mary to explain the abuse, Mary tells a story, replete with little pink dresses, booties, and marriage, that provides an ersatz refuge for readers to imagine a time and space where Precious was not being raped and abused but swathed in her parents' love. The text confirms the charming and seductive power of nostalgia, but inevitably the comfort of a sentimental past is unavailable to Ms. Weiss, the readers, and Precious because of Mary's untrustworthiness.

Mary's untrustworthiness hints at the novel's multidimensional genre positioning. With her fragile psychological state, Mary is emblematic of the unstable and unreliable character who helps induce mystery and suspense in psychological horror fiction. Sapphire's novel is rarely, if ever, classified as horror fiction in bookstores and libraries, but as it deromanticizes heteropatriarchy it also broadly aligns with the contours of horror fiction. Academia has a history of disparaging the genres of romance and horror, but it is generative to consider *Push* as a literary text that is also working within the genre of horror fiction because the categorization carves a space of vulnerability for Precious. Novels with themes similar to those in *Push* rarely get the "horror" designation because they do not include a zombie or psychotic serial killer and because Black female pain is often disregarded as unimportant or constructed as necessary in order to facilitate a larger lesson. Conversely, Black female characters in mainstream horror film and fiction are rarely central to the story and seldom survive by the narrative's end. Clarice

Starling, a central white female character in the 1988 novel *The Silence of the Lambs*, and Precious Claireece Jones are very different characters, but their dissimilarity does not preclude an understanding of *Push* as a novel that can be categorized under the broad umbrella of horror fiction. The graphic violence that Carl and Mary enact against Precious is repulsive and shocking enough to fall within the horror tradition and the hegemonic power of heteropatriarchy and its minions, Mary and Carl, are the fear-provoking "monsters" in this horrific tale. The horror genre frequently includes fantastical or supernatural elements, which Carl embodies as "Original Man" and "God." As monsters in horror fiction commonly do, Carl and Mary help tell readers something about the society in which Precious lives. Precious's subject position, miseducation, and trauma heightens fear about her survival because of society's contempt for Black girls and Black mothers as well as its inattention to schools, hospitals, and other institutions in Black communities. Sapphire's innovative genre manipulation works against desensitizing readers to the horrific violence that is frequently depicted against Black girls and women.

Black Female Artistic Production and Futurity

Sapphire's critique is bolstered by the novel's "memory" of the nationalist-modeled attacks on Black women writers who published work in the preceding decades. These attacks are similar to assessments of *Push* and haunt future writers and creative testimonies. *The Color Purple* and *Push* both use epistles, and Sapphire maintains that Alice Walker "kicked open the door" for her, so it is unsurprising that Precious and Ms. Rain sort through the web of debates surrounding *The Color Purple*, likely in anticipation of the criticism for *Push*.[65] After Precious confesses her love for *The Color Purple* because it gives her "strength," she learns from Ms. Rain that a "group of black men wanted to stop movie from the book. Say unfair picture" of Black men.[66] It is a moment encouraging a meditation on the past and futurity of Black female artistic production. Ms. Rain, Precious, and the Each One Teach One school name, like Sweet Honey in the Rock's "you young ones / you're the next ones" lyrics, theorize Black women's futurity beyond biological reproduction but made possible within a fertile landscape fostering creative tapestries of witnessing and testimony.[67]

Precious refuses to allow gendered critiques of *The Color Purple* mar her opinion, but her praise for Walker's novel does not shield *Push* from the kind of critical indictment that novels like *The Color Purple* and *The Bluest Eye* received, as Black male critics vehemently attacked both for their negative portrayals of Black men. One critic argued that unlike "happily married women" who did not need to unleash "pent up frustration," Black female writers of the 1970s owed their mounting success to their ability to satisfy Black women's "collective appetite for black male blood."[68] In outlining Black women's "pent up frustration," this disdain points to marriage as the central issue motivating Alice Walker's depiction of domestic violence, substantiating how marriage was overdetermined as a solution to representations of gender violence and abuse. One writer asserted that "Alice Walker has a high level of enmity toward Black men."[69] Another one accused Walker of having a penchant for "melodrama, militant self-pity, [and] guilt-mongering."[70] Black female critics insisted that Black male critics repeatedly condemned writers if they did not "see themselves reflected favorably" and if their texts did not uphold the "ideals of masculinity and femininity" buttressed by the nuclear family.[71]

Many readers complained that Precious was gratuitously saddled with problems, but her challenges were still insufficient in making Black female vulnerability and pain visible to some writers and critics. As the publicity for *Precious*, the film adaptation of *Push*, amplified, prominent critics echoed the earlier criticism of Walker and her peers. Just as critics compared Ntozake Shange's *for colored girls who have considered suicide when the rainbow is enuf* (1976) to D. W. Griffith's film *Birth of a Nation* (1915), Ishmael Reed insisted that *Precious* "makes D.W. Griffith look like a progressive."[72] Although Reed argues that *Precious* "includes the worst portrayal of Black women," he laments that Precious's father, Carl, "is the real victim of the movie."[73] Unrelenting in his ad hominem attacks, Reed claims that Black female professors who commend Precious are those "using university curriculum to get even with their fathers and teach courses in Black women's literature."[74] Black women's literary production, instruction, and testimony are not tied to intellectual goals, according to Reed, but are rooted in women's Freudian need for revenge against their fathers. In his review, Reed spends minimal time on the film's Black female characters or the classism, racism, ableism, and patriarchal violence Precious endures but goes on at length criticizing the film's negative representation of Black men, reaffirming his critical forefathers who were reluctant to identify literary merit in the fiction and poetry of Black women writers.

Testimony, Alternate Futures, and Shapeshifting Figures

Sapphire deconstructs heteropatriarchy and its monstrous distortions that have so ravaged Precious's life in order to refigure and accurately remember alternate possibilities of family formation. She draws attention to patterns, formations, kinship networks, negotiation, inventive relationship practices, and people left out of traditional narratives about Black family and political resistance. The heteronormativity and marriage typically emphasized in romance novels is replaced with homosocial relationships between Precious, Ms. Rain, and diverse classmates, whom she identifies as her "friends and family."[75] Critiquing nostalgia, Precious and her chosen family at Each One Teach One eschew "the solace of [heteronormative] family, religion, golden past, or organic community," as they bond over "shared class and gender oppression" and envision alternate futures for Black female subjectivity.[76] They are what Aimee Meredith Cox calls "shapeshifters" in the way that their testimonies "mobilize history, whether officially documented or bricolaged through recall and desire, to give new meaning to social contexts that engender cartographic capacities beyond particular physical or ideological sites."[77] The bricolaged Life Story project documented at the end of the novel, Ms. Blue Rain, and Each One Teach One's shapeshifting students reject the heteronormative model for characterizing Black female subjectivity and, through it, demonstrate reparative approaches for suturing what Black patriarchy and nationalist nostalgia have shattered.

Ms. Rain and her shapeshifting Each One Teach One students are a fictional representation of the radical political project Cathy J. Cohen imagines as dismantling queer political agendas that privilege a "homogenized" identity, rather than work toward an intersectional analysis of oppression that draws on "one's relation to power."[78] Cohen calls for maintaining the boundaries between heterosexual and queer identity but suggests a radical political link between, for example, disenfranchised Black heterosexual "welfare queens" and Black lesbians, because both occupy non-heteronormative positions in the eyes of the state.[79] Bolstering accord across and between nonnormative and marginal identities, such as those of Precious and her queer classmates and teacher, constructs progressive coalition building that calls greater attention to power, privilege, and oppression.

It is through an architecture of queer coalition building that the novel challenges the lifeless iconography of Malcolm X and the monstrous fathering of Carl and Farrakhan. Precious recounts the testimony of her friend and classmate Rita Romero watching her father "kill her mother in front her eyes."[80] Rhonda, another classmate, discloses that her brother raped her and "her mother fine out and put Rhonda, not brother, out."[81] The testimony of Precious, Rita, and Rhonda mobilize history and challenge heteronormativity as a site of privilege, defined by "'morally correct,' white, state-authorized, middle-class" heterosexual men, as it excludes poor, Black and brown men and women "portrayed as unable to raise their children with the right moral fiber; unable to find 'gainful' employment to support themselves and their 'illegitimate children'; and of course unable to manage 'effectively' the minimal assistance provided by the state."[82] Precious and her shapeshifting Each One Teach One family rupture heteronormativity through their familial relationship, class position, children born "out of wedlock," trauma, sexual violence, and dependence on the state. These experiences and identities all fall outside of what constitutes heteronormativity and "morally correct" citizenship, galvanizing radical queer coalition building.

Cohen's argument for the possibility of a radical queer politics is put to the test when Precious prepares to proudly outline Farrakhan's opposition to homosexuality to Ms. Rain and her Each One Teach One class. Ms. Rain quickly informs Precious that her enmity for homosexuals means that she also does not like Ms. Rain.[83] "Precious has difficulty in dismissing the nationalist philosophy that has thus far been her only comfort, yet she is faced with the reality of the philosophy's marked shortcomings."[84] Precious's adherence to Farrakhan's conservative gender politics clash with Ms. Rain's sexual identity and jeopardize her relationship with Ms. Rain, marking a significant watershed for her. Firing back at Precious, Ms. Rain reminds her that LGBTQ people are not the ones who raped her, are not the ones who "let [her] sit up not learn for sixteen years," and are not the ones selling "crack" in Harlem.[85] Precious admits, "It's true. Ms Rain the one who put the chalk in my hand, make me queen of the ABCs."[86] This paradigm-shifting scene challenges Precious's loyalty to Farrakhan's nationalist ideology, represented by his homophobic speech and conservatism, as Precious acknowledges Ms. Rain's role in teaching her to read and write and escape her mother's abuse. Ms. Blue Rain embodies the "waters / hidden from us" in Sweet Honey in the Rock's "Testimony" as a fluid, shapeshifting figure opening "doors and doors of locks" for Precious.[87]

Through this exchange, Sapphire makes visible to Precious, and to the reader, a radical queer coalition between Ms. Rain and Precious that supersedes the nostalgic fictions of heteropatriarchy. Sapphire's plot "destabilizes the excessive phallic authority awarded to black men under black nationalist philosophies that propagate standardized models of racial solidarity and heterosexuality."[88] In the course of developing love for and acceptance of Ms. Rain as well as herself, Precious inevitably distances herself from nationalist constructions of race, gender, and sexual identity. She writes, "At least when I look at the girls I see *them* and when they look they see ME, not what I looks like. But it seems like boyz just see what you looks like," reasserting her interiority and emotional evolution.[89] Ms. Rain is the catalyst for Precious's eventual question: "Where my Black love? Where my man love? Woman love? Any kinda love?" indicating that she is beginning to shun the conservative sexual politics of Farrakhan and embrace queer forms of love.[90] With a felled patriarchal leader and a chosen family reconstructed and refigured through radical queer politics, *Push* offers the possibility the word denotes, as Precious and her family present a testimony of failing and pushing and failing and pushing away from the constrictions, trauma, and violence of a nostalgia-based Black patriarchy.

CHAPTER FIVE

Viewer, I Married Him

> I take thee, to be my wedded husband, to have and to hold,
> from this day forward, for better or worse, for richer or poorer,
> in sickness and in health, to love and to cherish,
> until distance do us part.
> This is my solemn vow.

Riffing on Charlotte Brontë's dénouement in *Jane Eyre*, "Viewer, I Married Him" explores the route to marriage in Malcolm D. Lee's 1999 film *The Best Man* and Gina Prince-Bythewood's 2000 film *Love & Basketball*. As I mention in the invocation, African Americans have long been ingenious in constructing kinship and family despite the unwavering work of white supremacy, so it is exciting to examine a cinematic diptych that artfully depicts Black love as a radical act, asserting that Black women and men are worthy of love and desire. As canonical texts in African American culture, the mechanisms animating these beloved post–Civil Rights era cinematic depictions of marriage deserve a deeper consideration and exploration. Read together, the innovative genre refashioning and the sonic and visual vocabulary of both films mobilize a refrain of erasure and visibility for its female characters. Alongside this refrain, both films present a portrait of its male characters that adeptly cross-stitches the friction and elasticity within African American intimacy.

Produced by Spike Lee's 40 Acres and a Mule and set in New York City, *The Best Man* depicts an outwardly innocuous story about a homemaker, Mia Morgan (Monica Calhoun), and her college sweetheart, Lance Sullivan (Morris Chestnut), now a professional football player with the New York Giants. The two are anxiously preparing for their wedding day with an ensemble of friends, including the film's eponymous character, Harper Stewart (Taye Diggs). *The Best Man* soon relinquishes its secret: an incident from Mia's college years threatens to ruin her picture-perfect wedding day. Harper— Lance's best man—has written a semiautobiographical novel, *Unfinished Business*, which recounts a one-night stand between characters who are obviously paper thin versions of Mia and Harper. An advance copy falls into the hands of the groom, who recognizes the subjects of the book's pivotal sexual encounter as his fiancée and best man. Apoplectic, Lance cancels the

FIGURE 5.1 *The Best Man*, directed by Malcolm D. Lee (40 Acres and a Mule Filmworks/ Universal Pictures, 1999), DVD.

wedding without telling Mia. By the end of the film, however, "love conquers all," and Lance and Mia make their way to the altar.

As the central duplicity unfolds, the film scaffolds an additional conflict. In the New York City wedding setting, Harper is reunited with his old flame, Jordan Armstrong (Nia Long), who wants to renew their relationship, but Harper has a serious girlfriend, Robin (Sanaa Lathan), who is in Chicago but due to arrive shortly for the ceremony. The film builds suspense around Harper's choice as he entertains Jordan's request, but he ultimately proposes to Robin as Jordan watches from the sidelines. Thus, *The Best Man* ends not only with Mia and Lance's wedding but also with anticipation for Robin and Harper's impending matrimony (see figure 5.1).

Also produced by Spike Lee's 40 Acres and a Mule Filmworks, *Love & Basketball* chronicles the relationship between Monica Wright (Sanaa Lathan) and Quincy McCall (Omar Epps). Eleven-year-old Monica moves into an upper-middle-class Los Angeles neighborhood and soon meets her young neighbor, Quincy. He and Monica play basketball together and eventually embark on a monogamous romantic relationship, but Quincy ends their relationship during college because he believes that Monica is unsupportive as

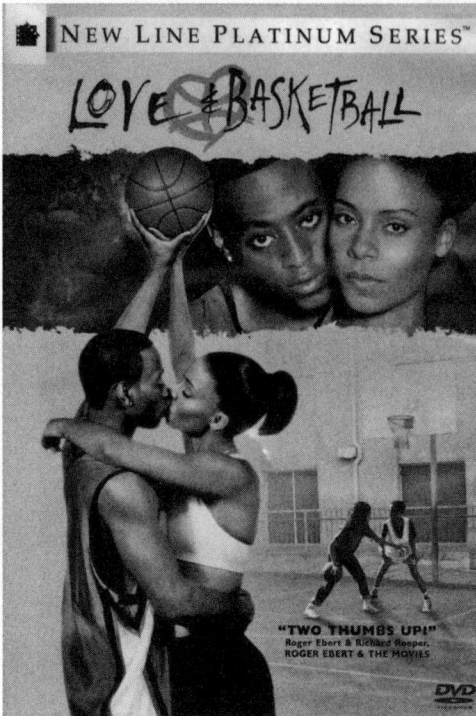

FIGURE 5.2 *Love & Basketball*, directed by Gina Prince-Bythewood (40 Acres and a Mule Filmworks/New Line Cinema, 2000), DVD.

he grapples with his father's infidelity. After having achieved stardom as a professional basketball player, Quincy gets engaged to another woman. Monica finally declares her love for Quincy, and the two end the film married, with Monica playing as a professional athlete in the Women's National Basketball Association (WNBA) (see figure 5.2).

Sonic culture, digital media, and reality television affirm the place of *Love & Basketball* and *The Best Man* in the African American cultural canon. In their 2005 song "Get You Right," the rhythm-and-blues/hip-hop group Pretty Ricky affectionately reference *Love & Basketball*, and hip-hop artist Rapsody endearingly cites the film in her 2013 song "She Got Game." Circulating memes on social media featuring scenes from the films—along with #Relationship-Goals, #BlackLove, and #ThisCouldBeUs as anchoring hashtags—further illustrate how these fictional tales serve as aspirational models of courtship and marriage for a new generation of cultural consumers. The decontextualized references in digital and sonic culture demonstrate the deep and profound political burden placed on African American women and men to live up to a heteronormative ideal as they amplify the cultural significance of these films and characters.

The Oprah Winfrey Network has taken advantage of this zeitgeist, releasing the 2017 docuseries *Black Love*. Mirroring #BlackLove, the show aims to feature the "joys, challenges and realities of love, marriage, and romance in the black community."[1] Scholars of popular culture shed light on this kind of cultural phenomenon, explaining that "though popular culture neither determines nor even necessarily reflects human experience, it does offer a vocabulary through which its viewers may come to understand and discuss their experience."[2] As cinematic monuments of African American matrimony, *The Best Man* and *Love & Basketball* generate a cultural vocabulary with a forceful impact on and significance for discourses of courtship and marriage.

What is more, *The Best Man* and *Love & Basketball* accomplish what few commercially successful films are able to achieve. The popularly known Bechdel Test, based on Alison Bechdel's comic strip, measures women's representation in fiction. To pass the test, a work must have two or more female characters who talk to each other about something other than a man. Although *The Best Man* fails the Bechdel Test, *Love & Basketball* fulfills its terms. Other cultural critics began building on Bechdel's assessment, adding race and proposing that a film must have two people of color who talk to each other about something other than white people. Unlike many commercially successful films, *The Best Man* and *Love & Basketball* meet these benchmarks. Finally, The DuVernay Test, named for Ana DuVernay, stipulates that a work must feature African Americans and other minorities who have "fully realized lives rather than serve as scenery in white stories."[3] Again, both films pass with flying colors.

The unique and heterogeneous characters of these iconic films as well as their well-timed release unquestionably buoyed their aesthetic and political import. The tableau of roles in *The Best Man* includes a professional football player, a homemaker, a television producer, a writer, a caterer, and a musician; this kaleidoscopic cast of middle-class characters challenged screenwriters, who used African American caricatures to deliver comic relief or liberate a white protagonist. Of the film's dramatic personae, film historian Donald Bogle maintains that "fifteen years earlier, these characters might have seemed implausible for a popular black film."[4] For the archive of romantic comedies with African American middle-class characters, the allure was bolstered by *The Best Man*'s celebration of Black love and stark contrast to films with sober depictions of violence and inequality in African American communities.[5] Malcolm D. Lee maintains that he wanted to write a screenplay in which "no one shoots anyone, no one does drugs."[6] Viewers and critics responded accordingly to Lee's intention to showcase a new portrait of

African American characters. The film received nine NAACP Image Award nominations, and Lee was a recipient of the Black Filmmakers Hall of Fame Award. Bogle calls *The Best Man* "refreshing," and Mia L. Mask attests that it is one of the best comedies released in 1999, exemplary of "quality craftsmanship in mainstream moviemaking."[7]

Likewise, audiences celebrated the release of *Love & Basketball* for myriad reasons. Not only was it a welcome deviation from gritty urban dramas, but it also honored Black love and desire, as it capitalized on the success of films such as Forest Whitaker's 1995 *Waiting to Exhale* and Theodore Witcher's 1997 *Love Jones*. Released just three years after the National Basketball Association (NBA) granted women the opportunity to play the sport professionally in the WNBA, *Love & Basketball* and its female lead generated strong cultural connections to its milieu. Moreover, Prince-Bythewood was one of just a few Black female filmmakers producing commercially successful films; thus, she as well as her Black female protagonist signified the need to make space for Black women with diverse career paths. Verifying the deterrents Black female directors continue to face in Hollywood, USC's Annenberg School for Communication and Journalism reports that there were "407 directors who premiered major movies and shows during 2014–2015. Only 53 were people of color. And only two, Amma Asante and Ava DuVernay, were black women."[8]

Reframing Dramedy and Masculine Motifs

The Best Man and *Love & Basketball* follow the basic romantic comedy narrative arc of boy meets girl, boy loses girl, boy and girl find love, but their masculine motifs and dramatic components present the most significant incongruity with the romantic-comedy formula, portending ulterior cinematic motives. Romantic comedies are typically linked to women by casting female leads, marketing to heterosexual female audiences, and featuring conflicts customarily associated with women.[9] *Love & Basketball* and *The Best Man*, through their titles, suggest a shift from the usual romantic-comedy focus on female characters to a deliberate interest in featuring male characters and attracting heterosexual male viewers.[10] The focus on basketball in *Love & Basketball*, like the emphasis on the groomsmen and football in *The Best Man*, seemingly subverts a female-centered genre but, in fact, bends to a burgeoning cross-gender trend in romantic-comedies in order to boost aspirations for marriage among African American heterosexual male viewers.

Film theorist Tamar Jeffers McDonald uses "homme-com" to identify the changing perspective in romantic-comedy from female to male point of view as well as its penchant for "the bodily, and particularly the sexual, elements within romance, the scatological and carnal motifs."[11] Exemplifying homme-com, *The 40-Year-Old Virgin* (2005) includes scenes of "erections, urination, masturbation, and . . . depilation."[12] *Swingers* (1996) and *Along Came Polly* (2004) are also representative of the homme-com style, but films featuring African American male protagonists—such as *The Wood* (1999) and *The Brothers* (2001) as well as *The Best Man* and *Love & Basketball*—retool this trend. *Love & Basketball* and *The Best Man* use their male characters and sports leitmotif to hail heterosexual male viewers, but *Love & Basketball* eschews most homme-com devices. *The Best Man* makes use of the carnal by depicting strippers at Lance's bachelor party but avoids homme-com emblems such as scatology and masturbation.

In an interview from 1999, Lee is adamant about *The Best Man*'s genre and tone: "The studio might think it's a comedy and the producers might say it's a comedy, but don't ever think of this movie as a comedy. . . . This is a drama."[13] Lee's impassioned abnegation of comedy and reclamation of drama as the film's narrative marrow is complicated. Despite its well-heeled post–civil rights characters and link to the romantic-comedy formula, the film buttresses the high political stakes for African American marriage in order to disprove a historical fiction of Black familial pathology, as it unearths the persistence of racism. Though he is not referencing *Love & Basketball*, Lee's keen defense of *The Best Man*'s dramatic core speaks to the ways in which both *Love & Basketball* and *The Best Man* must attract African American heterosexual male viewers without using the standard homme-com plot devices in order to represent marriage as a staid and politicized endeavor for heterosexual African American male viewers. The films dress marriage up as an auspicious venture by mitigating institutional racism for its middle-class characters, but by making marriage "dramatic" rather than comedic, the films insinuate that there is a surfeit of burdensome cultural and sociopolitical barriers to wedlock for African American men, signifying that late twentieth-century African American homme-coms cannot afford the levity that the genre bestows because of the racialized and gendered political burdens they carry.

The Best Man further destabilizes romantic-comedy and homme-com genre maneuvers through its use of the "rake" male lead, an archetype of the genre, with the purpose of making marriage more desirable to African American heterosexual male viewers.[14] The antithesis of the ideal suitor, the rake is defined by discomfiting personality characteristics, such as vanity, irresponsibility, or promiscuity, with the latter describing Lance's flaw. The rake's female partner or romantic interest is the catalyst for his change, compelling him to "make sacrifices to demonstrate his love to the heroine."[15] Karen Bowdre maintains that "in African American rom-coms the male lead is rarely put in a situation where he has to make a noble sacrifice or change his behavior in order to win the love of his life, thus proving his integrity and winning classical heroic status."[16]

Dovetailing with Bowdre's assertion, Lance, the quasi-rake in *The Best Man*, achieves integrity and classical heroic status without having to undergo substantial change. As a newly reformed Lothario and devout Christian, Lance is introduced at the beginning of the film as a character that has already made the kind of necessary metamorphosis common in the romantic-comedy genre and is now a famous, wealthy, and handsome football hero. Lance's groomsmen, especially the wanton Quentin (Terrance Howard), punctuate Lance's honor and decency. Lance's "sacrifice" consists of a flashback of contrition for his infinite sexual escapades and the grand gesture of forgiving his best man for having sex with his fiancée, Mia, during a time in which he was far from monogamous.

Lance and Harper quarrel over what is also Mia's deception, not simply Harper's, but Lance, as the moral arbiter, cancels the wedding, and he and Harper adjudicate the conflict without Mia's input. Mia and Lance are beginning the process of consecrating and legally fortifying their union, so it is odd that Lance does not include Mia in his decision. This narrative aperture highlights the ways in which African American women's private lives are always under surveillance and meticulously scrutinized without their input. Yet at the same time, it exposes additional problems and critical emotional gaps. Lance does not talk to Mia about her dishonesty because it may necessitate that he does the uncomfortable emotional labor of confronting his mendacity. Although the bromance between Lance and Harper is entertaining and prominently underscored, the film does not allow Lance to do the emotional labor of communicating with Mia about his deception and her affective scars, which might constitute another kind of "noble sacrifice" and progressive image of masculinity and marriage.

Quincy in *Love & Basketball* also never tells Monica that their relationship is over, then later sacrifices a relationship with his beautiful femme fiancée, Kyra Kessler (Tyra Banks), in order to marry Monica, the loyal but "plain Jane" girlfriend next door. Unlike Lance, Quincy suffers a serious basketball injury that compromises his career as a professional athlete. His physical vulnerability redeems him after his mistreatment of Monica and helps garner sympathy for him from viewers. His care of their son as Monica plays on the basketball court at the end of the film offers an image of fatherhood and marriage that endears "strong" African American female viewers who work outside the home and supposedly do not "need a man" to desire marriage and motherhood.

Nevertheless, Quincy's vulnerability astutely challenges "how central vulnerability has been to the construction of white womanhood and how stubborn the association of whiteness with vulnerability remains" in popular imaginary.[17] The film's emphasis on Monica as a professional athlete in the final frames suggests that Quincy has made a "noble sacrifice," particularly for a romantic comedy, and defies pathological narratives about absentee African American fathers and patriarchal husbands. It is an unconventional happily-ever-after dénouement that upends stereotypical representations of vulnerability and African American family formation.

As a narrative refrain, though, the homme-com sports motif equates heterosexual romantic relationships with athletic events, positing that love is a competitive sport and that the competition, whether acknowledged or not, is always between African American female characters. In *The Best Man*, Robin and Jordan unknowingly "compete" for Harper's affection in order to escape the social death of singlehood, mobilizing Black bridal pathos by upholding widespread claims about single African American women aching for marriage. In *Love & Basketball*, the triangulating competition is more explicit. Monica desires a relationship and is conveniently still single by the end of the film, though Quincy is not. In the final scenes, Monica asks Quincy to play against her in a basketball game in which she has an opportunity to win his "love," leaving Quincy's fiancée, Kyra, the hapless "loser" in their game. The film offers Quincy a choice between Monica and Kyra, while Murch (Harold Perrineau)—one of Lance's groomsman in *The Best Man*—has the power to choose between his girlfriend, Shelby (Melissa De Sousa), and a stripper named Candy (Regina Hall), who is also single. None of the female characters in either film, regardless of their intellect, beauty, loyalty, or class position, have the power to choose between two ardent romantic partners, showcasing their disadvantage and inflating myths of them desperately hankering for marriage.[18]

For Robin, Monica, and other female characters who ultimately "win," the victory of marriage is a costly one. According to the film's logic, African American men are allowed an inordinate number of sexual escapades, whereas African American women are expected to restrict their liaisons to one partner, an inevitable husband, in order to be considered "marriageable." Lance boasts of his sexual trysts, but with regard to Mia's sexual experiences, he erroneously proclaims to his groomsmen, "I'm the first, the last, and the only." Lance echoes Terry McMillan's Franklin whose first-person narration inaugurates and concludes *Disappearing Acts* as he yokes his and Mia's intimacy to his corporeal omnipotence. *Love & Basketball* offers a similar message; Quincy is Monica's first and only sexual partner throughout the film, though his sexual experience is not limited to Monica. In an interview about *The Best Man*, Sanaa Lathan laments, perhaps with some irony, "There's a double standard in this country. Every man wants to be a player who has slept with a thousand women. . . . But, on the flip side every woman is supposed to be virginal and untouched. It's so stupid. But that's the reality set up by pop culture, music, all these images perpetuated by the television."[19]

Unfinished Business, the literary appendage of *The Best Man*, augments the film's mission to incentivize marriage for African American heterosexual male spectators. *The Best Man*'s more palpable "unfinished business" is Harper's salacious penned confession about his and Mia's clandestine sexual encounter, as well as his decision about whether to restore a relationship with Jordan or continue his relationship with Robin. The romantic-comedy genre obliges the resolution of these "business" deals. Carved into Harper's book title, the film's more surreptitious message is that marriage is the unfinished business, or the final linchpin, of the American dream, particularly for middle-class African American men who are enjoying the spoils of the civil rights movement, exemplified by successful careers and affluent lifestyles. Part of the film's finishing touch is its postfeminist lexical and thematic tie to African American male viewers. Harper's book title, *Unfinished Business*, exploits the masculine connotation of "business" to define intimacy as a vehicle to rewrite and sell marriage as a public and advantageous investment for parsimonious and "risk-averse" African American men. The film's depiction of male characters as "classic heroes" who have the opportunity to "diversify their portfolio" and obtain and then choose between multiple women without substantial personal growth illustrates the deep-seated risk aversion.

Middle-class women's magazines often use meritocratic economic terms to discuss romance by suggesting that "instead of being 'stricken' or 'smitten' by love, a woman is responsible for her romantic successes and failures, that she must 'work hard' to secure a comfortable future for herself, and that she should guarantee that a relationship will provide an equitable exchange."[20] Print media with a predominantly Black readership followed the same pattern of galvanizing marriageocracy, but the analogies are perspicuous. *Ebony*'s 1990 article "How to Attract the Opposite Sex: It Takes More Than Good Looks to Be Successful in the Competitive Romance Market," *Crisis*'s 1999 article "Black & Single? Try Gauging Your Romantic Market Value," and *Ebony*'s 1999 article "When a Sister's Love Has a Price Tag Attached" are just a few instances of characterizing African American romance as a financial invest-ment, with the latter example unequivocally targeting male readers. These texts along with songs such as Parliament's 1977 "Wizard of Finance" and Gwen Guthrie's 1986 song "Ain't Nothing Goin' On But the Rent" play with the interpretations of romance and money and signify that financial stability can shape love and romance, especially for disenfranchised African American communities. Through monikers such as Murch, Lance's personification of his "fat ass" football contract, and Harper's book linking intimate relation-ships to business, *The Best Man* resists "love conquers all" bromides but im-plies that love has a price tag and that Black male "buyers" must get the largest "bottom" line for their investment.

Assuming that African American heterosexual female viewers are always ready for marriage because of the way society defines it as an "achievement" for women, *The Best Man* reinforces Black bridal pathos and fixates on en-couraging marriage among heterosexual African American men as it master-fully refutes hackneyed, pathological profiles of them as vehemently opposed to marriage—that is, as reluctant spouses and neglectful parents. About *The Best Man*, the *Washington Post* surmises, "You know these dudes. You grew up with them, went to school with them. Maybe even married one of them."[21] Another film review contends that *The Best Man* "challenges black men to love and forgive even through trying circumstances."[22] Far from anomalies, both *The Best Man* and *Love & Basketball* mimic discursive prescrip-tions enjoining African American men to "reclaim the black family" despite the "trying circumstances" they experience. As I discuss in other work, there is a cottage industry of heteronormative agitprop about the restoration of "the black family."[23] As they attempt to burke racist stereotypes and celebrate Black love, these relationship manuals and films minimize structural hin-drances such as unemployment, poverty, and incarceration, while correlat-ing relationship failures to culture and pathological behavior, cohering with a fictitious deracialized private sphere.

Silence and Erotic Sovereignty

Critics maintain that *The Best Man* works because it "is not trying to make a huge political statement about black relationships," and Malcolm D. Lee claims that the film is "not about race."[24] Lee leans on entertainment-industry parlance to unmoor banal designations of "black film" from demonized classifications of "protest art" and to unsettle the conflation of "race" with anything read as nonwhite or other. Whereas politicians use this deracialized jargon to mask the discriminatory ramifications of their policies, Lee marshals it as a way to shield his film against racist double standards for African American filmmakers. Film scholars confirm that "Hollywood (and related organizational systems and institutions that produce and distribute theater, literature, and film) employs racial categories to make investment decisions despite the fact that film executives continuously deny race ideology or racism's influence."[25]

In his declaration about race, however, Lee simultaneously adheres to narrow definitions of what constitutes the political. The messages etched in the written, sonic, and visual poetics of the films do not simply rehearse romantic comedy formula but make legible a complex negotiation of precarious erasure and visibility for the African American female characters. Though depicted through a flashback as an outspoken journalist during her undergraduate career, Mia is silenced for much of *The Best Man*. She has eighteen minutes of dialogue, totaling roughly 15 percent of the film's running time. The film's title makes clear its investment in exploring masculinity, but Mia's silence is still undeniably rare, especially for the depiction of an eager and excited fiancée in a romantic comedy.

Traditional romantic comedies with female protagonists frequently give its male characters, especially the principal male love interest, a significant amount of dialogue and screen time. That treatment is not reciprocated in *The Best Man*. Mia has been groomed into a taciturn companion from a confident and vengeful paramour, forewarning African American women to curtail their stereotypical brash, forthright characteristics in order to be crowned as "marriageable." It is no coincidence that Jordan, a candid and tenacious character who is bestowed more dialogue than Mia, ends the film without the monogamous partner she covets and is made to suffer the social death of a politicized and pathologized Black female singlehood.

In concert with the film's silencing, the film uses music to teach heterosexual male and female viewers that African American women's compliance with the nineteenth-century cult of true womanhood—"a metaphoric residue of whiteness," outlined by ideals of piety, purity, domesticity, and submissiveness—must be near perfect in order for her to be "worthy" of marriage.[26] Lee introduces Mia in the stark alabaster interior of her and Lance's mansion, signaling her fidelity to domesticity. In her first appearance in the film, Mia is adorned in pearl earrings, a pearl necklace, and a white sweater, shrouded in emblems of chastity and innocence. Decorated in ornamentation evincing her so-called propriety, Mia is shot at a low angle at the top of a grand staircase, apotheosizing her as a symbol of feminine perfection. As she descends the elegant sweep of staircase, the film burnishes the scene with Kenny Lattimore's song "Beautiful Girl," in which he sings, "I think I found myself an angel / A pretty girl who makes my life complete," consigning youthfulness, sanctity, and purity to Mia.[27] The first-person narration of Lattimore's nondiegetic sonic gloss informs viewers that Lance has the authority to define Mia as his infantilized, angelic, and pious possession.

The music and scene enunciate Mia's "true womanhood" for Lance's heteropatriarchal needs, demonstrating the film's fluency in the language of sociopolitical and cultural texts championing traditional forms of family. Nondiegetic scores often "map themselves onto the rhythm of the image, supporting the flow of narrative action without interrupting it."[28] In sync with the film's score, Lance admits to requiring that his wife be the consummate Madonna–whore and calls her an "angel" in his marriage vows. In a 1999 article, Malcolm D. Lee discloses that he wanted to depict Mia as an "angelic, floating from heaven, virginal character," affirming Sanaa Lathan's grievance about the pressure for women to be "virginal and untouched."[29] If "music is at once the container and transmitter of memory," *The Best Man*'s sonic and visual landscape works hard to align Mia with antiquated "true womanhood" norms to counteract the mark of pathology, deviance, and the "resonant echoes of slavery's memory" that Black female sexuality bears in the popular imaginary.[30] Slavery, then, has made African American women's attempts to live up to these inveterate standards of innocence and chastity Sisyphean.

Even as she is anointed as pure and largely silenced in the film, Mia does have her moment center stage during a flashback in which she is depicted as audacious in her rendezvous with Harper, a precarious compensation for her glaring silence in the film. This scene featuring Mia's tryst is an image seldom granted African American middle-class female characters. If allotted snippets of sexual expression, middle-class African American female characters are often already married or summarily denied marriage, exemplified by the unmarried and perhaps "unmarriageble" Jordan. The growing Black middle-class of the late 1980s and 1990s enabled a new stereotype of the "black lady" who rejected the "unbridled 'freaky' sexuality now attributed primarily to working-class Black women."[31]

The sonic sheath for Mia and Harper's dagger, or "lance," is D'Angelo's 1995 sinister magnum opus "Shit, Damn, Motherfucker."[32] The song's piercing interrogation, "Why are you sleeping with my woman?" as nondiegetic music captures Lance's feelings as he reads Harper's monograph recounting Mia and Harper's illicit event.[33] Mediated several times over with visual and oral texts, viewers see the encounter develop as he reads *Unfinished Business*, with Harper's voice-over chronicling the operatic unraveling of the union in painstaking detail. Scene and song—visual and oral texts—become entangled like the illicit lovers' bodies.

Lance's visualization, Harper's transcribed recollection, and D'Angelo's lacerating prose perforate Mia's hallowed veil of chastity and threaten to smother her, as well as conflate her carnal dexterity with the fetishized Madonna–whore. It is true that under the confusing labyrinth of voices and texts, Mia is primarily silent during the scene. It is also true that this scene is a product of Lance's imagination as he and the film put Mia, not Lance, on "trial" for the film's viewers. Although Lance's debauchery far exceeds Mia's one-time fling, spectators are never privy to an explicit, protracted restaging of his sexual escapades.

Because this scene sets out to visually and sonically indict Mia and is also a rare depiction of middle-class African American female characters, I read it not simply "for evidence of the wounds it inflicts on black women's flesh, but [also] for moments of racialized excitement," with the aim of illuminating the racialized and gendered compensation African American female characters negotiate in courtship and marriage, while uncovering the simultaneous possibility of pleasure enacted through the flesh.[34] By analyzing against the grain, I offer an alternative understanding and portrait of Mia that takes serious her silence and potential vociferous choreography, exploring how the "quiet subject negotiate[s] moments of subjection and power."[35] This exploration insists that "quiet is not an absence of articulation or utterance."[36]

In this scene, Mia confidently lets down her hair and begins kissing Harper (see figure 5.3). Her inaudible but self-possessed nomenclature with Harper is fruitful, accentuating D'Angelo's obscenity-laced song title. In this first frame of Mia's amatory debut, her drenched body is positioned upright, trumpeting her control and vigor. In an over-the-shoulder shot, spectators see the back of Harper's head, but Mia boldly faces viewers and her moans are audible, highlighting her striking presence against Harper's inconspicuousness. Though eventually omitted from the film, earlier screenplay drafts describing this scene insist that Mia "cannot be rejected" and have Mia explicitly requesting an "untraditional" sexual position.[37] The ebullience of this vignette, including its omissions and declarations, is exactly what positions Mia as an embodiment of "erotic sovereignty," or what Mireille Miller-Young limns as an attempt to "reterritorialize the always already exploitable black female body as a potential site of self-governing desire, subjectivity, dependence and relations with others, and erotic pleasure."[38]

FIGURE 5.3 Mia lets her hair down as she approaches Harper. *The Best Man*, directed by Malcolm D. Lee (40 Acres and a Mule Filmworks/Universal Pictures, 1999), DVD.

Mia's blackness makes her proximity to purity and divinity insufficient for heteropatriarchy, and her coquetry eventually proves to be a Faustian bargain, despite the film's happy ending. While Mia is afforded some sexual liberty in *The Best Man*, she collapses in pain as her body slowly deteriorates in the 2013 sequel *The Best Man Holiday*.[39] Not only does Mia die, but she is made ugly and suffers a slow and painful demise, marked by her emaciated frame, vomiting of blood, and patchy hair loss. Framed as aggressive cancer, Mia's histrionic death symbolizes the delayed and draconian atonement she must proffer for her erotic sovereignty and slavery's shadow of alleged Black female sexual excess. Lee's decision to kill Mia is an unconventional plot twist for a romantic comedy, and her death not only betrays the film's blithe and festive title but also imbues it with abhorrent, perverse meaning.

In an altogether different register, *Love & Basketball*'s Monica is a compelling character because she represents a new image of the romantic comedy protagonist. She challenges her mother's passive patriarchal affect but takes her mother's bold advice to pursue Quincy despite his engagement. Monica scoffs at traditional forms of feminine self-fashioning, which commercial films and Black bridal pathos often laud, while her confidence and aggression on the basketball court jettison respectability politics (see figure 5.4). She acquiesces to her mother's pleas to wear a dress on special occasions but is often outfitted in athletic clothes, with her hair in a disheveled ponytail, refusing the femme embellishments her peers embrace. When presented with the choice to comfort Quincy as he reckons with his father's infidelity

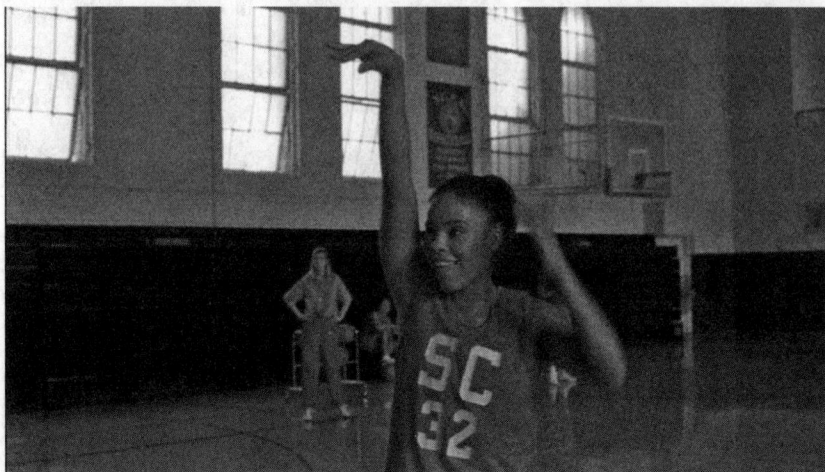

FIGURE 5.4 Monica exhibits confidence on the basketball court. *Love & Basketball*, directed by Gina Prince-Bythewood (40 Acres and a Mule Filmworks/New Line Cinema, 2000), DVD.

or to play in the next basketball game, she chooses to play basketball, hinting at a feminist challenge to her boyfriend's tacit ultimatum.

The markers of "feminism as a cultural force are apparent in romantic comedy, frequently expressed as discontent with misogynist masculinities and a narrative insistence that men too must change," and Monica represents this insistence to change.[40] She is an avatar for what Terri Simone Francis calls a "scary subjectivity," because she is an African American female character who rejects the terms of her oppression as not just wrong or unjust but as absurd, ridiculous, and stupid; she protects her vulnerability and subjectivity while rejecting her opponent's terms."[41] As a "scary subject," Monica ends the film triumphantly, playing professional basketball while Quincy watches from the stands and cares for their young son.

Monica represents a new image of the romantic comedy protagonist, but her characterization also adheres to some abysmal industry standards. Monica spends more time on-screen than Mia does in *The Best Man*, but the amount of dialogue she is allotted is surprisingly low. She has thirty-three minutes of dialogue, which is roughly 27 percent of the film's running title, in comparison to Mia's 15 percent. Though the romantic-comedy genre typically grants female characters more dialogue than do dramatic or action movies, *The Best Man* and *Love & Basketball* are not exceptional in the way that commercially successful films across a wide range of genres silence female

FIGURE 5.5 Young Monica looks affectionately at the bloody wound, or "kiss," on her cheek. *Love & Basketball*, directed by Gina Prince-Bythewood (40 Acres and a Mule Filmworks/New Line Cinema, 2000), DVD.

characters. Men typically speak twice as much as women in films—a systemic issue for most films produced in the United States.

Along with the silencing, early scenes in *Love & Basketball* reveal a disturbing portrait of Monica and Quincy. In the first quarter of the film, a bold eleven-year-old Monica plays basketball against Quincy in his backyard. She is close to scoring a point when Quincy pushes her to the ground, resulting in a bloody wound on her face, depicted in a tightly framed close-up, with New Edition's 1983 song "Candy Girl" as the nondiegetic sonic backdrop.[42] The quintet's falsetto voices croon, "You are my world / I need your love / each and every day," silencing Monica as it reverberates outmoded but familiar and dangerous conventions about boys using violence to show their affection to young girls.[43] This scene and its sonic shadow instantiate how romantic-comedies use music to render viewers "untroublesome (less critical, less wary) viewing subject[s]."[44] The ensuing images punctuate the regressive gender norms at play. Monica is depicted with a bloody abrasion on her cheek that resembles a kiss, and she smiles upon seeing the amatory wound in the mirror (see figure 5.5).

In a later scene, the two argue about Quincy transporting Monica to school on his bicycle. Quincy pushes Monica, with bandaged face from the earlier skirmish, off her bike and into a patch of multicolored impatiens, or aptly named "touch-me-nots," which frame Monica's dimly lit crumpled body

FIGURE 5.6 Young Monica in a patch of flowers after Quincy pushes her. *Love & Basketball*, directed by Gina Prince-Bythewood (40 Acres and a Mule Filmworks/ New Line Cinema, 2000), DVD.

(see figure 5.6). In this high-angle shot, Monica's prostration is juxtaposed against Quincy's power. Rufus and Chaka Khan's 1975 song "Sweet Thing," with Chaka singing "you are my heat / you are my fire," veils the depicted violence as a so-called warmhearted adolescent crush that will blossom, like the framing flora, into a beautiful, healthy marriage.[45] We might even think of these delicate flowers as a bucolic cradle nurturing a new kind of life—a new kind of way to be in the world.

The deployment of "Candy Girl" and "Sweet Thing" as sonic tourniquets operate as seemingly endearing palimpsests but also function as anesthetizing carols that silence Monica and assuage implicit fears about Monica's latent lesbian identity, a label often coterminous with female basketball players in the popular imaginary. The nondiegetic ballads also guilefully inlay a sonic ethos of innocence and adolescent naivete used to negate the stereotypical "angry" Black woman, hardened by life's difficulties, and perhaps the previous era's feminist movement. As it disavows angry Black women, the film offers Black women's sugarcoated flesh to men for consumption rather than for self-governing forms of straight or queer reciprocal love, partnership, or erotic sovereignty.

The film's culinary-inspired score speaks to political and cultural disparagement of alleged emasculating Black women and also coalesces with Miller-Young's deployment of "brown sugar."[46] As a metaphor, brown sugar "illuminate[s] circuits of domination over black women's bodies," and the ways in which the "process of refining cane sugar from its natural brown state into the more popular white, everyday sweetener reflects how black women, like brown sugar, represent a raw body in need of refinement and prone to manipulation."[47] The process of refining cane sugar is governed by a system of mass production that would make African American women's "bitter" and "hardened" bodies into "sweetened" and "candied" malleable products ready for marriage consumption.[48] In this scene, Monica's raw, recalcitrant body necessitates refinement and is eventually made pliable for Quincy's enjoyment and consumption.

As a way to counterbalance Monica's recalcitrance, vigor, and ambition, *Love & Basketball* depicts Monica as passive in her sexual encounter with Quincy. The "historical surveys of sex in Hollywood films demonstrate not only that depictions change as sexual attitudes and behaviors change within the wider culture but also that cinema is itself a site of ideological contestation, a kind of cultural proxy war over what kind of sexual morality should govern public and private life."[49] As a cultural proxy for sexual mores, Monica is depicted as a virgin, as Mia is, but Monica is not entrusted the freedom to initiate her first sexual encounter or the erotic sovereignty that Mia seizes. Quincy takes the reins. Partly mirroring Mia, Monica wears a white dress, accessorized with a set of white pearl earrings and necklace, at the beginning of their rendezvous, heralding her innocence and respectability. The film inserts Maxwell's cover of Kate Bush's ballad "This Woman's Work" as the nondiegetic sonic filter for their fleshly union.[50] Coinciding with the song's title, Monica nervously shields her breast as she assumes a traditional missionary position, buried under Quincy's body. This scene abruptly ends before any depictions of physical gratification, reinscribing the "proper" behavior for intimate encounters.

As an adult, Monica's return to basketball as a WNBA player after a successful but lonely career in an international league and an unfulfilling stint working at a bank parallels her return to Quincy after he has pledged his love to another woman. It is a hopeful ending for African American women who desire a gratifying career and a devoted husband and presents an appealing image for African American women who work outside the home and may not require the financial benefits characteristically associated with patriarchal marriage. Thus, it urges a reconsideration and restoration of marriage. As her surname, Wright, suggests, Monica seems to disturb and reinforce what it means to be the "right" kind of middle-class African American woman and wife.

Fading Out Single Women

These films bestow outwardly dissimilar female characters—Mia, a homemaker, and Monica, an athlete—with "happy endings," but the narrative arc also depends on a racialized and gendered punishment of its secondary characters, who are portrayed as the "wrong" kind of Black woman. Nona and Kyra in *Love & Basketball* and Shelby and Jordan in *The Best Man* embody an intersection of gender, race, sex, and class identities that ultimately prove to be too much and too little for heteropatriarchy to bear. Assuming that Black female spectators are always ready for marriage because of the way hegemonic cultural discourse defines it as an accomplishment, these characters must be made single, a supposed necessary but exacting sentence for ungovernable and insubordinate African American female characters.

For her pretentiousness and gender performance, Nona, Quincy's mother, is punished with her husband's infidelity and divorce. In a scene that appears early in the film, Nona is seen sneakily unwrapping a store-bought cake she will give to her new neighbors and duplicitously present as one she has toiled over in the kitchen. Nona's body, draped in a black, body-hugging wrap top, is fused with the heavily frosted pink cake being surreptitiously unwrapped, conveying her supposedly artificial and thickly frosted embodiment of Black womanhood. In a quip with Quincy, Zeke, Nona's husband, uses Nona's domestic subterfuge to underscore her haptic artifice, professing, "This is how your moms caught me. With the old fake and bake. Had me thinking I was catching a sister who could burn." Zeke insists that Nona's feigned culinary talents enraptured and duped him into marriage, painting her as a calculating and underhanded coquette. Zeke's innocuous ribbing, full of play and jest, emulates sexist and racist critiques of Black women who have supposedly used the "white woman's" feminist movement to get out of the kitchen where they belong, thereby calling into question their racial belonging and legibility.

Nona corroborates Zeke's assessment when she presents the cake to Monica's mother, Camille Wright, deceivingly claiming that she "loves to cook," as Quincy rolls his eyes and furls his brow in response to his mother's deceit. Nona, who mourns the increasing number of Black families moving into her pristine, white, upper-middle-class neighborhood, wears long synthetic hair, makeup, and ostentatious gold jewelry. *Love & Basketball*'s subtle and explicit critique of Nona reflects the widespread but meticulous scrutiny and disparagement of Black women's femininity, sartorial presentation, and racial illegibility via the superwoman archetype. The "superwoman/

strongblackwoman discourse assumes that a black woman has too many obligations, but she is expected to handle her business."[51] While contemporary popular culture suggests that "white women cannot have it all," Black women must "be everything for everyone else" and maintain "a sense of self."[52] Through her strategic but illusory domestic skills, Nona refuses the superwoman/strongblackwoman script and consequently must be punished with divorce.

Kyra, a flight attendant played by Tyra Banks, who is briefly cast as Quincy's fiancée and disruption to his and Monica's romance, is not completely unlike Nona. With model looks and a career stereotypically associated with beautiful women, Kyra, whose name is just one letter away from Tyra, evoking Tyra Banks's career as a model, is established as a sexy and attractive but discarded character, made to be single and unmarried. The film is able to use Quincy's rejection of Kyra as her punishment, despite her typically admirable sycophantic behavior, because her femme appearance means she is fated to become the contemptible, materialistic Nona. The film suggests that Kyra Kessler and Nona are complicit with white supremacy because they conform to a volley of so-called Eurocentric beauty standards and cultural values, such as coveting a white neighborhood, straightened hair/weave, and a spectacle of superficiality.

In *The Best Man*, Shelby and, to some extent, Jordan Armstrong are corollaries to *Love & Basketball*'s Nona and, as a result, suffer commensurate penalty of singlehood, one of the most severe modes of punishment and condemnation in a romantic comedy. Light-skinned, haughty, and well-heeled, Shelby, played by Melissa DeSousa, is the most despised character in *The Best Man*. In an interview, DeSousa verifies her character's snobbish affectation: "I'm a bitch to everyone. Everyone hates me."[53] Shelby's relationship with dark-skinned, dreadlocked, and milquetoast Murch, whose income is considerably lower than hers, represents a mésalliance. The film introduces viewers to Murch as he drives a minivan with his employer's name, Urban Youth Development, plastered on the side. His feminized vehicle and urban children signal his maternal and alleged emasculated positioning. Murch's job also demonstrates his commitment to underserved urban communities, attesting to his racial altruism.

For her arrogance and for further emasculating a so-called good Black man, Shelby is punished when Murch terminates their relationship in order to begin one with Candy, a stripper with a "heart of gold" who more explicitly represents a "sweet" malleable product ready for consumption. Rather abruptly, Murch trades in his bon vivant, Shelby, for Candy much like merchandise, a protracted homophone of his nickname. His name also amplifies Shelby's materialism, as he is her merchandise. Shelby ends the film in bed with Quentin, a lothario, but she has lost her devoted and benevolent prize, Murch.

Jordan Armstrong, the self-proclaimed superwoman, is less pompous and materialistic than Shelby or Nona but is a triangulating doppelgänger to Kyra, as both disrupt a central romantic pairing. Jordan is a beautiful and successful television producer who begins the film without a romantic partner, suggesting that Black women cannot, actually, have it all. A film review claims that "Jordan's life is similar to many well-established African American women without mates and many will identify with Jordan's issues," mobilizing Black bridal pathos by corroborating the prevailing assumption that Black women long to be brides and wives.[54] *The Best Man* is counting on the identification between character and viewer as it builds suspense that she and Harper will restore their relationship and marry, as Lance and Mia do. Harper makes it clear that he is in a relationship with Robin, but Jordan is forward with him about her desire to rekindle their romance.

Assertive in pursuing Harper, Jordan—the film's so-called strong Black woman—hastily kisses him when he mentions his relationship with Robin; invites him to come to her home after Lance's bachelor party, when he will hopefully be sexually aroused; and wears sexy lingerie in preparation for his arrival. Her surname, Armstrong, underscores her attempts to strong-arm Harper into reviving their romance and terminating his relationship with Robin. By the end of the film, Harper has considered both Jordan and Robin as romantic partners and opts to propose to Robin, his sensitive, devoted girlfriend, as Jordan watches from the sidelines. One of the film's "jokes" is Jordan's closeted lesbianism, which sanctions her punishment, while Robin's career as a caterer signifies her purported worth and imminent position as Harper's nurturing and dutiful wife. Analogous to Nona and Shelby, Jordan's penance constitutes a denial of the loving, monogamous relationship she desires and the opportunity to be crowned as wife. Jordan's transgression, in this case, is an amalgamation of her "superwoman" independence, success, confidence, and sex appeal, all reeking of feminist influence.

Final Frames

Although both films have become cultural icons, the praise they elicit may belie the complicated feelings they provoke. *The Best Man* and *Love & Basket-*

ball adroitly harness the aesthetic and utilitarian cornerstones of early twentieth-century uplift cinema, which "employed the medium of motion pictures to assert the humanity, respectability, modernity, and utility of African Americans . . . at a time when such propositions were, more often than not, challenged by cultural and political norms."[55] Like its predecessors, this modern cinematic offering functions "as an agent of positive self-definition for African American participants and spectators," signifying a model of #BlackLove.[56] As such, *The Best Man* and *Love & Basketball* decenter white characters as they expose the persistence of white supremacy.

This kind of critical nuance is repeated throughout the films. In chapter 2, I discuss how leaders and writers began championing a model of Black patriarchal power that upholds male authority but has excised the obligatory role of monetary support. *The Best Man*, with its characterization of Lance as a wealthy suitor, does not propose this form of patriarchal control. The film relocates dominance and subordination to other domains. Mia's erotic dexterity gestures toward a more expansive sexual life, but her painful death in the film's "celebratory" sequel suggests a precarious African American intimate sphere. By the end of *Love & Basketball*, Quincy is not able to offer the kind of financial support that Lance is able to provide in *The Best Man*, but Quincy is depicted holding his and Monica's child as she fulfills her passion playing for the WNBA, heralding a new characterization of the Black female protagonist. Both films reimagine new and old images of Black love and desire as they move between romanticizing and deromanticizing Black family formation and female silencing.

More recent romantic comedies with African American protagonists such as *Nappily Ever After* (2018) and *What Men Want* (2019) and have not garnered the kind of attention that *The Best Man* and *Love & Basketball* has in African American culture, but they have augmented space for Black female characters. Violet (Sanaa Lathan) in Netflix's *Nappily Ever After* talks for roughly fifty-three minutes or 54 percent of the film's running time and Alison Davis (Taraji P. Henson) in *What Men Want* speaks for fifty-four minutes or approximately 52 percent of the film's running time, indicating some quantitative progress for Black actresses since the release of *The Best Man* and *Love & Basketball*.

Nevertheless, *Nappily Ever After* and *What Men Want* rely on adaptation as they simultaneously impugn adaptive modes of navigating Black female subjectivity. *Nappily Ever After* is an adaptation of Trisha R. Thomas's novel of the same name and *What Men Want* is a modified version of the 2000 film

What Women Want, but both films upend the sartorial and domestic adaptations that its protagonists mobilize for social capital and professional advancement. As the title suggests, *Nappily Ever After* dramatizes a hair epiphany in which advertising executive Violet Jones abandons her "fake" hair and realizes the beauty of her "natural" hair as she shifts from pleasing men to self-acceptance. Though it harkens back to Bobby Jimmy and The Critters's 1989 song "Hair or Weave" and reduces Black women's use of weaves and protective styles to a hackneyed trope of superficiality rather than explores it as a landscape of creative expression, *Nappily Ever After* offers an unconventional resolution for a romantic comedy. In the final frames, instead of walking down the aisle on her wedding day, Violet walks alone outside claiming a sacred solitude, with Jamila Woods singing "I'm not lonely, I'm alone / And I'm holy by my own."[57]

In *What Men Want*, Alison Davis must give up pretending to be a wife and mother who parades a "fake" husband and son around as professional "accessories" in order to achieve career advancement as a sports agent. Like *Nappily Ever After*'s Violet, by the end of the film Alison's epiphany is characterized by her abandoning artifice and succumbing to her "genuine" feelings. She finally begins an authentic relationship with the man she falsely claimed to be her husband, ending her domestic theater. Alison does not conclude the film alone as Violet does, but establishes her professional independence by submitting her resignation and launching her own company. Both films gesture toward a contrived, shopworn "crisis" of inauthentic and artificial middle-class Black female characters, but trade on progressive cinematic depictions of professional and romantic autonomy.

Benediction

Will all of you witnessing these vows
do all in your power
to uphold these two persons in their marriage?

As I conclude, I circle back to the migrating women on the train in those early mornings, jostled about in the train car, anchored by fictional texts that explore the creative unveiling and veiling of Black female interiority. I also return to Lucille Clifton, who closes her poem "Black Women," illuminating this dexterity, writing: "We hid our ladyness / to save our lives."[1] The poem's resolution encloses the women in a cove of privacy and survival. This sacred dance of shadow, silhouette, and display rippled across the anchoring texts on the train. But, these texts were both anchor and estuary to other forms of knowledge for these commuting and communing women as they adopted fluid reading practices that cultivated liberating visions of world-making and survival. Just as the chorus of novels they read intertwined song lyrics, film, visual art, and television references, they read expansively, including fiction, self-help books, and periodicals. They curated both a syllabus and a road map for conceptualizing the intricacies of Black women's interiority and survival and the ways in which cultural production and the political landscape align and disconnect.

This labyrinth of political and popular commentary has migrated, but persists in twenty-first-century popular imaginaries. In 2000, Clinton strengthened Moynihan's legacy by awarding him the Presidential Medal of Freedom, while Donald Trump supporter Steve Harvey launched *The Steve Harvey Morning Show*, a weekday syndicated radio program during which he frequently offers "common sense" dating and marriage advice to his listeners. Harvey has perhaps been one of the most powerful voices to emerge since the 1996 Telecommunications Act; he exploited the figure of the single African American woman and was exploited by the political landscape as well as the mergers within and between the television, radio, and book publishing industry that I trace in the invocation. Just two years after his third marriage, Harvey released his 2009 book *Act Like a Lady, Think Like a Man: What Men Really Think about Love, Relationships, Intimacy, and Commitment*, which was published by Amistad (an imprint of Rupert Murdoch's HarperCollins Publishers) and inspired the 2012 romantic comedy *Think Like a Man*.

The same year Amistad/HarperCollins published Harvey's book, *Newsweek* published an article urging single Black women to seek dating advice from Disney's film *The Princess and the Frog* (2009), and the *Washington Post* published an article titled, "Bitch Is the New Black," profiling single, Black "lonely" women.[2] Following suit, *Nightline*'s December 22, 2009, segment featured single Black women, an event that stands as one of the few times Black women occupied a prominent space on *Nightline*.[3] The next year, the *New York Times* published an article insisting that Black women see fewer Black men at the altar.[4] This panic about Black women's intimate lives has also prompted a glut of misbegotten relationship experts—such as fashion model Tyson Beckford—to direct their advice to Black women and imply that Black women are invisible without a husband. Unfortunately, these kinds of didactic texts overshadow alarming reports about domestic or intimate partner violence, infant mortality, housing eviction, unequal pay, and student loan debt in African American communities.

Sonic culture also aggressively hails and demeans so-called lonely African American women. The painfully informal and lethargic marriage proposal, "we ain't getting no younger/we might as well do it," in Jagged Edge's 2000 rhythm and blues/soul single "Let's Get Married," flippantly summons "lonely" single women aching for marriage, registering it as an eleventh-hour desire.[5] Robert J. Patterson explains that "rhythm and blues music helps us to understand Black political and cultural desires and longings in light of neoliberalism's increased codification in America's racialized, gendered, and sexualized politics, policies, and economies."[6] Jagged Edge's ballad suggests that marriage is a socially and culturally requisite desire but also counters the notion of marriage as an irreproachable institution.

In *Marriage in Black* (2018), Katrina Bell McDonald and Caitlin Cross-Barnet lament how representations of Black relationships showcase "out-of-wedlock childbearing, divorce, individualism versus spousal and community partnership, father absenteeism, male infidelity, and greater socioeconomic advancement by wives than husbands."[7] These representations illuminate the ways in which racial isolation, loneliness, and a deracialized neoliberal echo chamber mined a well-worn groove of exploiting and policing "lonely" single African American women and familial "order" in African American communities, while overshadowing more unconventional forms of love and family.

An Unconscious Coupling | Marriage Surveillance and Spectacle

Tayari Jones's breathtaking novel *An American Marriage* (2018) reminds readers that "marriage is between two people, there is no studio audience," challenging the ways in which the image of matrimony has become much more about exhibition and spectacle.[8] As I have explained in previous work, spectacles ranging from *Basketball Wives* and *Bridalplasty* to *Surviving Marriage* and *Trading Spouses*—which cite family, marriage, and aspiring wives—have grown exponentially in the twenty-first century.[9] Each new reality-television drama approaches marriage differently, but collectively these visual spectacles, generated by major media giants, represent the expanding neoliberal backdrop and the national obsession with heteropatriarchy and its attendant connotations of social citizenship in the United States. While many of them are entertaining, frequently feature Black women as leading characters, and can defy "traditional models of partnership and motherhood, troubling conventional models of femininity," they also reduce the female characters to housewives or aspiring housewives, attempting to make real the patent fiction of the "normal" heterosexual family.[10]

Various programs have also begun grooming children and young adults for matrimony via the spectacle of the wedding ceremony, represented by shows such as the Learning Channel's pseudo-educational *Say Yes to the Prom*—a counterpart to *Say Yes to the Dress*—and the rise of the marriage-adjacent prom proposal, or "promposal." These programs and promposal spectacles mark joyous occasions and are more impassioned than Jagged Edge's 2000 ballad, but the language of "proposal" and saying "yes" to a dance tethers a disconcerting amount of gravity and pressure to what might merely be a party for some or an adolescent rite of passage for others. These words connote a mature commitment and engagement. In one promposal, a high school student uses a group of signs to write: "Alex–Will–You–Marry–LOL–J/K–Go-to-Prom–With me," drawing attention to ritual's marital subtext.[11] *Say Yes to the Dress* and promposals are more disturbing when considered alongside my analysis in chapter 2 where I unveil how Black female protagonists are routinely disallowed a childhood and adolescence and are prematurely coerced into marriage. This spectacle of bridal cosplay is also worrisome when read in tandem with research about child marriage showing that "an estimated quarter-million children, at least, as young as 10, were married in the United States between 2000 and 2010."[12]

Shows such as *The Real Housewives of Beverly Hills* and *The Real Housewives of Orange County* shun traditional images of the housewife for something far more extravagant in order to inspire young adults and women who may be less enamored with heteronormative relationships. These shows and settings supplant the responsibilities that typically constitute domestic work with consumerism, luxury, and leisure. I do not want to nostalgically praise the labor-intensive housework performed by 1950s housewives, but I do want to point out how these programs simultaneously capitalize on the "housewife" title but uncouple it from the emotional and domestic labor that is characteristically associated with being a housewife such as managing feelings, cooking, cleaning, and childcare. Using a postfeminist gesture, these shows center female characters and narratives of "empowerment" and "having it all" as they sell marriage to its female viewers by redefining it as a vehicle for wealth and autonomy. These franchises often embrace "popular feminism," where feminism is celebrated for its 'focus on the individual empowered woman.'"[13]

Media consumption has changed dramatically since those early morning train rides in Chicago, but there are interesting parallels in the way that texts by McMillan and her peers and programs such as Bravo Network's *Real Housewives of Atlanta* harness a verisimilar conceit, dramatize the romantic lives of diverse characters, and make visible the lives of single African American women. Much like some of the fictional characters I examine in the preceding chapters, reality television "housewife" characters are forced to negotiate condemnation for "imperfect" marriages or for being mistresses, being divorced, or failing to get hitched to a long-term beau. Shows predominantly cast with Black women, such as *Real Housewives of Atlanta* and *Basketball Wives*, are often subjected to heightened scrutiny. Discussions about who is a wife, who is divorced, and who is a mistress dominate gossip blogs with the aim of amplifying schadenfreude and branding unmarried women with the contemptible scarlet letter.

The Real Housewives of Atlanta and other new forms of visual culture are emblematic of the way that marital status signals social and literal death, echoing nineteenth-century African American women and men who understood marriage as a matter of literal life and death. A few months after the 2014 murder of Michael Brown in Ferguson, Missouri, galvanized Black communities across the country under the banner of Black Lives Matter, bizarre posters began to surface in Atlanta. The posters advertised *The Real Housewives of Atlanta*, then in the middle of its seventh season. The text above the eight Black women who star in the show read, "Black Wives Matter," a play on the bourgeoning racial justice movement's rallying cry (see figure B.1). It is an image insinuating that conventional family structure,

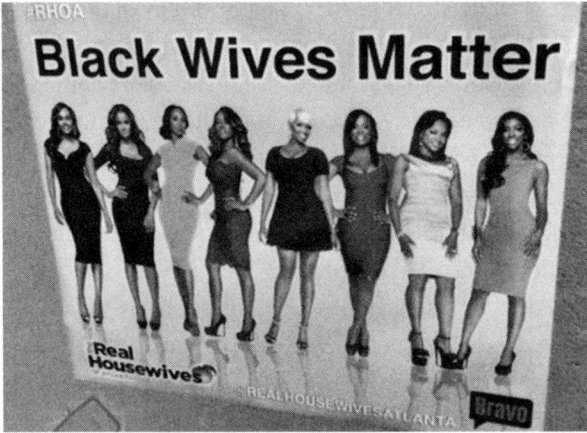

FIGURE B.1
Black Wives
Matter poster.
January 2015.

Let's be honest...
If Sandra Bland
had a husband,
she would
probably be alive
today.
Marriage matters.
Who's your
protector?

MAN LEADS Manual

FIGURE B.2 A 2015 meme exploiting
Sandra Bland's death, disseminated by Ro
Élori Cutno, author of *Man Leads . . . :
Woman Follows, Everyone Wins*. Self-
published, CreateSpace, 2013.

represented by African American women's roles as wives, has usurped political organizing against the state.

Later that summer, in the wake of the assault, jailing, and subsequent
death of Sandra Bland, a viral meme featuring her photo declared, "Let's be
honest . . . If Sandra Bland had a husband, she would probably be alive
today. Marriage matters. Who's your protector?" (see figure B.2). If "memes
are just born-digital nuggets of cultural norms," this one articulates a dangerous precept.[14] Operating as an ominous threat, this startling image touts
heteropatriarchal family as a kind of Black power that can combat state violence, consigning marriage an impossible responsibility and burden. Read
together, this diptych asserts the primacy of wedlock as a corrective not only
for Black women's romance woes and declining marriage rates, but also for

their experiences of gendered racism, reflecting a half century of the politicization of wedlock as a balm for racial inequality.

In 2015, the U.S. Supreme Court ruled that marriage cannot be denied to same-sex couples in the *Obergefell v. Hodges* case, and "there is a more visible range of "alternative routes open; they wind around combinations of love, sex, partnership, parenthood, work and friendship, at different speeds."[15] These various combinations do not, nonetheless, placate the demand for more legal protection against LBGTQ hate crimes, which are steadily rising. This increase has occurred alongside a recent swell of gender-reveal celebrations and spectacles, with themes such as "Glitter or Guns" and "Mustaches or Lashes" (because apparently babies sexed as male do not have eyelashes). In sync with this trend, there has been an upsurge in sexist messages on baby clothes such as "Pretty Like Mommy" and "Smart Like Daddy" as well as "Mr. & Mrs.," "His & Hers" or "Wife" emblazoned on coffee mugs, wine tumblers, jewelry, aprons, and T-shirts in discount, specialty, and high-end department stores.[16]

It is a strange zeitgeist considering that marriage rates are falling and millennials are "marrying much later than any generation before them."[17] *Say Yes to the Prom*, and the increase of promposals, gender reveal celebrations, and the aforementioned forms of material culture seem to fill a void that the spectacle of the wedding ceremony has left and they may be a comforting way for some to deal with the country's political circus and spectacle. This phenomenon could also be a way for people to counteract the growing bluesy feelings of despair, inadequacy, and loneliness that I discuss in the invocation. Unfortunately, many of these messages also convey harmful political ideals and appear to be an attempt to coax more people to walk down the aisle. They often endorse traditional gender roles and counter the slow but increasing public attention paid to LGBTQ people. They signify the ways in which cultural production can invigorate "the notion that marriage is both an ideal worth pursuing and an example of highly respectable behavior [that] has not gone out of fashion."[18]

Unveiling and Disavowal

Although reader reception is beyond the scope of this book, it is important to note, especially in the context of Harvey and other new forms of racist heteropatriarchal cultural production, that book clubs provide an indispensable space for intellectual, creative, and political enrichment. Janice Radway traces the cultural importance of the Book-of-the-Month Club from its start in 1926, and Elizabeth McHenry explains that nineteenth-century African American literary societies—such as the Bethel Literary and Historical Association in Washington, D.C., and the Boston Literary and Historical Association—formed in order to disavow white supremacy by advancing the "evolution of a black public sphere and politically conscious society."[19] Continuing the legacy of these literary societies, Jean Weathers inaugurated the You Go Girl African American Book Club in Chicago three years before Oprah's Book Club selected its first novel. The You Go Girl African American Book Club's unique membership of housewives, college students, teachers, postal workers, computer specialists, and authors mirrors the diverse characters in Black popular fiction. Club members discuss fiction by Black authors and have met famous authors, verifying that Black authors understand how book clubs constitute a vital Black public and political sphere. The inclusion of discussion questions in many of the novels by popular writers confirm that authors and publishers are attentive to the importance of these resuscitated book clubs. "As cultural producers, critics, and members of an audience, the women are positioned to intervene strategically in the imaginative construction, critical interpretation, and social condition of black women."[20]

Proliferating in urban and suburban communities and working-class, middle-class, and upper-middle-class neighborhoods, these clubs lift the veil on Black women's lives in more public spaces. The novels and book clubs also make available an occasion for Black women experiencing isolation in their work environments and neighborhoods to build community and form chosen family with other women, as the fictional characters they read about ostensibly do. As technology advanced rapidly during the late twentieth and early twenty-first centuries, access to discussion boards on websites such as the African American Literature Book Club (aalbc.com) began to enhance and expand book club membership, book sales, and politicized discussions about Black women's intimacy. The You Go Girl African American Book Club and Glory Edim's more recently established Well-Read Black Girl Book Club also give readers an opportunity to speak about the relationships between racism, sexism, class, and intimacy without the fear of being silenced. They can become modes of survival.

These African American book clubs, like many other book clubs across the country, offer another way to consider how portraits of marriage in the popular and political imaginary are an essential mode of reassessing family formation. This is particularly meaningful as younger generations grapple with the decision to start traditional families amid rising student-loan debt and a growing housing crisis. These conversations shed light on the ways in which the preoccupation with gendered roles, such as the housewife—made popular by contemporary reality television—still matters and must contend with an increasing number of young adults innovatively refashioning old and new forms of kinship and family.

Acknowledgments

Generous support for this project came in many different forms. I am honored to be a recipient of the American Association of University Women's American Postdoctoral Research Leave Fellowship and the Woodrow Wilson Career Enhancement Fellowship. I would not have been able to complete my book without these two prestigious awards. I was also grateful to have been selected as a fellow in the Summer Institute on Tenure and Professional Advancement Program at Duke University and invited to be a distinguished scholar-in-residence at Brown University's Pembroke Center for Teaching and Research on Women. These opportunities and spaces allowed me to refine my research and learn from scholars across diverse fields.

I am appreciative of the brilliant intellectual matchmakers who helped me wed my research interests to an urgent scholarly intervention early in the writing process. Immense gratitude goes to members of my dissertation committee who helped make the English Department my disciplinary home and insisted on the importance of this project, including Madhu Dubey, Natasha Barnes, Helen Heran Jun, Judith Kegan Gardiner, and Nancy Cirillo. I also appreciate the energizing encouragement from Sharon P. Holland and Vainis Aleksa. It was a pleasure to work across campus with Constance Dallas and learn about her remarkable research on African American families. I am thankful to the African American Studies Department as well as the support provided by their Grace Holt Memorial Award. It was a privilege to receive the Diversifying Faculty in Illinois Fellowship and the University of Illinois at Chicago's Abraham Lincoln Graduate Fellowship. I would be remiss if I did not thank the English Department at Middle Tennessee State University for hosting me as a dissertation fellow.

Leaving my beloved Chicago and migrating to New England was both difficult and exciting, but institutional support—such as the Five College Dissertation Fellowship and Amherst College's Robert E. Keiter 1957 Postdoctoral Fellowship were indispensable. I also enjoyed having the opportunity to share my work among colleagues as a Center for Humanistic Inquiry Fellow and a Crossroads in the Study of the Americas fellow. Amherst College's publication subvention support, External Faculty Mentoring Program, Gregory S. Call Academic Internship Program, and Faculty Research

Award Program were also beneficial as I completed my research. Amherst College colleagues within and outside my department were kind enough to read portions of my manuscript early in the writing process, including Michele Barale, Amrita Basu, Rick Griffiths, Amelie Hastie, Marisa Parham, and Pooja Rangan. Spread out across the Five College Consortium and Pioneer Valley, Iyko Day, Paula J. Giddings, Joya Misra, and Elizabeth Pryor were similarly generous with their time and attention to portions of the project.

Aliyyah Abdur-Rahman, Sandy Alexandre, and Kimberly Juanita Brown were crucial interlocutors who carefully read the entire manuscript. I am honored that they made space in their schedules to meet with me and provide detailed feedback on my work. I was invigorated by Kimberly's scholarly sustenance and my membership in The Dark Room: Race and Visual Culture Studies Collective.

I am grateful to have had Herman Beavers, Shanna Benjamin, Marlo D. David, Ann duCille, Sari Edelstein, James Ford III, Stephanie Harzewski, Holly Jackson, Joo Ok Kim, Robert J. Patterson, Zandria F. Robinson, and Courtney Thorsson read portions of my manuscript and offer insightful feedback and mentorship. I feel lucky to have had Tera W. Hunter's mentorship along this journey and hope our conversations will continue. I am indebted to Candice M. Jenkins for consistently offering supportive comments and guidance, which enriched my thinking throughout this process.

Many thanks to my editor, Jessica Newman; Mark Simpson-Vos, the Gender and American Culture series editors, the University of North Carolina Press community; and the two anonymous readers for the manuscript. I thank the Andrew W. Mellon Foundation; Shawn Theodore; the Jacob Lawrence estate; and the staff members at Northwestern University's Charles Deering McCormick Library of Special Collections, the University of Virginia's Albert and Shirley Small Special Collections Library, the John D. Rockefeller Jr. Library at Brown University, the California State University Library–Long Beach, and Amherst College's Robert Frost Library.

Other forms of support were also invaluable as I worked on this project. Nellie Boucher, Nicola M. Courtright, Sonya Donaldson, Stacie Selmon McCormick, and Richard Yarborough were invariably charitable with their time and advice.

The obstacles to raising two young African American boys while completing this project occasionally seemed insurmountable, but I am thrilled to have the opportunity to love and nurture two such imaginative people with fascinating but distinct personalities. They have been my light as inspiration and motivation. I am forever grateful for the love from my mother and father, who galvanized my deep love of fiction, film, and music. I would not have been able to do this without my mother's love and care. I treasure the love from my amazing grandparents, aunt, brother, uncles, nieces, in-laws, "play" aunts, friends, and extended kinship networks.

My deepest, most heartfelt gratitude goes to my loving partner, who has also been an amazing father and friend for this entire process, from undergraduate essays to book publication.
I love you and cherish our bond, always.

This is my solemn vow.

Notes

Invocation

1. Hunter, *Bound in Wedlock*, 293.
2. Wall, *Worrying the Line*, 7.
3. Jenkins, *Private Lives, Proper Relations*, 4.
4. Edmondson, "The Black Romance," 192.
5. Jacobs, *Incidents*, 164.
6. Brontë, *Jane Eyre*, 419.
7. Clifton, "Black Women," 3.
8. Tate, *Domestic Allegories of Political Desire*, 32.
9. Painter, *Sojourner Truth*, 229.
10. Foster, *'Til Death or Distance*, 70.
11. Hunter, *Bound in Wedlock*, 293–94.
12. Hunter, 296.
13. Moynihan, *Negro Family*, 6–7.
14. David Brooks, "The Professor Goes to Washington," *New York Times*, October 15, 2010, 112–15.
15. Staples, "Myth of Black Macho," 29–30.
16. Rushdy, *Remembering Generations*, 13.
17. L. Norment, "What Black Men Should Know," 132.
18. See Madhubuti, "Confusion By Any Other Name."
19. Williams, "Black Woman's Book," section C, 11.
20. Ali, *Blackman's Guide*, 169.
21. *CBS Reports*.
22. Iton, *In Search of the Black Fantastic*, 104.
23. Marsh et al., "Emerging Black Middle Class," 754.
24. Jun, *Race for Citizenship*, 125.
25. David, *Mama's Gun*, 10.
26. Harvey, *A Brief History of Neoliberalism*, 165.
27. Threadcraft, *Intimate Justice*, 32.
28. Alexandre, *Properties of Violence*, 134.
29. Perry, *Vexy Thing*, 104.
30. Du Bois, *Souls of Black Folk*, chap. 11, chap. 1; Du Bois, *The Negro-American Family*, 127–30.
31. Du Bois, *Souls of Black Folk*, chap. 9.
32. M. Alexander, *New Jim Crow*, 56.
33. Richie, *Arrested Justice*, 56.
34. Richie, 112.
35. David, *Mama's Gun*, 16.

36. Personal Responsibility and Work Opportunity Reconciliation Act of 1996, Pub. L. No. 104–193, 110 Stat. 2105 (1996).

37. Jodeci, "Feenin'," Track 3 on *Diary of a Mad Band*. Uptown | MCA Records, 1993.

38. Warner, *Trouble with Normal*, 117.

39. Traister, *All the Single Ladies*, 29.

40. "Verizon's Worrisome Cable Deals," *New York Times*, December 24, 2011.

41. Timothy Egan, "A Refuge for Racists," *New York Times*, June 26, 2015.

42. Jonathan Kandell, "S.I. Newhouse Jr., Who Turned Condè Nast Into a Magazine Powerhouse, Dies at 89," *New York Times*, October 1, 2017.

43. Jonathan Kandell, "S.I. Newhouse Jr., Who Turned Condè Nast Into a Magazine Powerhouse, Dies at 89," *New York Times*, October 1, 2017.

44. Greco, Rodríguez, and Wharton, *Culture and Commerce*, 11.

45. Celello, *Making Marriage Work*, 6.

46. Celello, 3.

47. Graham, "Black Is Gold," 73.

48. Graham, 73.

49. C. L. Jackson, "From Writer to Reader," 661.

50. McMillan, email to Karen Hunter, Louise Burke, and Carolyn Reidy, October 10, 2007, available at http://forum.blackhairmedia.com/terry-mcmillan-mad-as -heck-over-superhead-books_topic96026.html.

51. Edmondson, "The Black Romance," 207.

52. C. L. Jackson, "From Writer to Reader," 663.

53. Adrienne Rich, "Credo of a Passionate Skeptic," *Los Angeles Times*, March 11, 2001, http://articles.latimes.com/2001/mar/11/books/bk-36077.

54. Morris, *Close Kin*, 11.

55. Blackburn, review of *Sula*.

56. Domini, "Roots and Racism," 20.

57. McDowell, *Changing Same*, 6.

58. See Awkward, "Chronicling Everyday Travails."

59. Rambsy II, "Re-representing," 71.

60. McMillan, "Interview," 41.

61. Edmondson, "The Black Romance," 206.

62. P. A. Banks, *Represent*, 2.

63. Mehren, "Friction over Fact versus Fiction."

64. Carby, *Reconstructing Womanhood*, 61.

65. C. L. Jackson, "From Writer to Reader," 663.

66. E. M. Jackson, "Images of Black Males," 20–26.

67. "Exhaling and Inhaling," 1996.

68. See, for example, Jarrett, "Vicious Lynching," 6.

69. Daniel Max, "McMillan's Millions," *New York Times*, August 9, 1992.

70. Daniel Max, "McMillan's Millions," *New York Times*, August 9, 1992.

71. *Norton Anthology of African American Literature*, 2571–72.

72. *Norton Anthology of African American Literature*, 2571.

73. *Norton Anthology of African American Literature*, 2nd ed., xxxiii.

74. Daniel Max, "McMillan's Millions," *New York Times*, August 9, 1992.

75. Bragg, *Reading Contemporary African American Literature*, x.

76. Edmondson, "The Black Romance," 193.

77. Morrison, *Source of Self-Regard*, 59.

78. See Tompkins, *Sensational Designs*.

79. Harzewski, *Chick Lit and Postfeminism*, 145.

80. Perry, *Prophets of the Hood*, 112.

81. Neal, *Soul Babies*, 2–3.

82. Neal, 2–3.

83. Patterson, *Destructive Desires*, 3

84. Patterson, 3.

Chapter One

1. McMillan, *Waiting to Exhale*, chap. 3.

2. Lordi, *Black Resonance*, 6, 8.

3. Redmond, *Anthem*, 1.

4. Brooks, "'It's Not Right,'" 33.

5. Baker, "Fairy Tales," Track 9 on *Compositions*, Elektra, 1990.

6. Baker, "Fairy Tales," Track 9 on *Compositions*, Elektra, 1990.

7. Brooks, "'It's Not Right,'" 38.

8. Brooks, 38.

9. Kelly Barnhill, "Bringing Favorite Fairy Tales Up to Date," *New York Times*, May 16, 2019.

10. Baker, "Fairy Tales," Track 9 on *Compositions*, Elektra, 1990.

11. Womack and Womack, "Baby, I'm Scared of You," Track 3 on *Love Wars*, 1984.

12. Womack and Womack, "Baby, I'm Scared of You," Track 3 on *Love Wars*, 1984.

13. Wanzo, "Black Love," 6.

14. Gaines, *Uplifting the Race*, 231.

15. Davis, "Don't Worry," 26.

16. Richards, *Terry McMillan*, 19.

17. Tate, *Domestic Allegories*, 7.

18. C. M. Jenkins, *Private Lives*, 23–24.

19. Wall, *Worrying the Line*, 7.

20. McMillan, *Disappearing Acts*, 6.

21. McMillan, 36.

22. Roach, *Happily Ever After*, 66.

23. Hurston, *Dust Tracks*, 204.

24. McMillan, *Disappearing Acts*, 268.

25. McMillan, 1.

26. McMillan, 221–28.

27. McMillan, 150.

28. Naylor, "Love and Sex," 273.

29. Hartman, "Belly of the World," 169.

30. McMillan, *Disappearing Acts*, 408.

31. Valerie Sayers, "Someone to Walk over Me," *New York Times*, August 6, 1989.

32. McMillan, *Disappearing Acts*, 394.
33. Hine, *Hine Sight*, xxviii.
34. Hine, 915.
35. Baker, "Fairy Tales," Track 9 on *Compositions*, Elektra, 1990.
36. McMillan, *Disappearing Acts*, 202.
37. Dawson and Van Fleet, *African American Literature*, 297.
38. Cleaver, *Soul on Ice*, 189; Kgositsile, "Towards Our Theater," 147.
39. McMillan, *Disappearing Acts*, 204.
40. Ali, *Blackman's Guide*, 53.
41. N. Norment, "Addison Gayle," 377.
42. McMillan, *Disappearing Acts*, 157.
43. McMillan, 294.
44. Porter, *Conspiracy*, 106–7.
45. McMillan, *Disappearing Acts*, 360.
46. McMillan, 360.
47. Dubey, *Black Women Novelists*, 17.
48. Alexander-Floyd, *Gender, Race, and Nationalism*, 78.
49. McMillan, *Disappearing Acts*, 116.
50. Collins, *Black Sexual Politics*, 144; Crenshaw, "Whose Story Is It Anyway?," 416.
51. Hammonds, "Black (W)holes," 20.
52. McMillan, *Disappearing Acts*, 294.
53. Lorde, *Sister Outsider*, 121.
54. McMillan, *Disappearing Acts*, 42.
55. McMillan, 295.
56. McMillan, 282.
57. Melancon, *Unbought and Unbossed*, 82.
58. McMillan, *Disappearing Acts*, 282.
59. McMillan, 283.
60. McMillan, 283.
61. Roach, *Happily Ever After*, 95.
62. Wolcott, *Remaking*, 7.
63. McMillan, *Disappearing Acts*, 104, 102.
64. McMillan, 117.
65. McMillan, 104.
66. Ellerby, "Deposing," 109.
67. McMillan, *Breaking Ice*, xxiv.
68. A. Y. Clarke, *Inequalities of Love*, 3.
69. Baker, "Fairy Tales," Track 9 on *Compositions*, Elektra, 1990.
70. Richards, *Terry McMillan*, 101.
71. McMillan, *Breaking Ice*, xv.
72. Leder and Heffron, *Complete Handbook of Novel Writing*, 421.
73. Dandridge, "Debunking," 121.
74. Canty, "McMillan Arrives," 96.
75. hooks, *Reel to Real*, 436.
76. Majors and Levant, "You Can Breathe Now," 48.

77. Majors and Levant, 50, 54.

78. Majors and Levant, 52.

79. Hull, Scott, and Smith, *All the Women*, 17.

80. C. M. Jenkins, *Private Lives*, 115.

81. C. M. Jenkins, 106.

82. C. M. Jenkins, 116.

83. Naylor, "Love and Sex," 274.

84. Naylor, 271.

85. Levy-Hussen, *How to Read*, 101.

86. McMillan, *Waiting to Exhale*, chap. 5.

87. McMillan, chap. 5.

88. McMillan, chap. 2.

89. Krentz, *Dangerous Men*, 8.

90. McMillan, "What We've Lost," 2.

91. Baker, "Fairy Tales," Track 9 on *Compositions*, Elektra, 1990.

92. E. R. Edwards, *Charisma*, 135.

93. E. R. Edwards, 135.

94. McMillan, *Waiting to Exhale*, chap. 10.

95. McMillan, chap. 28.

96. McMillan, chap. 18.

97. McMillan, chap. 18.

98. McMillan, chap. 18.

99. Krentz, *Dangerous Men*, 5.

100. hooks, *Reel to Real*, 437.

101. McMillan, *Waiting to Exhale*, chap. 11.

102. McMillan, chap. 19.

103. Beavers, "African American Women Writers and Popular Fiction," 267.

104. McMillan, *Waiting to Exhale*, chap. 19.

105. Juffer, *Single Mother*, 32.

106. McMillan, "Interview," 41.

107. Patterson, "Is It Just Baby F(Ph)at?," 32.

108. McMillan, *Waiting to Exhale*, chap. 19.

109. Shaw, *Embodiment of Disobedience*, 9.

110. Enchantment, "Gloria," by E. Stokes and E. Johnson, United Artists, 1976.

111. Baker, "Fairy Tales," Track 9 on *Compositions*, Elektra, 1990.

112. Baker, "Fairy Tales," Track 9 on *Compositions*, Elektra, 1990.

113. David, *Mama's Gun*, 142.

114. McMillan, *Waiting to Exhale*, chap. 4.

115. McMillan, chap. 4.

116. Baker, "Fairy Tales," Track 9 on *Compositions*, Elektra, 1990.

117. McMillan, *Waiting to Exhale*, chap. 23.

118. McMillan, chap. 23.

119. Baker, "Fairy Tales," Track 9 on *Compositions*, Elektra, 1990.

120. Leder and Heffron, *Complete Handbook of Novel Writing*, 419.

121. Williams, "*Waiting to Exhale*," 90.

122. Thompson, *Beyond the Black Lady*, 2–3.

123. McMillan, *Waiting to Exhale*, chap. 3.

124. Dandridge, "Debunking," 133.

125. Dandridge, 133.

126. McMillan, *Waiting to Exhale*, chap. 27.

127. Juffer, *Single Mother*, 30.

128. Wanzo, "Black Love," 14.

129. Roach, *Happily Ever After*, 66.

130. Juffer, *Single Mother*, 17.

131. McMillan, *Waiting to Exhale*, chap. 4.

132. Baker, "Fairy Tales," Track 9 on *Compositions*, Elektra, 1990.

133. Baker, "Fairy Tales," Track 9 on *Compositions*, Elektra, 1990.

134. Baker, "Fairy Tales," Track 9 on *Compositions*, Elektra, 1990.

135. Blake, *Black Love*, 13.

136. E. R. Edwards, *Charisma*, xv.

137. Naylor, "Love and Sex," 274.

Chapter Two

1. E. F. White, "Africa on My Mind," 117.

2. E. F. White, 118.

3. McClintock, *Imperial Leather*, 359.

4. Randolph, *Florynce "Flo" Kennedy*, 5.

5. Farmer, *Remaking Black Power*, 91.

6. Ransby and Matthews, "Black Popular Culture," 526.

7. Kelley, "Stormy Weather," 68.

8. Gifford, *Pimping Fictions*, 2.

9. Gifford, 4.

10. Gifford, 156.

11. Lubiano, "Black Ladies," 335.

12. Collins, *Black Feminist Thought*, 74.

13. Sam Roberts, "Black Women See Shrinking Pool of Black Men at the Marriage Altar," *New York Times*, June 4, 2010, New York ed., A12.

14. Durham, Cooper, and Morris, "The Stage Hip-Hop Feminism Built," 732.

15. D. Smith, "Black Talk," 189.

16. Watkins, "Black Is Back," 197.

17. Cheney, *Brother's Gonna Work It Out*, 63.

18. Public Enemy, "Sophisticated Bitch," Track 2 on *Yo! Bum Rush the Show*, Def Jam Columbia Records, 1987.

19. Public Enemy, "Sophisticated Bitch," Track 2 on *Yo! Bum Rush the Show*, Def Jam Columbia Records, 1987.

20. Public Enemy, "Sophisticated Bitch," Track 2 on *Yo! Bum Rush the Show*, Def Jam Columbia Records, 1987.

21. Lubiano, "Black Nationalism," 245.

22. Miller-Young, *A Taste for Brown Sugar*, 4–5.

23. Lubiano, "Black Nationalism," 236.

24. Souljah, *The Coldest Winter Ever*, front matter.

25. Beavers, "African American Women Writers and Popular Fiction," 269.

26. Public Enemy, "Sophisticated Bitch," Track 2 on *Yo! Bum Rush the Show*, Def Jam Columbia Records, 1987.

27. Collins, *Black Sexual Politics*, 126.

28. Souljah, *The Coldest Winter Ever*, 4.

29. Pollard, "The P-Word Exchange," 116.

30. Pollard, 11.

31. Pollard, 9.

32. Lubiano, "Black Nationalism," 244.

33. Souljah, *The Coldest Winter Ever*, 12.

34. Public Enemy, "Sophisticated Bitch," Track 2 on *Yo! Bum Rush the Show*, Def Jam Columbia Records, 1987.

35. R. M. Williams, "Living at the Crossroads," 144.

36. Lubiano, "Black Nationalism," 274.

37. Dunbar, "Hip Hop," 107.

38. Keyes, "Empowering Self," 256.

39. Taylor, *Promise of Patriarchy*, chap. 10.

40. Keyes, "Empowering Self," 257.

41. Souljah, *The Coldest Winter Ever*, 9.

42. McClintock, *Imperial Leather*, 354.

43. Souljah, *The Coldest Winter Ever*, 164, 247.

44. Neal, *Soul Babies*, 3.

45. Souljah, *The Coldest Winter Ever*, 47.

46. E. F. White, *Dark Continent*, 118.

47. Dunn, "New Black Cultural Studies," 90.

48. "Who Is Sister Souljah?," 13.

49. Souljah, *The Coldest Winter Ever*, 31.

50. Dunn, "New Black Cultural Studies," 93.

51. E. F. White, *Dark Continent*, 133.

52. Porter, *Conspiracy*, 35.

53. Souljah, *The Coldest Winter Ever*, 438.

54. Souljah, 468–69, 176.

55. Souljah, *No Disrespect*, 150.

56. Spillers, "Interstices," 164.

57. Stuart, "Kemba's Nightmare," 4.

58. Graaff, *Street Literature*, 125.

59. Souljah, *The Coldest Winter Ever*, 424.

60. Pittman, "Black Women Writers," 67.

61. Wright, *Physics of Blackness*, 46, 74.

62. Souljah, *The Coldest Winter Ever*, 494.

63. Lubiano, "Black Nationalism," 243.

64. Public Enemy, "Sophisticated Bitch," Track 2 on *Yo! Bum Rush the Show*, Def Jam Columbia Records, 1987.

65. Griffin, "Ironies of the Saint," 218.

66. Griffin, 219.

67. Souljah, *The Coldest Winter Ever*, 39.

68. Tyree, *Flyy Girl*, 392.

69. Public Enemy, "Sophisticated Bitch," Track 2 on *Yo! Bum Rush the Show*, Def Jam Columbia Records, 1987.

70. Souljah, *No Disrespect*, 77.

71. Ford, *Liberated Threads*, 5

72. Ongiri, *Spectacular Blackness*, 29.

73. Matthews, "'No One Ever Asks,'" 271.

74. Tyree, *Flyy Girl*, 399.

75. Graff, *Street Literature*, 124.

76. Tyree, *Flyy Girl*, 400.

77. Liz Robbins, "Billboard Opposing Abortion Stirs Debate," *New York Times*, February 23, 2011.

78. Public Enemy, "Sophisticated Bitch," Track 2 on *Yo! Bum Rush the Show*, Def Jam Columbia Records, 1987.

79. Tyree, *Flyy Girl*, 408.

80. Tyree, 408.

81. Tyree, 408.

82. Tyree, 408.

83. Tyree, 409.

84. Woods, *True to the Game*, chap. 1.

85. Woods, chap. 1.

86. Woods, chap. 1.

87. Woods, chap. 2.

88. Woods, chap. 2.

89. Mussell, "Beautiful and Damned," 85.

90. Woods, *True to the Game*, chap. 7.

91. Woods, 127.

92. Woods, chap. 1, chap. 9.

93. Woods, chap. 10.

94. Woods, chap. 1.

95. Public Enemy, "Sophisticated Bitch," Track 2 on *Yo! Bum Rush the Show*, Def Jam Columbia Records, 1987.

96. Lubiano, "Black Nationalism," 240.

97. Woods, *True to the Game*, chap. 19.

98. Lubiano, "Black Nationalism," 240.

Chapter Three

1. Franklin, *What's Love Got to Do with It?*, 118.

2. Curwood, *Stormy Weather*, 3.

3. Weems, *Desegregating the Dollar*, 60.

4. Parker, *Department Stores and the Black Freedom Movement*, 3.

5. Cooks, "Speech on the 'Black Black' Campaign," 88.

6. Cooks, 92.

7. Anderson, *Our Black Year*, 17.

8. Botham, *Almighty God Created the Races*, 3.

9. Jackson, "Black or White," Track 8 on *Dangerous*, Epic Sony, 1991.

10. Dunning, *Queer in Black and White*, 27.

11. NdegèOcello, "Soul on Ice," Track 8 on *Plantation Lullabies*, Maverick, 1993.

12. Kitt, *The Color of Love*, 47.

13. Kitt, 47.

14. Kitt, 95.

15. Kitt, 11, 95.

16. Kitt, 92.

17. Kitt, 93.

18. Kitt, 25–26.

19. Later in the novel, Jordan discovers that Kimberly is multiracial. She rejects being categorized as black or African American.

20. Dickey, *Milk in My Coffee*, 293.

21. Dickey, 32.

22. Dickey, 78.

23. Dickey, 73.

24. Dickey, 28.

25. Dickey, 40.

26. Dickey, 27.

27. Nelson, *Straight, No Chaser*, 108.

28. Nelson, 108.

29. Nelson, 108.

30. Briscoe, *Sisters and Lovers*, 211.

31. Briscoe, 242.

32. Illouz, *Consuming the Romantic Utopia*, 2.

33. Kitt, *The Color of Love*, 66.

34. Dickey, *Milk in My Coffee*, 38.

35. Jackson, "Black or White," Track 8 on *Dangerous*, Epic Sony, 1991.

36. Kitt, *The Color of Love*, 59.

37. Kitt, 116.

38. Collins, *Black Sexual Politics*, 265.

39. Jones-Rodgers, *They Were Her Property*, 205.

40. Dickey, *Milk in My Coffee*, 107.

41. Dickey, 22.

42. Dickey, 259.

43. Kitt, *The Color of Love*, 196.

44. Collins, *Black Sexual Politics*, 103–4.

45. Jackson, "Black or White," Track 8 on *Dangerous*, Epic Sony, 1991.

46. NdegèOcello, "Soul on Ice," Track 8 on *Plantation Lullabies*, Maverick, 1993.

47. Kitt, *The Color of Love*, 120.

48. Kitt, 396.

49. Moran, *Interracial Intimacy*, 105.

50. Giddings, *When and Where I Enter*, 319.

51. NdegèOcello, "Soul on Ice," Track 8 on *Plantation Lullabies*, Maverick, 1993.

52. Dickey, *Milk in My Coffee*, 46.

53. Jackson, "Black or White," Track 8 on *Dangerous*, Epic Sony, 1991.

54. Jackson, "Black or White (Official Video)," YouTube video, 11:01, posted on November 14, 2016, https://www.youtube.com/watch?v=pTFE8cirkdQ.

55. Cleaver, *Soul on Ice*, 189.

56. Dickey, *Milk in My Coffee*, 76.

57. Dickey, 82.

58. NdegèOcello, "Soul on Ice," Track 8 on *Plantation Lullabies*, Maverick, 1993.

59. Kitt, *The Color of Love*, 24.

60. Kitt, 203–4.

61. Quoted in Weems, *Desegregating*, 74.

62. Anderson, *Our Black Year*, xi.

63. Dickey, *Milk in My Coffee*, 17.

64. Dickey, 14.

65. Dickey, 14.

66. NdegèOcello, "Soul on Ice," Track 8 on *Plantation Lullabies*, Maverick, 1993.

67. Dickey, *Milk in My Coffee*, 73.

68. Dickey, 118.

69. Dickey, 15–16.

70. C. Y. Clarke, "Lesbianism," 246.

71. Jackson, "Black or White," Track 8 on *Dangerous*, Epic Sony, 1991.

72. Dickey, *Milk in My Coffee*, 80.

73. Dickey, 237.

74. Jackson, "Black or White," Track 8 on *Dangerous*, Epic Sony, 1991.

75. Dickey, *Milk in My Coffee*, 236.

76. Dickey, 293.

77. NdegèOcello, "Soul on Ice," Track 8 on *Plantation Lullabies*, Maverick, 1993.

78. Dickey, *Milk in My Coffee*, 239.

79. Hamilton, Goldsmith, and Darity, "Shedding 'Light' on Marriage," 46.

80. R. R. Banks, *Is Marriage for White People?*, 112.

81. Judice, *Interracial Marriages*, 58.

82. Judice, 58–59.

83. Moran, *Interracial Intimacy*, 115.

84. Daileader, *Racism, Misogyny*, 15.

85. Cottom, *Thick: And Other Essays*, 149.

86. Moran, *Interracial Intimacy*, 125.

Chapter Four

1. B. Smith, "Toward a Black Feminist Criticism," 20.

2. Gomez, "But Some of Us Are Brave," 290.

3. I discuss this as a problem in my essay on Dee Rees's 2011 film *Pariah*. See Henderson, "Rebirth of Queer."

4. Giles, "Beginner's Pluck," 72–73.

5. Sweet Honey in the Rock also currently has one male guitarist.

6. Rosemary Mahoney, "Don't Nobody Want Me. Don't Nobody Need Me," review of *Push*, by Sapphire, *New York Times*, July 7, 1996, 9.

7. E. R. Edwards, *Charisma*, xv.

8. E. R. Edwards, xv.

9. Sapphire, *Push*, 66.

10. Ransby and Matthews, "Black Popular Culture," 528.

11. A. Davis, "Meditations," 42.

12. Edwards, *Charisma*, xv.

13. Sapphire, *Push*, 34.

14. Sapphire, 34.

15. Sweet Honey in the Rock, "Testimony," Track B2 on *We All . . . Everyone of Us*, Flying Fish, 1983.

16. B. Smith, *Truth That Never Hurts*, 173.

17. B. Smith, 171.

18. H. L. Gates, "The Charmer," 30, 42.

19. H. L. Gates, 171.

20. Sweet Honey in the Rock, "Testimony," Track B2 on *We All . . . Everyone of Us*, Flying Fish, 1983.

21. Louis Farrakhan, "'Ugly Woman' by the Charmer, Louis Farrakhan," YouTube video, 3:00, posted by Glenroy Joseph, June 25, 2011, https://www.youtube.com/watch?v=nUPxElXRTtQ.

22. Taylor, *Promise of Patriarchy*, 107.

23. Taylor, 118.

24. The Department of Supreme Wisdom, *The Supreme Wisdom Lessons by Master Fard Muhammad*, 14.

25. Lubiano, "Black Nationalism," 232.

26. Farrakhan, *A Torchlight for America*, 103.

27. Farrakhan, 103.

28. Farrakhan, 104.

29. Farrakhan, 106–7.

30. "Minister Louis Farrakhan Talks Issues That Directly Effect [sic] the Black Community and More (Part 2 of 3)," YouTube video, 25:29, uploaded by Hiphopsince1987tv, September 10, 2015, www.youtube.com/watch?v=Y-PXMA70T80.

31. Sapphire, *Push*, 34.

32. Sapphire, 12.

33. Sapphire, 112.

34. Sapphire, 6.

35. Sweet Honey in the Rock, "Testimony," Track B2 on *We All . . . Everyone of Us*, Flying Fish, 1983.

36. Farrakhan, *A Torchlight for America*, 102–3.

37. Griffin, "Conflict and Chorus," 120.

38. Sapphire, *Push*, 24.

39. Morris, *Close Kin*, 113.

40. Farrakhan, *A Torchlight for America*, 103.

41. The Five Percent Nation believes that only 5 percent of the world knows the "real truth about existence," including the idea that black men are "Gods" and black women are "Queens" and the "Earth" is to be fertilized with "seeds" (children). It is a belief in accord with popular and scholarly Afrocentric accounts of the often ignored existence of African kings and queens, such as fourteenth-century Egyptian queen Nefertiti. It is a fascinating counternarrative, but it often supplants historical narratives tracing less majestic but equally valuable stories about poor, enslaved African people.

42. Sapphire, *Push*, 81.

43. Miyakawa, *Five Percenter Rap*, 64.

44. Sapphire, *Push*, 67.

45. Coontz, *Way We Never Were*, xiii.

46. Monroe, "Louis Farrakhan's Ministry of Misogyny and Homophobia," 278.

47. Alexander-Floyd, *Gender, Race, and Nationalism*, 5.

48. Quadagno, *Color of Welfare*, 178.

49. Sapphire, *Push*, 76–77.

50. Harkins, *Everybody's Family Romance*, xi.

51. Alexander-Floyd, *Gender, Race, and Nationalism*, 124–25.

52. Bolen, *Child Sexual Abuse*, 30.

53. Bolen, 30.

54. Merriam Webster's Time Traveler Web site, July 23, 2019.

55. Personal Responsibility and Work Opportunity Act of 1996, Pub. L. No. 104–93, 110 Stat. 2105 (1996).

56. Sapphire, *Push*, 24.

57. Sapphire, 80.

58. Sweet Honey in the Rock, "Testimony," Track B2 on *We All . . . Everyone of Us*, Flying Fish, 1983.

59. Sweet Honey in the Rock, "Testimony," Track B2 on *We All . . . Everyone of Us*, Flying Fish, 1983.

60. Sapphire, *Push*, 133.

61. Sapphire, 131–32.

62. Sapphire, 132.

63. Sapphire, 132.

64. Sapphire, 132.

65. Rountree, "Overcoming Violence," 139.

66. Sapphire, *Push*, 82–83.

67. Sweet Honey in the Rock, "Testimony," Track B2 on *We All . . . Everyone of Us*, Flying Fish, 1983.

68. Staples, "Myth of Black Macho," 27.

69. D. Bradley, "Telling the Black Woman's Story," 36.

70. Crouch, "Aunt Medea," 39.

71. McDowell, *Changing Same*, 126.

72. I. Reed, "The Selling of 'Precious,'" http://www.counterpunch.org/2009/12/04/the-selling-of-quot-precious-quot/.

73. I. Reed.

74. I. Reed.

75. Sapphire, *Push*, 95.

76. Dubey, *Black Women Novelists*, 65.

77. Cox, *Shapeshifters*, 28.

78. C. J. Cohen, "Punks, Bulldaggers, and Welfare Queens," 22, 34.

79. C. J. Cohen, 42.

80. Sapphire, *Push*, 94.

81. Sapphire, 94.

82. C. J. Cohen, "Punks, Bulldaggers, and Welfare Queens," 41.

83. Sapphire, *Push*, 81.

84. Morris, *Close Kin*, 121.

85. Sapphire, *Push*, 81.

86. Sapphire, 81.

87. Sweet Honey in the Rock, "Testimony," Track B2 on *We All . . . Everyone of Us*, Flying Fish, 1983.

88. Abdur-Rahman, *Against the Closet*, 140.

89. Sapphire, *Push*, 95.

90. Sapphire, 82.

Chapter Five

1. Oliver and Oliver, *Black Love*. http://www.oprah.com/app/black-love.html.

2. Radner and Stringer, "Speaking the Name of the Father in the Neo-Romantic Comedy," 135.

3. Manohla Dargis, "Sundance Fights Tide with Films Like 'The Birth of a Nation,'" *New York Times*, January 29, 2016.

4. Bogle, *Toms, Coons*, 329.

5. Examples include *Boyz n the Hood* (1991), *New Jack City* (1991), *Juice* (1992), *South Central* (1992), *Menace II Society* (1993), and *Higher Learning* (1995).

6. "Friends Reunite," 38.

7. Bogle, *Toms, Coons*, 364; Mask, "Buppy Love in an Urban World," 44.

8. Strachan, "What It's Like to Be a Black Woman in White Hollywood."

9. Examples include *10 Things I Hate About You* (1999), *Runaway Bride* (1999), and *How to Lose a Guy in 10 Days* (2003).

10. Producers also cast male actors with whom male viewers might be familiar in order to capture heterosexual male interest. *Love & Basketball*'s male lead, Omar Epps, would possibly be recognizable to male viewers from his role as Q in *Juice* (1992), with Q acting as a subtle link to his role as Quincy in *Love & Basketball*. (Epps would later play the role of Malik Williams in *Higher Learning* [1995].) Similarly, Morris Chestnut would most likely be familiar to male viewers from his role as Ricky Baker in *Boyz n the Hood* (1991).

11. McDonald, "Homme-Com," 147.

12. McDonald, 153.

13. Kevin Brown, "Around Town with Kevin Brown: Afro A&E Talks with Film-maker Malcolm Lee," *Afro-American Red Star* (Washington, DC), October 22, 1999, B4.

14. Unemployed, condescending, and a womanizer, Troy (Ethan Hawke) in *Reality Bites* (1994) is an example of the romantic comedy rake. His sacrifice is his father's death, which finally motivates him to profess his love for Lelaina (Winona Ryder).

15. Bowdre, "Romantic Comedies and the Raced Body," 109.

16. Bowdre, 109.

17. Hagelin, *Reel Vulnerability*, 15.

18. Cultivating the cinematic landscape, a quarrel about a shared love interest in Brandy and Monica's hit duet "The Boy Is Mine" illustrates the appeal of female competition for black male suitors in the popular imaginary. In 1998, just a year before *The Best Man* was released, the song spent thirteen weeks at the top of the Billboard Hot 100 chart.

19. Kaia Shivers, "*The Best Man*—the Members of the Wedding Party," *Los Angeles Sentinel*, October 21, 1999, B6.

20. Illouz, *Consuming the Romantic Utopia*, 195.

21. Lonnae O'Neal Parker, "*The Best Man*: A Joyous Occasion," *Washington Post*, October 22, 1999, N46.

22. "*The Best Man*," review of *The Best Man*, directed by Malcolm D. Lee, *Hyde Park Citizen* (Chicago), October 28, 1999, 21.

23. See Henderson, "Black Political and Popular Culture," 198–208.

24. Claudia Eller, "Company Town; The Biz; Filmmaker Hopes All-Black Film Will Make It to the Mainstream," *Los Angeles Times*, September 24, 1999, 1; Allister Harry, "Simply the Best: He's Spike Lee's Cousin but Malcolm D. Lee's Debut Movie, *The Best Man*, Marks Him Out as a Future Star in His Own Right," *Evening Standard* (London), June 29, 2000, 33.

25. Ndounou, *Shaping the Future*, 7.

26. Cruz, *The Color of Kink*, 4.

27. Lattimore, "Beautiful Girl," Track 7 on *The Best Man* (Music from the Motion Picture). Sony BMG Music Entertainment, 1999.

28. Herzog, *Dreams of Difference*, 6.

29. Marsha Mitchell-Bray, "*The Best Man*, an Instant Black Film Classic," *Los Angeles Sentinel*, October 21, 1999, B4.

30. Wall, *Worrying the Line*, 10; K. J. Brown, *Repeating Body*, 8.

31. Collins, *Black Sexual Politics*, 139.

32. D'Angelo, "Shit, Damn, Motherfucker," Track 5 on *Brown Sugar*. Virgin Records America, 1995.

33. D'Angelo, "Shit, Damn, Motherfucker," Track 5 on *Brown Sugar*. Virgin Records America, 1995.

34. Nash, *Black Body in Ecstasy*, 1.

35. Quashie, *Sovereignty of Quiet*, 9.

36. Campt, *Listening to Images*, 4.

37. Lee, "The Best Man," 91–92.

38. Miller-Young, *Taste for Brown Sugar*, 16.

39. Lee, *The Best Man Holiday*, Universal City, CA: Universal Pictures, 2014, DVD.

40. Tasker, *"Enchanted,"* 69.

41. Francis, "She Will Never Look," 100.

42. New Edition, "Candy Girl," Track 6 on *Candy Girl*. Warlock Records, 1983.

43. New Edition, "Candy Girl," Track 6 on *Candy Girl*. Warlock Records, 1983.

44. Gorbman, *Unheard Melodies*, 58.

45. Khan, "Sweet Thing," Track 6 on *Rufus featuring Chaka Khan*. Rufus band, ABC Records ABCD-909, 1975.

46. Miller-Young, *Taste for Brown Sugar*, 4.

47. Miller-Young, 4–5.

48. Michael Elliott and Rick Famuyiwa's 2002 romantic comedy film *Brown Sugar* pushes this metaphor to its logical end.

49. Kelly, *Abstinence Cinema*, 5.

50. Maxwell, "This Woman's Work," by Kate Bush. Track 13 on *Love & Basketball* (Music from the Motion Picture). Columbia Records, 2000.

51. Springer, "Divas," 252.

52. Springer, 252.

53. "Friends Reunite," *Jet*, 38.

54. Shivers, "The Best Man," B6.

55. Field, *Uplift Cinema*, 16.

56. Field, 16.

57. Woods, "Holy (Reprise)," Track 26 on *Nappily Ever After* soundtrack. Netflix, 2018.

Benediction

1. Clifton, "Black Women," 3.

2. Samuels, *"The Princess and the Frog*: Disney's Mixed-Race Royalty"; D. L. Brown, "Profile of Helena Andrews."

3. Davis and Karar, "Single, Black, Female."

4. Sam Roberts, "Black Women See Shrinking Pool of Black Men at the Altar," *New York Times*, June 4, 2010.

5. Jagged Edge, "Let's Get Married," Track 7 on *J. E. Heartbreak*. So So Def Recordings and Sony Music Entertainment, Inc., 2000.

6. R. J. Patterson, *Destructive Desires*, 2.

7. McDonald and Cross-Barnet, *Marriage in Black*, 135.

8. T. Jones, *An American Marriage*, 72.

9. Henderson, "Black Political and Popular Culture," 202.

10. R. J. Gates, *Double Negative*, 150.

11. Hess, "The Awkward Charm of the Promposal," *New York Times*, April 8, 2016.

12. Reiss, "Despite Progress, Child Marriage Is Still Legal in All 50 States," *New York Times*, July 26, 2017.

13. Banet-Weiser, *Empowered*, 17.

14. Cottom, *Thick*, 45.

15. Traister, *All the Single Ladies*, 9.

16. Dell'Antonia, "Sexist Messages on Baby Clothes," *New York Times*, November 22, 2011.

17. Parker-Pope, "Should We All Take the Slow Road to Love?," *New York Times*, July 2, 2019.

18. Morris, *Close Kin*, 2.

19. McHenry, *Forgotten Readers*, 3.

20. Bobo, *Black Women as Cultural Readers*, 27.

Bibliography

Abdur-Rahman, Aliyyah I. *Against the Closet: Black Political Longing and the Erotics of Race*. Durham: Duke University Press, 2012.

"About the Romance Genre." Romance Writers of America: The Voice of Romance Writers. Accessed August 20, 2016. www.rwa.org/p/cm/ld/fid=578.

Abramovitz, Mimi, and Ann Withorn. "Playing by the Rules: Welfare Reform and the New Authoritarian State." In *Without Justice for All: The New Liberalism and Our Retreat from Racial Equality*, edited by Adolph Reed, 151–74. Boulder, CO: Westview Press, 1999.

Ahmed, Sara. *The Promise of Happiness*. Durham, NC: Duke University Press, 2010.

Akbar, Na'im. *Visions for Black Men*. Tallahassee: Mind Productions, 2006.

Alexander, Amy, ed. *The Farrakhan Factor: African-American Writers on Leadership, Nationhood, and Minister Louis Farrakhan*. New York: Grove Press, 1998.

Alexander, Michelle. *The New Jim Crow: Mass Incarceration in the Age of Colorblindness*. New York: New Press, 2010.

Alexander-Floyd, Nikol G. *Gender, Race, and Nationalism in Contemporary Black Politics*. New York: Palgrave Macmillan, 2007.

Alexandre, Sandy. *The Properties of Violence: Claims to Ownership in Representations of Lynching*. Jackson: University Press of Mississippi, 2012.

Ali, Shahrazad. *The Blackman's Guide to Understanding the Blackwoman*. Philadelphia: Civilized Publications, 1989.

Anderson, Maggie. *Our Black Year: One Family's Quest to Buy Black in America's Racially Divided Economy*. New York: PublicAffairs, 2012.

Awkward, Michael. "Chronicling Everyday Travails and Triumphs." Review of *Mama*, by Terry McMillan. *Callaloo*, no. 36 (Summer 1988): 649–50.

Baker, Anita. "Fairy Tales." Track 9 on *Compositions*. Atlantic Recording Corporation, 1990.

Bambara, Toni Cade, ed. *The Black Woman: An Anthology*. New York: Washington Square Press, 1970.

Banet-Weiser, Sarah. *Empowered: Popular Feminism and Popular Misogyny*. Durham, NC: Duke University Press, 2018.

Banks, Patricia A. *Represent: Art and Identity among the Black Upper-Middle Class*. New York: Routledge, 2010.

Banks, Ralph Richard. *Is Marriage for White People? How the African American Marriage Decline Affects Everyone*. New York: Plume, 2014.

Baraka, Amiri. "The Myth of a 'Negro Literature.'" In *Within the Circle: An Anthology of African American Literary Criticism from the Harlem Renaissance to the Present*, edited by Angelyn Mitchell, 165–71. Durham, NC: Duke University Press, 1994.

Barnhill, Kelly. "Bringing Favorite Fairy Tales Up to Date." *New York Times*, May 16, 2019.

Beale, Frances. "Double Jeopardy: To Be Black and Female." In *The Black Woman: An Anthology*, edited by Toni Cade Bambara, 109–22. New York: Washington Square Press, 2005.

Beavers, Herman. "African American Women Writers and Popular Fiction: Theorizing Black Womanhood." *The Cambridge Companion to African American Women's Literature*, edited by Angelyn Mitchell and Danille K. Taylor, 262–77. Cambridge: Cambridge University Press, 2009.

Blackburn, Sara. Review of *Sula*, by Toni Morrison. *New York Times Book Review*, December 30, 1973, 3.

Blake, Felice D. *Black Love, Black Hate: Intimate Antagonisms in African American Literature*. Columbus, OH: Ohio State University Press, 2018.

Bobby Jimmy & the Critters. "Hair or Weave." YouTube video, 3:42, posted by kennylavish, August 10, 2010. https://www.youtube.com/watch?v=aFlxqltj1EI.

Bobo, Jacqueline. *Black Women as Cultural Readers*. New York: Columbia University Press, 1995.

Bogle, Donald. *Toms, Coons, Mulattoes, Mammies, and Bucks: An Interpretive History of Blacks in American Films*. 5th ed. New York: Bloomsbury, 2016.

Bolen, Rebecca. *Child Sexual Abuse: Its Scope and Our Failure*. New York: Springer, 2001.

Botham, Fay. *Almighty God Created the Races: Christianity, Interracial Marriage, and American Law*. Chapel Hill: University of North Carolina Press, 2009.

Bowdre, Karen. "Romantic Comedies and the Raced Body." In *Falling in Love Again: Romantic Comedy in Contemporary Cinema*, edited by Stacey Abbott and Deborah Jermyn, 104–15. London: I.B. Tauris, 2009.

Bowser, Benjamin P. *The Black Middle Class: Social Mobility and Vulnerability*. Boulder, CO: Lynne Rienner, 2007.

Bradley, David. "Telling the Black Woman's Story." *New York Times Magazine*, January 1984, 34.

Bradley, Deborah. "Black Writers Turn a New Leaf: Romance Novels." *Sun Sentinal*, September 5, 1994. https://www.sun-sentinel.com/news/fl-xpm-1994-09-05-9409070333-story.html.

Bragg, Beauty. *Reading Contemporary African American Literature: Black Women's Popular Fiction, Post–Civil Rights Experience, and the African American Canon*. Lanham, MD: Lexington Books, 2015.

Briscoe, Connie. *Sisters and Lovers*. New York: Ballantine, 1994.

Brontë, Charlotte. *Jane Eyre*. Mineola: Dover Books, 2002. First published 1847 by Smith, Elder & Co. of London.

Brook, Heather. "'Die, Bridezilla, Die!': Bride Wars (2009), Wedding Envy, and Chick Flicks." In *Feminism at the Movies: Understanding Gender in Contemporary Popular Cinema*, edited by Hilary Radner and Rebecca Stringer, 227–40. New York: Routledge, 2011.

Brooks, Daphne. "'It's Not Right but It's Okay': Contemporary Black Women's R&B and the House That Terry McMillan Built." *Souls: A Critical Journal of Black Politics, Culture, and Society* 5, no. 1 (Winter 2003): 32–45.

Brown, DeNeen L. "Profile of Helena Andrews, Author of a Book about Successful but Lonely Young Black Women." *Washington Post*, December 10, 2009, http://www.washingtonpost.com/wp-dyn/content/article/2009/12/09/AR2009120904546.html.

Brown, Kimberly Juanita. *The Repeating Body: Slavery's Visual Resonance in the Contemporary*. Durham, NC: Duke University Press, 2015.

Butterfield, Fox. "Study Finds Big Increase in Black Men as Inmates since 1980." *New York Times*, August 28, 2002.

Cameo. "Candy." By Larry Blackmon and Tomi Jenkins. Track 2 on *Word Up!* UMG Recordings, 1986.

Campbell, Bebe Moore. *Brothers and Sisters*. New York: Berkley Books, 2005.

Campt, Tina M. *Listening to Images*. Durham, NC: Duke University Press, 2017.

Canty, Donnela. "McMillan Arrives." Review of *Waiting to Exhale*, by Terry McMillan. *English Journal* 85, no. 4 (April 1996): 86–87.

Carby, Hazel. *Reconstructing Womanhood: The Emergence of the Afro-American Woman Novelist*. New York: Oxford University Press, 1987.

CBS Reports: The Vanishing Family: Crisis in Black America. Narrated by Bill Moyers, January 25, 1986.

Celello, Kristin. *Making Marriage Work: A History of Marriage and Divorce in the Twentieth-Century United States*. Chapel Hill: University of North Carolina Press, 2009.

Cheney, Charise L. *Brothers Gonna Work It Out: Sexual Politics in the Golden Age of Rap Nationalism*. New York: New York University Press, 2005.

Chideya, Farai. *Don't Believe the Hype: Fighting Cultural Misinformation about African Americans*. New York: Plume, 1995.

Clarke, Averil Y. *Inequalities of Love: College Educated Black Women and the Barriers to Romance and Family*. Durham, NC: Duke University Press, 2011.

Clarke, Cheryl Y. "Lesbianism: An Act of Resistance." In *This Bridge Called My Back: Writings by Radical Women of Color*, edited by Cherríe Moraga and Gloria E. Anzaldúa, 128–37. New York: Kitchen Table Press, 1981.

Cleaver, Eldridge. *Soul on Ice*. New York: Dell, 1968.

Clifton, Lucille. "Black Women." In *The Collected Poems of Lucille Clifton, 1956–2010*, edited by Kevin Young and Michael S. Glaser, 3. Rochester, NY: BOA Editions, 2012.

Cohen, Cathy J. "Punks, Bulldaggers, and Welfare Queens: The Radical Potential of Queer Politics?" In *Black Queer Studies: A Critical Anthology*, edited by E. Patrick Johnson and Mae G. Henderson, 21–51. Durham, NC: Duke University Press, 2005.

Cohen, Philip N. *The Family: Diversity, Inequality, and Social Change*. New York: W. W. Norton, 2014.

Collins, Patricia Hill. *Black Feminist Thought: Knowledge, Consciousness, and the Politics of Empowerment*. New York: Routledge, 2000.

———. *Black Sexual Politics: African Americans, Gender, and the New Racism*. New York: Routledge, 2004.

Cooks, Carlos. "Speech on the 'Buy Black' Campaign." In *Modern Black Nationalism: From Marcus Garvey to Louis Farrakhan*, edited by William L. Van Deburg, 85–92. New York: New York University Press, 1997.

Coontz, Stephanie. *The Way We Never Were: American Families and the Nostalgia Trap*. New York: Basic Books, 1992.

Cosby, Bill, and Alvin Poussaint. *Come on, People: On the Path from Victims to Victors*. Nashville, TN: Thomas Nelson, 2007.

Cott, Nancy F. *Public Vows: A History of Marriage and the Nation*. Cambridge, MA: Harvard University Press, 2002.

Cottom, Tressie McMillan. *Thick: And Other Essays*. New York: New Press, 2019. Kindle.

Cox, Aimee Meredith. *Shapeshifters: Black Girls and the Choreography of Citizenship*. Durham, NC: Duke University Press, 2015.

Craig-Henderson, Kellina. *Black Men in Interracial Relationships: What's Love Got to Do with It?* New Jersey: Transaction, 2006.

Crenshaw, Kimberlé. "Whose Story Is It Anyway? Feminist and Antiracist Appropriations of Anita Hill." In *Race-ing Justice, En-gendering Power: Essays on Anita Hill, Clarence Thomas, and the Construction of Social Reality*, edited by Toni Morrison, 402–40. New York: Pantheon, 1992.

Crouch, Stanley. "Aunt Medea." Review of *Beloved*, by Toni Morrison. *New Republic*, October 19, 1987, 38–43.

———. *Notes of a Hanging Judge: Essays and Reviews, 1979–1989*. New York: Oxford University Press, 1991.

Cruz, Ariane. *The Color of Kink: Black Women, BDSM, and Pornography*. New York: New York University Press, 2016.

Curwood, Anastasia C. *Stormy Weather: Middle-Class African American Marriages between the Two World Wars*. Chapel Hill: University of North Carolina Press, 2013.

Daileader, Celia R. *Racism, Misogyny, and the Othello Myth: Inter-racial Couples from Shakespeare to Spike Lee*. New York: Cambridge University Press, 2005.

Dandridge, Rita B. "Debunking the Beauty Myth with Black Pop Culture in Terry McMillan's *Waiting to Exhale*." In *Language, Rhythm, and Sound: Black Popular Cultures into the Twenty-First Century*, 121–33. Pittsburgh: University of Pittsburgh Press, 1997.

D'Angelo. "Shit, Damn, Motherfucker." Track 5 on *Brown Sugar*. Virgin Records America, 1995.

Daniels, Lee, dir. *Precious*. 2009; USA: Lionsgate, 2009. DVD.

David, Marlo D. *Mama's Gun: Black Maternal Figures and the Politics of Transgression*. Columbus: Ohio State University Press, 2016.

Davis, Angela. "Black Nationalism: The Sixties and the Nineties." In *The Angela Y. Davis Reader*, edited by Joy James, 289–96. Malden, MA: Blackwell, 1998.

———. "Meditations on the Legacy of Malcolm X." In *Malcolm X: In Our Own Image*, edited by Joe Wood, 36–47. New York: St. Martin's Press, 1992.

———. *Women, Race, and Class*. New York: Vintage, 1983.

Davis, Linsey, and Hana Karar. "Single, Black, Female—and Plenty of Company." *ABC News*. December 22, 2009.

Davis, Thulani. "Don't Worry, Be Buppie: Black Novelists Head for the Mainstream." *Village Voice Literary Supplement*, May 1990: 26–29.

Dawson, Alma, and Connie Van Fleet. *African American Literature: A Guide to Reading Interests*. Westport: Libraries Unlimited, 1997.

Dell'Antonia, K. J. "Sexist Messages on Baby Clothes." *New York Times*, November 22, 2011.

Department of Supreme Wisdom. *The Supreme Wisdom Lessons by Master Fard Muhammad*. Greenville, SC: CreateSpace Independent Publishing Platform, 2009.

Dickey, Eric Jerome. *Milk in My Coffee*. New York: NAL Trade, 2000.

Domini, John. "Roots and Racism: An Interview with Ishmael Reed." *Boston Phoenix*, April 5, 1977, 20.

Dubey, Madhu. *Black Women Novelists and the National Aesthetic*. Bloomington: Indiana University Press, 1994.

Du Bois, W. E. B. *The Negro-American Family*. Chicago: University of Chicago Press, 1978. First published 1909 by Atlanta University (Georgia).

———. *The Souls of Black Folk*. Chicago: A. C. McClurg, 1903. Kindle.

duCille, Ann. *The Coupling Convention: Sex, Text, and Tradition in Black Women's Fiction*. New York: Oxford University Press, 1993.

Duggan, Lisa. *The Twilight of Equality? Neoliberalism, Cultural Politics, and the Attack on Democracy*. Boston: Beacon Press, 2003.

Dunbar, Eve. "Hip Hop (feat. Women Writers): Reimagining Black Women and Agency through Hip Hop Fiction." In *Contemporary African American Literature: The Living Canon*, edited by Lovalerie King and Shirley Moody-Turner, 91–112. Bloomington: Indiana University Press, 2013.

Dunn, Stephanie. "The New Black Cultural Studies: Hip Hop Ghetto Lit, Feminism, Afro-Womanism, and Black Love in *The Coldest Winter Ever*." *Fire!!! The Multimedia Journal of Black Studies* 1, no. 1 (2012): 83–99.

Dunning, Stefanie K. *Queer in Black and White: Interraciality, Same Sex Desire, and Contemporary African American Culture*. Bloomington: Indiana University Press, 2009.

Durham, Aisha, Brittney C. Cooper, and Susana M. Morris. "The Stage Hip-Hop Feminism Built: A New Directions Essay." *Signs: Journal of Women in Culture and Society* 38, no. 3 (2013): 721–37.

Edmondson, Belinda. "The Black Romance." *Women's Studies Quarterly* 35 (Spring–Summer 2007): 191–211.

Edwards, Audrey. "Terry McMillan: Waiting to Inhale." *Essence*, October 1992, 77.

Edwards, Erica R. *Charisma and the Fictions of Black Leadership*. Minneapolis: University of Minnesota Press, 2012.

———. "Sex After the Black Normal." *differences: A Journal of Feminist Culture Studies* 26, no. 1 (2015): 141–67.

Egan, Timothy. "A Refuge for Racists." *New York Times*, June 26, 2015.

Ellerby, Janet Mason. "Deposing the Man of the House: Terry McMillan Rewrites the Family." *MELUS* 22, no. 2 (1997): 105–17.

"Exhaling and Inhaling: Was the Movie Fair to Black Men and Black Women?" *Ebony*, April 1996, 116–27.

Farmer, Ashley D. *Remaking Black Power: How Black Women Transformed an Era*. Chapel Hill: University of North Carolina Press, 2017.

Farrakhan, Louis. "Farrakhan Describes Cycle of Domestic Violence." *Washington Post*, June 27, 1994: A 22.

———. *The Teachings 2.0: Twitter Sayings of the Honorable Minister Louis Farrakhan*. Vol. 1. Compiled by Jesse Muhammad. Chicago: FCN Publishing, 2013.

———. *A Torchlight for America*. Chicago: FCN Publishing, 1993.

Ferguson, Roderick A. *Aberrations in Black: Toward a Queer of Color Critique*. Minneapolis: University of Minnesota Press, 2004.

Ferriss, Suzanne, and Mallory Young, eds. *Chick Lit: The New Woman's Fiction*. New York: Routledge, 2006.

Field, Allyson Nadia. *Uplift Cinema: The Emergence of African American Film and the Possibility of Black Modernity*. Durham, NC: Duke University Press, 2015.

Ford, Tanisha C. *Liberated Threads: Black Women, Style, and the Global Politics of Soul*. Chapel Hill: University of North Carolina Press, 2017.

Forman, Murray, and Mark Anthony Neal, eds. *That's the Joint! The Hip Hop Studies Reader*. New York: Routledge, 2004.

Foster, Frances Smith. *'Til Death or Distance Do Us Part: Love and Marriage in African America*. New York: Oxford University Press, 2010.

Francis, Terri Simone. "She Will Never Look: Film Spectatorship, Black Feminism, and Scary Subjectivities." In *Reclaiming the Archive: Feminism and Film History*, edited by Vicki Callahan, 98–125. Detroit: Wayne State University Press, 2010.

Franklin, Donna L. *Ensuring Inequality: The Structural Transformation of the African American Family*. New York: Oxford University Press, 1997.

———. *What's Love Got to Do with It? Understanding and Healing the Rift between Black Men and Black Women*. New York: Simon & Schuster, 2001.

Frazier, E. Franklin. *The Negro Family in the United States*. Chicago: University of Chicago Press, 1939.

"Friends Reunite for a Wedding and Scandalous Secrets Are Revealed in *The Best Man*." *Jet*, October 25, 1999, 36–39.

Gaines, Kevin. *Uplifting the Race: Black Leadership, Politics, and Culture in the Twentieth Century*. Chapel Hill: University of North Carolina Press, 1996.

Garner, Dwight. "Sistahood Is Lucrative." *Salon*, September 23, 1996. https://www .salon.com/1996/09/23/blacklit/.

Gates, Henry Louis, Jr. "The Charmer." In *The Farrakhan Factor: African-American Writers on Leadership, Nationhood, and Minister Louis Farrakhan*, edited by Amy Alexander, 18–51. New York: Grove Press, 1998.

Gates, Henry Louis, Jr., and Nellie Y. McKay, eds. *Norton Anthology of African American Literature*. New York: W. W. Norton, 1997.

———, eds. *Norton Anthology of African American Literature*. 2nd ed. New York: W. W. Norton, 2004.

Gates, Racquel J. *Double Negative: The Black Image and Popular Culture*. Durham, NC: Duke University Press, 2018.

Gerald, Carolyn F. "The Black Writer and His Role." In *African American Literary Criticism, 1773-2000*, edited by Hazel Arnett Ervin, 129–34. New York: Twayne, 1999.

Gerhart, Ann. "Terry McMillan's Epilogue to *Groove Affair*." *Washington Post*, June 29, 2005, http://www.washingtonpost.com/wp-dyn/content/article/2005/06 /28/AR2005062801718.html.

Giddings, Paula J. *When and Where I Enter: The Impact of Black Women on Race and Sex in America*. New York: Perennial, 1996.

Gifford, Justin. *Pimping Fictions: African American Crime Literature and the Untold Story of Black Pulp Publishing*. Philadelphia: Temple University Press, 2013.

Giles, Jeff. "Beginners' Pluck." *Newsweek*, June 3, 1996, 72–73.

Gilmore, Glenda Elizabeth. *Gender and Jim Crow: Women and the Politics of White Supremacy in North Carolina, 1896–1920*. Chapel Hill: University of North Carolina Press, 1996.

Glickman, Simon. "Souljah, Sister 1964–." In *Contemporary Black Biography*. Accessed April 4, 2011. https://www.encyclopedia.com/education/news-wires -white-papers-and-books/souljah-sister-1964.

Gomez, Jewelle. "But Some of Us Are Brave Lesbians: The Absence of Black Lesbian Fiction." In *Black Queer Studies: A Critical Anthology*, edited by E. Patrick Johnson and Mae G. Henderson, 289–97. Durham, NC: Duke University Press, 2005.

Gorbman, Claudia. *Unheard Melodies: Narrative Film Music*. Bloomington: Indiana University Press, 1987.

Graaff, Kristina. *Street Literature: Black Popular Fiction in the Era of Mass Incarceration*. American Studies, vol. 263. Heidelberg: Universitätsverlag, 2015.

Graham, Maryemma. "Black Is Gold: African American Literature, Critical Literacy, and Twenty-First-Century Pedagogies." In *Contemporary African American Literature: The Living Canon*, edited by Lovalerie King and Shirley Moody-Turner, 55–90. Bloomington: Indiana University Press, 2013.

Graham, Renee. "Getting Out the Vote for Black Films." *Boston Globe*, October 26, 1999, E 1:1.

Greco, Albert N., Clara E. Rodríguez, and Robert M. Wharton. *The Culture and Commerce of Publishing in the 21st Century*. Redwood City, CA: Stanford Business Books, 2006.

Green, Joyce. "Black Romanticism." In *The Black Woman: An Anthology*, edited by Toni Cade Bambara, 171–78. New York: Washington Square Press, 2005.

Gregory, Ted. "Adding Up One Family's Year of Buying Black." *Chicago Tribune*, January 11, 2010.

Griffin, Farah Jasmine. "Conflict and Chorus: Reconsidering Toni Cade's *The Black Woman: An Anthology*." In *Is It Nation Time? Contemporary Essays on Black Power and Black Nationalism*, edited by Eddie S. Glaude Jr., 113–29. Chicago: University of Chicago Press, 2002.

———. "'Ironies of the Saint': Malcolm X, Black Women, and the Price of Protection." In *Sisters in the Struggle: African American Women in the Civil Rights–Black Power Movement*, edited by Bettye Collier-Thomas and V. P. Franklin, 214–29. New York: New York University Press, 2001.

Gunne, Sorcha, and Zoe Brigley Thompson, eds. *Feminism, Literature, and Rape Narratives: Violence and Violation*. New York: Routledge, 2009.

Hagelin, Sarah. *Reel Vulnerability: Power, Pain, and Gender in Contemporary American Film and Television*. New Brunswick, NJ: Rutgers University Press, 2013.

Haley, Alex. *The Autobiography of Malcolm X: As Told to Alex Haley*. New York: Ballantine, 1964.

Hamilton, Darrick, Arthur H. Goldsmith, and William Darity Jr. "Shedding 'Light' on Marriage: The Influence of Skin Shade on Marriage for Black Females." *Journal of Economic Behavior and Organization* 72, no. 1 (October 2009): 30–50.

Hammonds, Evelyn. "Black (W)Holes and the Geometry of Black Female Sexuality." *differences: A Journal of Feminist Cultural Studies* 6, no. 2 (1994): 127–45.

Hamri, Sanaa, dir. *Something New*. 2006. USA: Gramercy, 2006. DVD.

Harkins, Gillian. *Everybody's Family Romance: Reading Incest in Neoliberal America*. Minneapolis: University of Minnesota Press, 2009.

Hartman, Saidiya. "The Belly of the World: A Note on Black Women's Labors." *Souls: A Critical Journal of Black Politics, Culture, and Society* 18, no. 1 (2016): 166–73.

———. "Venus in Two Acts." *Small Axe: A Caribbean Journal of Criticism* 12, no. 2 (2008): 1–14.

Harvey, David. *A Brief History of Neoliberalism*. Oxford: Oxford University Press, 2005.

Harzewski, Stephanie. *Chick Lit and Postfeminism*. Charlottesville: University of Virginia Press, 2011.

———. "Tradition and Displacement in the New Novel of Manners." In *Chick Lit: The New Woman's Fiction*, edited by Suzane Ferris and Mallory Young, 29–46. New York: Routledge, 2006.

Henderson, Aneeka A. "Black Political and Popular Culture: The Legacy of Richard Iton." *Souls: A Critical Journal of Black Politics, Culture and Society* 16, nos. 3–4 (2014): 198–208.

———. "The Rebirth of Queer: Exile, Kinship, and Metamorphosis in Dee Rees's *Pariah*." In *African American Culture and Society after Rodney King: Provocations and Protests, Progression and "Post-Racialism,"* edited by Jo Metcalf and Carina Spaulding, 141–55. London: Ashgate, 2015.

Herbert, Bob. "Impossible, Ridiculous, Repugnant." *New York Times*, October 6, 2005. http://query.nytimes.com/gst/fullpage.html?res=9C04E6DF1E30F935A3575 3C1A9639C8B63.

Herzog, Amy. *Dreams of Difference, Songs of the Same: The Musical Moment in Film*. Minneapolis: University of Minnesota Press, 2009.

Hess, Amanda. "The Awkward Charm of the Promposal." *New York Times*, April 8, 2016.

Hill, Donna. "The Beat Goes On" (guest post), edited by Carleen Brice. *White Readers Meet Black Authors* (blog). February 9, 2010. http://welcomewhitefolks.blogspot .com/2010/02/guest-post-by-author-donna-hill.html.

Hine, Darlene Clark. *Hine Sight: Black Women and Re-construction of American History*. New York: Carlson, 1994.

Hirshberg, Lynn. "The Audacity of *Precious*." *New York Times*, October 21, 2009. http://www.nytimes.com/2009/10/25/magazine/25precious-t?pagewanted=1.

Hong, Grace Kyungwon. *Death beyond Disavowal: The Impossible Politics of Difference*. Minneapolis: University of Minnesota Press, 2015.

hooks, bell. *Reel to Real: Race, Sex, and Class at the Movies*. New York: Routledge, 1996.

Hull, Gloria T., Patricia Bell Scott, and Barbara Smith, eds. *All the Women Are White, All the Blacks Are Men, but Some of Us Are Brave: Black Women's Studies*. New York: Feminist Press, 1982.

Hunter, Tera W. *Bound in Wedlock: Slave and Free Black Marriage in the Nineteenth Century*. Cambridge, MA: Harvard University Press, 2017.

Hurston, Zora Neale. *Dust Tracks on a Road: An Autobiography*. New York: HarperCollins, 2010. Kindle.

————. *Their Eyes Were Watching God*. New York: HarperCollins, 1937.

————. "What White Publishers Won't Print." In *Within the Circle: An Anthology of African American Literary Criticism from the Harlem Renaissance to the Present*, edited by Angelyn Mitchell, 117–21. Durham, NC: Duke University Press, 1994.

Illouz, Eva. *Consuming the Romantic Utopia: Love and Cultural Contradictions of Capitalism*. Berkeley: University of California Press, 1997.

Iton, Richard. *In Search of the Black Fantastic: Politics and Popular Culture in the Post–Civil Rights Era*. New York: Oxford University Press, 2008.

Jackson, Candice Love. "From Writer to Reader: Black Popular Fiction." In *The Cambridge History of African American Literature*, edited by Maryemma Graham and Jerry W. Ward Jr., 655–79. New York: Cambridge University Press, 2011.

Jackson, Edward M. "Images of Black Males in Terry McMillan's *Waiting to Exhale*." *MAWA Review* 8 (June 1993): 20–26.

Jackson, Michael. "Black or White (Official Video)." YouTube video, 11:01, posted on November 14, 2016. https://www.youtube.com/watch?v=pTFE8cirkdQ.

————. "Black or White." Track 8 on *Dangerous*. Epic Sony, 1991.

Jackson, Mick, dir. *The Bodyguard*. 1992. USA: Kasdan, 1992. DVD.

Jacobs, Harriet. *Incidents in the Life of a Slave Girl*. Mineola: Dover, 2001.

Jagged Edge. "Let's Get Married." Track 7 on *J. E. Heartbreak*. So So Def Recordings and Sony Music Entertainment Inc., 2000.

Jarrett, Vernon. "A Vicious Lynching Delights Audience." Review of *For Colored Girls Who Have Considered Suicide When the Rainbow Is Enuf*, by Ntozake Shange. *Chicago Tribune*, January 1, 1978, 6.

Jenkins, Candice M. *Private Lives, Proper Relations: Regulating Black Intimacy*. Minneapolis: University of Minnesota Press, 2007.

Jodeci. "Feenin'." Track 3 on *Diary of a Mad Band*. Uptown | MCA Records. 1993.

Johnson, John H. *The Negro Handbook*. Chicago: Johnson, 1966.

Jones, Jacqueline. *Labor of Love, Labor of Sorrow: Black Women, Work, and the Family from Slavery to the Present*. New York: Basic, 1985.

Jones, Tayari. *An American Marriage*. Chapel Hill: Algonquin Books of Chapel Hill, 2019.

Jones, Vanessa E. "Wedding Black Professionals, Relationships." *Boston Globe*, October 28, 1999, D.

Jones-Rodgers, Stephanie E. *They Were Her Property: White Women as Slave Owners in the American South*. New Haven, CT: Yale University Press, 2019.

Judice, Cheryl. *Interracial Marriages between Black Women and White Men*. Amherst, NY: Cambria Press, 2008.

Juffer, Jane. *Single Mother: The Emergence of the Domestic Intellectual*. New York: New York University Press, 2006.

Jun, Helen Heran. *Race for Citizenship: Black Orientalism and Asian Uplift from Pre-emancipation to Neoliberal America*. New York: New York University Press, 2011.

Kandell, Jonathan. "S.I. Newhouse Jr., Who Turned Condè Nast Into a Magazine Powerhouse, Dies at 89." *New York Times*, October 1, 2017.

Kelley, Robin D. G. "Stormy Weather: Reconstructing Black (Inter)Nationalism in the Cold War Era." In *Is It Nation Time?: Contemporary Essays on Black Power and Black Nationalism*, edited by Eddie S. Glaude, 67–90. Chicago: University of Chicago Press, 2002.

Kelly, Casey Ryan. *Abstinence Cinema: Virginity and the Rhetoric of Sexual Purity in Contemporary Film*. New Brunswick, NJ: Rutgers University Press, 2016.

Kennedy, Dana. "How Stella Got Her Groove." *Entertainment Weekly*, May 3, 1996, http://www.ew.com/article/1996/05/03/how-stella-got-her-groove-back-2/.

Kennedy, Randall. *Interracial Intimacies: Sex, Marriage, Identity, and Adoption*. New York: Pantheon, 2003.

Keyes, Cheryl L. "Empowering Self, Making Choices, Creating Spaces: Black Female Identity via Rap Music Performance." *Journal of American Folklore* 113, no. 449 (2000): 255–69.

Kgositsile, Keorapetse W. "Towards Our Theater: A Definitive Act." In *Black Expression: Essays by and about Black Americans in the Creative Arts*, edited by Addison Gayle Jr., 146–48. New York: Weybright and Talley, 1970.

Khan, Chaka. "Sweet Thing." Track 6 on *Rufus featuring Chaka Khan*. Rufus band, ABC Records ABCD-909, 1975.

Kitt, Sandra. "About Sandra Kitt." Accessed September 1, 2011. http://www.sandrakitt.com/about-sandra-kitt/.

———. *Close Encounters*. New York: Signet, 2000.

———. *The Color of Love*. New York: Signet, 1995.

Kratz, Corrine A. "On Telling/Selling a Book by Its Cover." *Cultural Anthropology* 9, no. 2 (1994): 179–200.

Krentz, Jayne Ann. *Dangerous Men and Adventurous Women: Romance Writers on the Appeal of the Romance*. Philadelphia: University of Pennsylvania Press, 1992.

Larson, Aaron. "Fathers' Rights and Child Custody Law." July 8, 2016. http://www.expertlaw.com/library/child_custody/fathers_rights.html.

Lattimore, Kenny. "Beautiful Girl." Track 7 on *The Best Man (Music from the Motion Picture)*. Sony BMG Music Entertainment, 1999.

Leder, Meg, and Jack Heffron. *The Complete Handbook of Novel Writing*. Cincinnati, OH: Writer's Digest Books, 2002.

Lee, Malcolm D. "The Best Man" (screenplay draft). October 29, 1998. California State University Library, Long Beach.

———, dir. *The Best Man*. Universal Pictures, 1999.

———, dir. *The Best Man Holiday*. 2013; Universal City, CA: Universal Pictures, 2014. DVD.

Lee, Spike, dir. *Jungle Fever*. 1991. USA: 40 Acres and a Mule Filmworks, 1991. DVD.

Levy-Hussen, Aida. *How to Read African American Literature: Post–Civil Rights Fiction and the Task of Interpretation*. New York: New York University Press, 2016.

Liddell, Janice. "Agents of Pain and Redemption in Sapphire's Push." In *Arms Akimbo: Africana Women in Contemporary Literature*, edited by Yakini B. Kemp and Janice Liddell, 135–46. Gainesville: University Press of Florida, 1999.

Lindsey, Kay. "Poem." In *The Black Woman: An Anthology*, edited by Toni Cade Bambara, 13. New York: Washington Square Press, 1970.

Lomax, Tamura. *Jezebel Unhinged: Loosing the Black Female Body in Religion and Culture*. Durham, NC: Duke University Press, 2018. Kindle.

Lorde, Audre. *Sister Outsider: Essays and Speeches*. Trumansburg, NY: Crossing Press, 2007.

Lordi, Emily J. *Black Resonance: Iconic Women Singers and African American Literature*. New Brunswick, NJ: Rutgers University Press, 2013.

Lubiano, Wahneema. "Black Ladies, Welfare Queens, and State Minstrels: Ideological War by Narrative Means." In *Race-ing Justice Engendering Power: Essays on Anita Hill, Clarence Thomas, and the Construction of Social Reality*, edited by Toni Morrison, 323–63. New York: Pantheon, 1992.

———. "Black Nationalism and Black Commonsense: Policing Ourselves and Others." In *The House That Race Built: Black Americans, U.S. Terrain*, 232–53. New York: Pantheon, 2007.

———, ed. *The House That Race Built: Black Americans, U.S. Terrain*. New York: Pantheon, 2007.

Lucas, Demetria L. "Real Talk: Are White Men the Answer?" *Essence*, August 9, 2011. https://www.essence.com/news/real-talk-are-white-men-the-answer/.

Madhubuti, Haki, ed. *Confusion By Any Other Name: Essays Exploring the Negative Impact of* The Blackman's Guide to Understanding the Blackwoman. Chicago: Third World Press, 1990.

———. *Earthquakes and Sun Rise Missions: Poetry and Essays of Black Renewal*. Chicago: Third World Press, 1984.

Majors, Richard, and Ronald F. Levant. "You Can Breathe Now: A Psychological Response to *Waiting to Exhale*." *Journal of African American Men* 2, no. 4 (Spring 1997): 47–57.

Marsh, Kris, William A. Darity, Philip N. Cohen, Lynne M. Casper, and Danielle Salters. "The Emerging Black Middle Class: Single and Living Alone." *Social Forces* 86, no. 2 (2007): 735–62.

Martin, Reginald. "Ishmael Reed—Poet Author." African American Literature Book Club. Accessed October 8, 2010, https://aalbc.com/authors/author.php?author_name=Ishmael+Reed.

Mask, Mia. "Buppy Love in an Urban World." *Cineaste* 25, no. 2 (2000): 41–45.

Matthews, Tracye. "'No One Ever Asks, What a Man's Place in the Revolution Is': Gender and the Politics of the Black Panther Party, 1966–1971." *The Black Panther Party Reconsidered*, edited by Charles E. Jones, 267–305. Baltimore, MD: Black Classic Press, 1998.

Max, Daniel. "McMillan's Millions." *New York Times*, August 9, 1992.

Maxwell. "This Woman's Work," by Kate Bush. Track 13 on *Love & Basketball (Music from the Motion Picture)*. Columbia Records, 2000.

McAdoo, Harriette Pipes, ed. *Black Families*. Thousand Oaks, CA: Sage, 1997.

McClintock, Anne. *Imperial Leather: Race, Gender, and Sexuality in the Colonial Contest*. New York: Routledge, 1995.

McCracken, Scott. *Pulp: Reading Popular Fiction*. Manchester, UK: Manchester University Press, 1998.

McDonald, Katrina Bell, and Caitlin Cross-Barnet. *Marriage in Black: The Pursuit of Married Life among American-Born and Immigrant Blacks*. New York: Routledge, 2018.

McDonald, Tamar Jeffers. "Homme-Com: Engendering Change in Contemporary Romantic Comedy." *Falling in Love Again: Romantic Comedy in Contemporary Cinema*, edited by Stacey Abbott and Deborah Jermyn, 146–59. London: I.B. Tauris, 2009.

McDowell, Deborah. *The Changing Same: Black Women's Literature, Criticism, and Theory*. Bloomington: Indiana University Press, 1995.

McHenry, Elizabeth. *Forgotten Readers: Recovering the Lost History of African American Literary Societies*. Durham, NC: Duke University Press, 2002.

McMillan, Terry, ed. *Breaking Ice: An Anthology of Contemporary African American Fiction*. New York: Penguin Books, 1990.

———. Correspondence to her editor, n.d. Alan Cheuse Papers. Small Special Collections, University of Virginia.

———. *Disappearing Acts*. New York: New American Library, 1989. Kindle.

———. *Five for Five: The Films of Spike Lee*. New York: Stewart, Tabori & Chang, 1991.

———. *How Stella Got Her Groove Back*. New York: Viking, 1996.

———. "How Terry McMillan Got Her Groove Back." By Cassandra Spratling. *Knight-Rider/Tribune News Service*, May 22, 1996.

———. "An Interview with Terry McMillan." By Molly Giles. *Poets and Writers* 20, no. 6 (November/December 1992): 32–43.

———. *Mama*. New York: Washington Square Press, 1987.

———. *Waiting to Exhale*. New York: Penguin, 1992. Kindle.

———. "What We've Lost." Speech presented at the American Booksellers Association Convention, Anaheim, CA, May 25, 1992.

Mehren, Elizabeth. "Friction over Fact versus Fiction: Books: An Ex-Lover of author Terry McMillan Claims a Character in 'Disappearing Acts' Is a Distorted Portrait of Him. His Suit Chills the Writing World." *Los Angeles Times*, October 29, 1990.

Melancon, Trimiko. *Unbought and Unbossed: Transgressive Black Women, Sexuality, and Representation*. Philadelphia: Temple University Press, 2014.

Merriam-Webster's Time Traveler Web site. Accessed July 23, 2019, http://www.merriam-webster.com/time-traveler.

Miller-Young, Mireille. *A Taste for Brown Sugar: Black Women in Pornography*. Durham, NC: Duke University Press, 2015.

Miyakawa, Felicia M. *Five Percenter Rap: God Hop's Music, Message, and Black Muslim Mission*. Bloomington: Indiana University Press, 2005.

Monroe, Irene. "Louis Farrakhan's Ministry of Misogyny and Homophobia." *The Farrakhan Factor: African-American Writers on Leadership, Nationhood, and Minister Louis Farrakhan*, edited by Amy Alexander, 275–98. New York: Grove Press, 1998.

Moran, Rachel F. *Interracial Intimacy: The Regulation of Race and Romance*. Chicago: University of Chicago Press, 2003.

Morris, Susana M. *Close Kin and Distant Relatives: The Paradox of Respectability in Black Women's Literature*. Charlottesville: University of Virginia Press, 2014.

Morrison, Toni. "Rootedness: The Ancestor as Foundation." In *Black Women Writers (1950–1980): A Critical Evaluation*, edited by Mari Evans, 339–45. New York: Anchor Books/Doubleday, 1984.

———. *The Source of Self-Regard: Selected Essays, Speeches, and Meditations*. New York: Knopf, 2019.

———. *Sula*. New York: Plume, 1973.

Moynihan, Daniel Patrick. *The Negro Family: The Case for National Action*. Washington, DC: Government Printing Office, 1965.

Mussell, Kay J. "Beautiful and Damned: The Sexual Woman in Gothic Fiction." *Journal of Popular Culture* 9, no. 1 (1975): 84–89.

Nash, Jennifer C. *The Black Body in Ecstasy: Reading Race, Reading Pornography*. Durham, NC: Duke University Press, 2014.

"Nation of Islam." Southern Poverty Law Center. Accessed August 20, 2016. www .splcenter.org/fighting-hate/extremist-files/group/nation-islam.

Naylor, Gloria. "Love and Sex in the Afro-American Novel." In *Women in Romance: A Reader*, edited by Susan Ostrov Weisser, 271–75. New York: New York University Press, 2001.

NdegèOcello, Me'Shell. "Soul on Ice." Track 8 on *Plantation Lullabies*. Maverick, 1993.

Ndounou, Monica White. *Shaping the Future of African American Film: Color-Coded Economics and the Story behind the Numbers*. New Brunswick, NJ: Rutgers University Press, 2014.

Neal, Mark Anthony. *Soul Babies: Black Popular Culture and the Post-Soul Aesthetic*. New York: Routledge, 2002.

Nelson, Jill. *Straight, No Chaser: How I Became a Grown-Up Black Woman*. New York: Penguin Books, 1999.

Neubeck, Kenneth J., and Noel A. Cazenave. *Welfare Racism: Playing the Race Card against America's Poor*. New York: Routledge, 2001.

New Edition. "Candy Girl." Track 6 on *Candy Girl*. Warlock Records, 1983.

"Nia Long on the Quintessential Black Woman." *Los Angeles Sentinel* (October 1999): B4.

Norment, Lynn. "What Black Men Should Know about Black Women." *Ebony*. August 1983, 132–38.

Norment, Nathaniel, ed. "Addison Gayle: Interviewed by Saundra Towns." In *The Addison Gayle Jr. Reader*, 359–80. Urbana: University of Illinois Press, 2009.

Obama, Barack. *Dreams from My Father: A Story of Race and Inheritance*. New York: Three Rivers Press, 2004.

Oliver, Codie, and Tommy Oliver. *Black Love*. Oprah Winfrey Network, 2017.

Omolade, Barbara. *The Rising Song of African American Women*. New York: Routledge, 1994.

Ongiri, Amy Abugo. *Spectacular Blackness: The Cultural Politics of the Black Power Movement and the Search for a Black Aesthetic*. Charlottesville: University of Virginia Press, 2010.

Osborne, Gwendolyn E. "It's All about Love: Romance Readers Speak Out." African American Literature Book Club. February 1, 2011. https://aalbc.com/authors /article.php?id=1907.

Painter, Nell Irvin. *Sojourner Truth: A Life, a Symbol*. New York: W. W. Norton, 1996.

Parker, Traci. *Department Stores and the Black Freedom Movement: Workers, Consumers, and the Civil Rights from the 1930s to the 1980s*. Chapel Hill: University of North Carolina Press, 2019.

Parker-Pope, Tara. "Should We All Take the Slow Road to Love?," *New York Times*, July 2, 2019.

Patterson, Courtney J. "Is It Just Baby F(Ph)at? Black Female Teenagers, Body Size, and Sexuality." In *Black Female Sexualities*, edited by Trimiko Melancon and Joanne M. Braxton, 27–40. New Brunswick, NJ: Rutgers University Press, 2015.

Patterson, James T. *Freedom Is Not Enough: The Moynihan Report and America's Struggle over Black Family Life—from LBJ to Obama*. New York: Basic Books, 2010.

Patterson, Robert J. *Destructive Desires: Rhythm and Blues Culture and the Politics of Racial Equality*. New Brunswick, NJ: Rutgers University Press, 2019.

Perry, Imani. *Prophets of the Hood: Politics and Poetics in Hip Hop*. Durham, NC: Duke University Press, 2004.

———. *Vexy Thing: On Gender and Liberation*. Durham, NC: Duke University Press, 2018.

Philips, Chuck. "'I Do Not Advocate . . . Murdering': 'Raptivist' Sister Souljah Disputes Clinton Charge." *Los Angeles Times*. June 17, 1992. http://articles.latimes .com/1992-06-17/entertainment/ca-573_1_sister-souljah.

Pittman, Coretta. "Black Women Writers and the Trouble with *Ethos*: Harriet Jacobs, Billie Holiday, and Sister Souljah." *Rhetoric Society Quarterly* 37, no. 1 (2006): 43–70.

Pollard, Cherise. "The P-Word Exchange: Representing Black Female Sexuality in Contemporary Urban Fiction." In *Black Female Sexualities*, edited by Trimiko Melancon and Joanne M. Braxton, 113–26. New Brunswick, NJ: Rutgers University Press, 2015.

Porter, Michael. *The Conspiracy to Destroy Black Women*. Chicago: African American Images, 2001.

Prince-Bythewood, Gina, dir. *Disappearing Acts*. 2000. USA: Amen Ra Films, HBO Films, 2001. DVD.

Public Enemy. "Fight the Power." Track 20 on *Fear of a Black Planet*. Def Jam Recordings, 1990.

———. "Sophisticated Bitch." Track 2 on *Yo! Bum Rush the Show*. UMG Recordings, 1987.

Quadagno, Jill. *The Color of Welfare: How Racism Undermined the War on Poverty*. New York: Oxford University Press, 1994.

Quashie, Kevin. *The Sovereignty of Quiet: Beyond Resistance in Black Culture*. New Brunswick, NJ: Rutgers University Press, 2012.

Radner, Hilary, and Rebecca Stringer. "Speaking the Name of the Father in the Neo-Romantic Comedy: *13 Going on 30* (2004)." In *Feminism at the Movies: Understanding Gender in Contemporary Popular Cinema*, edited by Hilary Radner and Rebecca Stringer, 134–48. New York: Routledge, 2011.

Radway, Janice A. *Reading the Romance: Women, Patriarchy, and Popular Literature*. Chapel Hill: University of North Carolina Press, 1991.

Rambsy, Howard, II. "Re-representing 'Black Boy': The Evolving Packaging History of Richard Wright's Autobiography." *Southern Quarterly* 46, no. 2 (2009): 71–83.

Ramsdell, Kristin. *Romance Fiction: A Guide to the Genre*. Englewood, CO: Libraries Unlimited, 1999.

Randolph, Sherie M. *Florynce "Flo" Kennedy: The Life of a Black Feminist Radical*. Chapel Hill: University of North Carolina Press, 2015. Kindle.

Ransby, Barbara, and Tracye Matthews. "Black Popular Culture and the Transcendence of Patriarchal Illusions." In *Words of Fire: An Anthology of African American Feminist Thought*, edited by Beverly Guy-Sheftall, 526–36. New York: New Press, 1995.

"Rap and Race." *Newsweek*, June 28, 1992. https://www.newsweek.com/rap-and -race-199550.

Redmond, Shana L. *Anthem: Social Movements and the Sound of Solidarity in the African Diaspora*. New York: New York University Press, 2014.

Reed, Adolph. "The Liberal Technocrat." *Nation*, February 6, 1988.

Reed, Ishmael. "The Selling of *Precious*." *CounterPunch*, December 4–6, 2009, http://www.counterpunch.org/2009/12/04/the-selling-of-quot-precious-quot/.

Reid, E. Shelley. "Beyond Morrison and Walker: Looking Good and Looking Forward in Contemporary Black Women's Studies." *African American Review* 34, no. 2 (2000): 313–28.

Reiss, Fraidy. "Despite Progress, Child Marriage Is Still Legal in All 50 States," *New York Times*, July 26, 2017.

Richards, Paulette. *Terry McMillan: A Critical Companion*. Westport, CT: Greenwood Press, 1999.

Richie, Beth E. *Arrested Justice: Black Women, Violence, and America's Prison Nation*. New York: New York University Press, 2012.

Roach, Catherine M. *Happily Ever After: The Romance Story in Popular Culture*. Bloomington: Indiana University Press, 2016.

Robbins, Liz. "Billboard Opposing Abortion Stirs Debate." *New York Times*, February 23, 2011.

Roberts, Sam. "Black Women See Shrinking Pool of Black Men at the Marriage Altar." *New York Times*, June 4, 2010, New York edition, A12.

Roiphe, Katie. "Making the Incest Scene: In Novel after Novel, Writers Grope for Dark Secrets." *Harper's*, November 1995, 65–71.

Romance Writers of America. March 4, 2012. http://www.rwa.org/cs/home.

Rountree, Wendy A. "Overcoming Violence: Blues Expression in Sapphire's *Push*." *Atenea* 24, no. 1 (2004): 133–42.

Rushdy, Ashraf H. A. *Remembering Generations: Race and Family in Contemporary African American Fiction*. Chapel Hill: University of North Carolina Press, 2001.

Samuels, Allison. "*The Princess and the Frog*: Disney's Mixed Race Royalty."
 Newsweek, November 18, 2009. http://www.newsweek.com/princess-and-frog
 -disneys-mixed-race-royalty-76767.

Sapphire. *Push*. New York: Knopf, 1996.

Sayers, Valerie. "Someone to Walk over Me." *New York Times*, August 6, 1989,
 http://www.nytimes.com/1989/08/06/books/someone-to-walk-over-me.html.

Scott, Ellen C. *Cinema Civil Rights: Regulation, Repression, and Race in the Classical
 Hollywood Era*. New Brunswick, NJ: Rutgers University Press, 2015.

Scott, Karen. "Millenia Black's Suit against Penguin Has Been Resolved to 'Her
 Resolution' . . ." *It's My Blog and I'll Say Want I Want To!* (blog). Accessed
 September 2, 2011. http://karenknowsbest.com/2008/05/13/millenia-blacks-suit-
 against-penguin-has-been-resolved-to-her-satisfaction/.

Seale, Bobby. *Seize the Time: The Story of the Black Panther Party and Huey P. Newton*.
 Baltimore, MD: Black Classic Press, 1991.

Shaw, Andrea Elizabeth. *The Embodiment of Disobedience: Fat Black Women's Unruly
 Political Bodies*. Lanham, MD: Lexington Books, 2006.

Shivers, Kaia. "*The Best Man*—the Members of the Wedding Party. *Los Angeles
 Sentinel*. October 21, 1999, B6.

Smith, Barbara. "Toward a Black Feminist Criticism." *Radical Teacher*, no. 7
 (March 1978): 20–27.

———. *The Truth That Never Hurts: Writings on Race, Gender, and Freedom*.
 New Brunswick, NJ: Rutgers University Press, 2000.

Smith, Danyel. "Black Talk and Hot Sex." In *Total Chaos: The Art and Aesthetics of
 Hip-Hop*, edited by Jeff Chang, 188–97. New York: Civitas Books, 2008.

Smith, Tom W. "Ethnic Images." *GSS Topical Report*, no. 19. National Opinion
 Research Center. University of Chicago.

Smith, Wendy. "Terry McMillan: The Novelist Explores African American Life from the
 Point of View of a New Generation." *Publishers Weekly* 239, no. 11 (May 1992): 50.

Souljah, Sister. *The Coldest Winter Ever*. New York: Pocket Books, 1999. Kindle.

———. *No Disrespect*. New York: Vintage Books, 1996.

Spillers, Hortense J. "Interstices: A Small Drama of Words." In *Black, White, and in
 Color: Essays on American Literature and Culture*, 152–75. Chicago: University of
 Chicago Press, 2003.

Springer, Kimberly. "Divas, Evil Black Bitches, and Bitter Black Women: African
 American Women in Postfeminist and Post–Civil Rights Popular Culture." In
 Interrogating Postfeminism: Gender and the Politics of Popular Culture, edited by Diane
 Negra and Yvonne Tasker, 249–76. Durham, NC: Duke University Press Books,
 2007.

Stallings, L. H. *Mutha' Is Half a Word: Intersections of Folklore, Vernacular, Myth, and
 Queerness in Black Female Culture*. Columbus: Ohio State University Press, 2007.

Stanley, Amy Dru. *From Bondage to Contract: Wage Labor, Marriage, and the Market in
 the Age of Slave Emancipation*. Cambridge: Cambridge University Press, 1998.

Staples, Robert. "The Myth of Black Macho: A Response to Angry Black Feminists."
 Black Scholar 10, nos. 6–7 (1979): 24–33.

Stepto, Robert B. "Teaching African American Literature: Survey or Tradition." *Afro-American Literature: The Reconstruction of Instruction*, edited by Dexter Fisher and Robert B. Stepto, 8–24. New York: MLA, 1979.

Strachan, Maxwell. "What It's Like to Be a Black Woman in White Hollywood." *Huffington Post*, March 15, 2016. https://www.huffpost.com/entry/female-black -directors-hollywood_n_56cfbde9e4b0bf0dab31a4b9.

Stuart, Reginald. "Kemba's Nightmare." In *The Best of Emerge Magazine*, edited by George E. Curry, 71–90. New York: Ballantine Books, 2003.

Sweet Honey in the Rock. "Testimony." Track B2 on *We All . . . Everyone of Us*. Flying Fish, 1983.

Tami. "Social Capital and Denying the Pain of Black Women." *What Tami Said* (blog). March 29, 2010. http://www.whattamisaid.com/2010/03/social-capital-and -denying-pain-of.html.

Tasker, Yvonne. "*Enchanted* (2007) by Postfeminism: Gender, Irony, and the New Romantic Comedy." In *Feminism at the Movies: Understanding Gender in Contemporary Popular Cinema*, edited by Hilary Radner and Rebecca Stringer, 64–79. New York: Routledge, 2011.

Tate, Claudia. *Domestic Allegories of Political Desire: The Black Heroine's Text at the Turn of the Century*. New York: Oxford University Press, 1992.

Taylor, Ula Y. *The Promise of Patriarchy: Women and the Nation of Islam*. Chapel Hill: University of North Carolina Press, 2017. Kindle.

Thompson, Lisa B. *Beyond the Black Lady: Sexuality and the New African American Middle Class*. Urbana: University of Illinois Press, 2009.

Threadcraft, Shatema. *Intimate Justice: The Black Female Body and the Body Politic*. New York: Oxford University Press, 2016.

Tompkins, Jane. *Sensational Designs: The Cultural Work of American Fiction, 1790–1860*. New York: Oxford University Press, 1985.

"Toni Morrison Special." *Start the Week*. BBC Radio 4. December 8, 2003. Accessed March 4, 2012. http://www.bbc.co.uk/radio4/factual/starttheweek_20031208.shtml.

Traister, Rebecca. *All the Single Ladies: Unmarried Women and the Rise of an Independent Nation*. New York: Simon & Schuster, 2016.

Truth, Sojourner. "Address to the American Equal Rights Association." New York City, May 9, 1867.

Tyree, Omar. *Flyy Girl*. New York: Scribner, 1993. Kindle.

Van Deburg, William, ed. *Modern Black Nationalism: From Marcus Garvey to Louis Farrakhan*. New York: New York University Press, 1997.

Wall, Cheryl A. *Worrying the Line: Black Women Writers, Lineage, and Literary Tradition*. Chapel Hill: University of North Carolina Press, 2005.

Wanzo, Rebecca. "Black Love Is Not a Fairytale." *Poroi: An Interdisciplinary Journal of Rhetorical Analysis and Invention* 7, no. 2 (2011): 1–18.

Warner, Michael. *The Trouble with Normal: Sex, Politics, and the Ethics of Queer Life*. New York: Free Press, 1999.

Watkins, S. Craig. "Black Is Back and It's Bound to Sell: Nationalist Desire and the Production of Black Popular Culture." In *Is It Nation Time? Contemporary Essays on*

Black Power and Black Nationalism, edited by Eddie S. Glaude, 189–214. Chicago: University of Chicago Press, 2002.

Weems, Robert E. Jr. *Desegregating the Dollar: African American Consumerism in the Twentieth Century*. New York: New York University Press, 1998.

White, E. Frances. "Africa on My Mind: Gender, Counter Discourse and African-American Nationalism." *Journal of Women's History* 1, no. 2 (1990): 73–97.

———. *Dark Continent of Our Bodies: Black Feminism and the Politics of Respectability*. Philadelphia: Temple University Press, 2001.

"Who Is Sister Soulja? She States: 'I'm a Rapper, Activist, Organizer, Lecturer.'" *Jet*, July 6, 1992, 12–13.

Williams, Dana Brunvand. "*Waiting to Exhale* by Terry McMillan." Review of *Waiting to Exhale*. *Western American Literature* 28, no. 1 (1993): 90.

Williams, Lena. "Black Woman's Book Starts a Predictable Storm," *New York Times*, October 2, 1990.

Williams, Rhonda M. "Living at the Crossroads: Explorations in Race, Nationality, Sexuality, and Gender." In *The House That Race Built*, edited by Wahneema Lubiano, 136–56. New York: Pantheon, 1997.

Wolcott, Victoria. *Remaking Respectability: African American Women in Interwar Detroit*. Chapel Hill: University of North Carolina Press, 2001.

Womack and Womack. "Baby, I'm Scared of You." Track 3 on *Love Wars*. Elektra,1984.

Woods, Jamila. "Holy (Reprise)." Track 26 on *Nappily Ever After Soundtrack*. Netflix, 2018.

Woods, Teri. *True to the Game*. New York: Grand Central, 1998. Kindle.

Woodson, Carter G. *The Mis-Education of the Negro*. Trenton: Africa World Press, 1933.

Wright, Michelle. *Physics of Blackness: Beyond the Middle Passage Epistemology*. Minneapolis: University of Minnesota Press, 2015.

Index

Page numbers appearing in italics refer to illustrations.

empowerment, Black female, 11, 60, 62, 77, 166

Empowerment Experiment, 97, 109

Enchantment, 58

Ensemble (Saint James), 21, 24

EPMD, 71

Epps, Omar, 141, 187n10

Equal Pay Act, 14

erotic sovereignty, 152–53, 156, 157

Fair Housing Act of 1968, 15

fairy tales, 33–34, 41, 49, 60, 65

"Fairy Tales" (Baker), 33–34, 40, 48, 50, 54–55, 59, 60, 63, 65

family: as an enabler for abuse, 117, 127, 132; Black power and, 11, 167; Black reconstruction of, 49, 149; deterioration of Black, 6–7, 10; Farrakhan and, 122, 128, 129, 132–33; legislation and funding for, 11–13, 15, 130, 132; monetary value and, 93–94; traditional, 129–31; unconventional historical Black, 5, 129

Family Law Act of 1969, California's, 15

Farrakhan, Louis: about, 122–23; *Flyy Girl* and, 89; Million Man March and, 132; *Push* and, 120–23, 124, 125, 127–29, 130–31, 138; *Torchlight for America*, 30, 123–27, 128; traditional family and, 129–31

Fatherhood Initiatives, 130

F C N Publishing Company, 123

"Feenin'" (Jodeci), 14, 71

feminism: Black Power movement and, 67; as a cultural force, 154; personal narrative of, 18, 26, 166

fetishization of white women, 105, 109, 111–12

fiction's relationship with music, 32–33, 70–71

Files, Lolita, 20, 22, 24

Five Percent Nation, 128, 186n41

Flyy Girl (Tyree): background and overview of, 65–66, 67–68, 84–85; class and, 84–85; cultural allusion in,

87–89; protection in, 85–87; sophisticated bitch image in, 84, 85; yield to conservative gender politics in, 89–90

Food and Drug Administration, 14

40 Acres and a Mule Filmworks, 140, 141, 141–42

40-Year-Old Virgin, The, 145

Fox, Vivica A., 90

Fox Entertainment Group, 15–16

Fox News Channel, 15–16

Francis, Terri Simone, 154

Frazier, E. Franklin, 6

Freedmen's Bureau, 4–5, 97

freedom and white woman, 108

Friedman, Milton, 97

friend groups, Black, 45–48

Gates, Henry Louis, Jr., 122

gender: Farrakhan and, 89, 122, 124, 126, 128, 131; nationalism and, 66–67; norms of, 38–39, 46, 92, 107, 132; oppression, 37, 102, 137; privilege and hierarchy and, 40–41, 69–70, 93, 120. *See also* racialized gendered politics

genderqueer, 132

gender reveal celebrations, 168

genres: in film, 140, 144–46, 148, 154–55; crime fiction, 68–71; hip-hop fiction, 70–71; horror fiction, 134–35; romance novels, 1, 41, 48, 54, 62, 134; street or urban fiction, 13, 71, 82, 88

George, Nelson, 29

"Get You Right" (Pretty Ricky), 142

Gifford, Justin, 68

"Gloria" (Enchantment), 58

Goines, Donald, 71

"Gold Digger" (EPMD), 71

"Gold Digger" (Ludacris), 71

"Gold Digger" (West), 71

gold digger image, 45, 65–66, 71–73, 75–77, 78, 93–94. *See also* sophisticated bitch image

Golden, Marita, 25

Gomez, Jewelle, 117

PRWORA and, 12–13; in *True to the Game*, 92

marry Black covenant, 95, 96, 98, 99–102, 104

marrying down, 113

marrying up: background and overview of, 65–66; in *Coldest Winter Ever*, 75, 76, 81, 82; in *Flyy Girl*, 87, 89; in *True to the Game*, 91

masculine motifs, 144–46, 187n10

masculine veneer: about, 10–11, 66; in *Coldest Winter Ever*, 75, 81, 86; in *Disappearing Act*, 36–37; Farrakhan and, 122; in *True to the Game*, 92–93

Mask, Mia L., 144

Maxwell, 157

McClintock, Anne, 66–67, 78

McDonald, Katrina Bell, 164

McDonald, Tamar Jeffers, 144–45

McHenry, Elizabeth, 168–69

McMillan, Terry: background and overview of, 1, 7, 17–18, 28–29, 32–34; *Breaking Ice*, 27; cover art for books by, 20–21, 22–25; defamation case against, 25; *Disappearing Acts* (*See Disappearing Acts* (McMillan)); literary histories and, 26–28; literary to popular migration of, 19–20, 22, 25–26, 29; *Mama*, 19, 24; "Quilting on the Rebound," 27–28; visual culture and, 24–25; *Waiting to Exhale* (*See Waiting to Exhale* (McMillan)

Mecham, Evan, 53

media, 15–16

median marital age, 15

meritocracy: in *Coldest Winter Ever*, 83; in "Fairy Tales," 34; marriageocracy and, 8; in McMillan, 34, 40, 41–42, 44; neoliberalism and, 14; in print media, 148–49

Middle-Atlantic Writers Association Review, 26

middle-class, Black: art consumption of, 25; identity and, 44, 49, 61; meritocracy and, 44, 148; porous boundaries of, 84–85, 113; relationships and, 1–2, 49, 73, 95, 114; sexual behavior and, 61; socioeconomic achievement and, 69–70, 84; stereotypes and, 151. *See also* class

Middle Passage (Johnson), 27

Migration Series (Lawrence), 22–24, 23

Milk in My Coffee (Dickey): background and overview of, 96, 100–102, 183n19; female beauty in, 109–10; idealization of white partners in, 107–8; interracial asymmetrical stakes in, 104, 105–6, 107; interracial intimacy in, 114–15; racial coquette in, 112; serendipitous meetings in, 102–3

Miller-Young, Mireille, 152, 156–57

Million Man March, 132

misogyny, racialized, 68, 88, 126

Mo'Nique, 120

Moran, Rachel F., 115

Morrison, Toni, 18, 26, 28

Mosely, Walter, 74

"Mother Africa," 77

movement, 32

Moyers, Bill, 7

Moynihan, Daniel Patrick, 6, 7, 28–29, 43, 163

Muhammad, Elijah, 122–23

Murdoch, Rupert, 15

Murphy, Eddie, 95

Murray, Pauli, 6

music: in *Best Man*, 150–52; fiction's relationship with, 32–33, 70–71; hip-hop and, 14, 33, 70–74, 119; individualism in industry of, 119; rhythm and blues and, 33, 50–51, 71, 164. *See also specific musicians and songs*

Nappily Ever After (movie), 161–62

Nappily Ever After (Thomas) (book), 161

Nas, 71

nationalism, 66–67, 78; African American Nationalism, 66, 86; Black American commonsense, 66, 73–74,

nationalism (cont.)
75–76, 77, 86, 90; Black Power
movement and, 44, 67, 98, 100, 112,
131; racial uplift and, 87, 89
Nation of Islam, 77, 89, 122–23, 128
natural beauty, 86–87
Naylor, Gloria: McMillan and, 27, 58;
Women of Brewster Place, 52, 58; on
writings on Black women, 38, 52, 64
NdegèOcello, Me'Shell, 98–99, 106, 108,
110, 112, 114
Neal, Mark Anthony, 29
Negro Family in the United States, The
(Frazier), 6
Negro Family: The Case for National Action,
The (Moynihan), 6, 7, 28–29, 43
Negro Handbook, The (Johnson), 97, 109,
110
Nelson, Jill, 103
neoliberalism: background and
overview of, 7–8, 9–10; buy Black and
marry Black covenants and, 96–97,
98; culture of despair and, 14, 164;
legislation and, 11–13, 15; in McMillan,
32, 40–42, 50; patriarchy and, 53, 76,
165; personal responsibility and, 62,
79, 83, 88; victimization and, 69;
violent inequality of, 72, 73
New American Library, 51
New Edition, 155, 156
Newhouse, Samuel Irving, Jr., 16
Newsday, 7
Newsweek, 7, 164
New York Times: on marriage, 69–70, 164;
McMillan and, 27, 39, 51; on *Push*,
120; on *Sula*, 18
Nightline, 164
noble sacrifices, 146, 147
No Disrespect (Souljah), 81, 86
North American Free Trade Agreement
(NAFTA), 70
Norton Anthology of African American
Literature, 27–28
nostalgia, Black political: background
and overview of, 9–11; buy/marry

Black covenants and, 98–99, 100, 101;
character naming and, 127–29;
iconography and, 55, 72–73, 74, 97,
120–22; in McMillan, 58–59, 62;
memory and, 133–34; neoliberalism
and, 9–10, 74; for patriarchal family,
129–31, 137, 138–39; as a remedy, 53;
Torchlight for America and, 123, 125
Notorious B.I.G., 71

Obergefell v. Hodges, 168
oligopolies, 15–17
oppression: identity and, 137; marry
Black covenant and, 98, 101, 102, 104;
in McMillan, 35, 37, 38, 39, 40–41, 42,
44, 51; Souljah and, 79
Oprah's Book Club, 169
Oprah Winfrey Network, 143
Original Man, 123, 126–27, 135
Othellophilia, 114
outsourcing policing and incarceration,
11

Parliament, 149
patriarchy: as an abuse enabler, 66, 91,
117–18, 127–29, 130–33; in *Best Man*,
151, 153, 161; Black bridal pathos and,
10, 37; Farrakhan and, 122, 124, 126,
127, 130, 132; government and,
11–12, 13, 30, 70, 130, 132–33; horror
genre and, 134, 135; incarceration
and, 82; literary criticism and, 52, 53,
54, 56; marrying up and, 76–77, 87,
93–94; masculine veneer and, 10–11,
37; nostalgia and, 120–21, 122, 124,
129–30, 138; political histories and,
6–7; protection and, 85, 87, 88, 93;
racial solidarity and, 45; shapeshifting
and, 137, 138–39; Souljah and, 81,
82–83; spectacle and, 165, 167–68; in
Waiting to Exhale, 56, 57
Patterson, Robert J., 164
Penguin Books, 27, 99
Penguin Random House, 19, 51
Penguin USA, 25

Perry, Imani, 29

"personal is political," 18, 26

personal responsibility: in *Coldest Winter Ever*, 76, 77, 79, 83, 86, 88, 94; government and, 12–13, 132; in McMillan, 40–41, 43, 44, 62; victim blaming and, 67

Personal Responsibility and Work Opportunity Reconciliation Act (PRWORA), 12–14, 132

Poets and Writers, 27

policing and surveillance of Black women, 52, 68–69, 70, 85–87, 92, 122, 146

political nostalgia. *See* nostalgia, Black political

popular culture, Black, 3, 29, 143

popular feminism, 166

Porter, Michael, 42–43, 80

Precious, 120–21, 136

pregnancy, teenage, 7

Pretty Ricky, 142

Prince-Bythewood, Gina. *See Love & Basketball* (Prince-Bythewood)

Princess and the Frog, The, 164

Prisoner's Wife, A (Bandele), 84

private sphere, 3, 11, 26

promiscuity of Black girls and women, 72–74, 107

promposal celebrations, 165, 168

proposals, marriage, 1–2, 4, 49, 89–91, 114

protection: as constabulary language, 68; gender norms and, 92, 93–94, 106, 127; health care and, 88; patriarchal, 75, 82, 85–87, 93, 132; from racism, 113–14; self-blame and, 127

PRWORA (Personal Responsibility and Work Opportunity Reconciliation Act), 12–14, 132

Public Enemy: about, 14, 72–73, 97; "By the Time I Get to Arizona," 53, 55; "Sophisticated Bitch," 72–74, 76–77, 82, 84, 86–87, 89, 92–93

public sphere, 11, 169

punishment of single women, 158–60

Push (Sapphire): background and overview of, 117–19, 120; government foreshadowing in, 130; as horror fiction, 134–35; image and iconography in, 120–23; male criticism of, 135–36; marriage as a monstrosity in, 132–33; naming in, 127–29; nostalgia motif in, 133–34; rejection of heteronormativity in, 137–39; sexual child abuse in, 130–31, 132; *Torchlight* as a template for, 124, 125, 127

PUSH acronym, 119

Quality Paperback Book Club, 20

quasi-autobiographical Black crime fiction, 68

queer coalition building, 137–38

queer women: discursive terrains for, 46; fear for family and, 16; first print appearances of, 132; marriage and, 10; organizations for, 67, 70; in *Push*, 118, 137–39

"Quilting on the Rebound" (McMillan), 27–28

racial coquette, 112

racial identity, 25, 41, 112–14, 123

racial inequality, 6, 9–10, 168

racialized gendered politics, 15, 38, 40, 43–44, 67–68, 84–85, 87, 89

racialized misogyny, 68, 88, 126

racial uplift, 35, 89

racism: as cause of violence against women, 43, 51; female escape from, 69–70; gender and, 37–38, 39–40, 43, 104, 168; interracial relationships and, 35, 105, 113–14, 115; minimization of, 41, 44; mitigation of, 145, 150; nationalism and, 66

Radway, Janice, 168

"rakes," 145–46, 188n14

Rambsy, Howard, II, 20

Random House, 16. *See also* Penguin Random House